TEACHING FOR
DEEP
UNDERSTANDING

TEACHING FOR DEEP UNDERSTANDING

WHAT EVERY EDUCATOR SHOULD KNOW

KENNETH LEITHWOOD
PAT McADIE
NINA BASCIA
ANNE RODRIGUE

CORWIN PRESS
A SAGE Publications Company
Thousand Oaks, California

For information:

Corwin Press
A Sage Publications Company
2455 Teller Road
Thousand Oaks, California 91320
www.corwinpress.com

Sage Publications Ltd.
1 Oliver's Yard
55 City Road
London EC1Y 1SP
United Kingdom

Sage Publications India Pvt. Ltd.
B-42, Panchsheel Enclave
Post Box 4109
New Delhi 110 017 India

Printed in the United States of America.

Library of Congress Cataloging-in-Publication Data

Teaching for deep understanding: What every educator should know /
Kenneth Leithwood . . . [et al.].
      p. cm.
Includes bibliographical references and index.
ISBN 1-4129-2695-5 (cloth) — ISBN 1-4129-2696-3 (pbk.)
   1. Critical thinking—Study and teaching. 2. Curriculum planning.
I. Leithwood, Kenneth A. II. Title.
LB2395.35.L43 2006

371.39—dc22   2005034513

This book is printed on acid-free paper.

06   07   08   09   10   9   8   7   6   5   4   3   2   1

Acquisitions Editor:	Elizabeth Brenkus
Editorial Assistant:	Desirée Enayati
Production Editor:	Diane S. Foster
Copy Editor:	Jackie Tasch
Typesetter:	C&M Digitals (P) Ltd.
Proofreader:	Scott Oney
Indexer:	Molly Hall
Cover Designer:	Michael Dubowe

Contents

About the Editors

Kenneth Leithwood is Professor of Educational Leadership and Policy at OISE/UT. His research and writing about school leadership, educational policy, and organizational change is widely known and respected by educators throughout the English-speaking world. His recent books include *Making Schools Smarter* (2nd edition, Corwin Press, 2002), *Understanding Schools as Intelligent Systems*, and *Changing Leadership for Changing Times*. Dr. Leithwood was the senior author of *The Schools We Need Report* (with Michael Fullan and Nancy Watson) and co-principal investigator (with Lorna Earl, Michael Fullan, and Nancy Watson) of the recent external evaluation of England's National Literacy and Numeracy Strategies.

Pat McAdie is a Research Officer with the Elementary Teachers' Federation of Ontario. She has served in a research capacity in teacher federations for more than 20 years, working on a variety of issues, including gender equity, collective bargaining, assessment, privatization of education, and education change. Ms. McAdie has published in *Canadian Woman Studies, Orbit,* and *Our Schools/Our Selves,* as well as various teacher union publications.

Nina Bascia is Professor and Chair of the Department of Theory & Policy Studies at OISE/UT. Her research focuses on teachers' work and careers and how policy and organizational factors affect them. She has written and edited several books including *Unions in Teachers' Professional Lives, The Sharp Edge of Educational Change* (with Andy Hargreaves), and the *International Handbook of Educational Policy* (with Alister Cumming, Amanda Datnow, Ken Leithwood, and David Livingstone).

Anne Rodrigue is a bilingual educator who presently works as an executive staff officer with the Elementary Teachers' Federation of Ontario. Her recent doctoral work examined how Canadian teacher unions conceptualized and articulated their professional mandate. She has presented at national and international conferences on teacher professionalism, accountability, teacher work, and teacher unions.

About the Contributors

Clive Beck is a Professor in the Department of Curriculum, Teaching and Learning at OISE/UT, where he teaches in both the graduate and preservice programs. He is a past president of the Philosophy of Education Society of North America. His main areas of research and writing are teaching and teacher education. His books include *Better Schools* and *Learning to Live the Good Life*.

Larry Bencze (BSc, MSc, BEd, PhD) is Associate Professor in Science Education at the Ontario Institute for Studies in Education at the University of Toronto. Prior to this, he worked as a secondary school science teacher for eleven years and a science consultant for a school district. His research program involves development and studies of students' opportunities to be engaged in realistic contexts of knowledge building in science and technology, along with relevant pedagogical considerations.

Carl Bereiter is a professor emeritus and special adviser to the Chief Information Officer and the Education Commons at OISE/UT.

David Booth is Professor Emeritus and Scholar in Residence in the Curriculum, Teaching and Learning Department in the Ontario Institute for Studies in Education at the University of Toronto. He is an internationally respected authority on both literacy and arts in education and has authored many teacher reference books and textbooks in all areas of curriculum development. He has won several awards for his classroom teaching and is widely sought after as a speaker about the teaching of reading and the arts.

Jim Cummins teaches in the Department of Curriculum, Teaching and Learning at OISE/UT. His research focuses on the challenges and opportunities of teaching in classrooms where cultural and linguistic diversity is the norm. Among his publications is *Negotiating Identities: Education for Empowerment in a Diverse Society*.

Lorna M. Earl, PhD, is the Head of the International Centre of Educational Change and Associate Professor in the Department of Theory and Policy Studies at OISE/UT. She has a long-standing interest in classroom assessment and how it can influence changes in learning and teaching.

Mark Evans is Director of the Secondary Teacher Education Program and Senior Lecturer in the Department of Curriculum, Teaching and Learning, OISE/UT. He has been involved in a variety of curriculum reform initiatives, teacher education projects, and research studies with teachers and schools locally, nationally, and internationally (e.g., Pakistan, Hong Kong, England, European Union, Russia). Most recently, his work has focused on pedagogical perspectives and practices related to political learning and citizenship education. He has written numerous articles, texts, and learning resources.

Michel Ferrari is an Associate Professor in the Department of Human Development and Applied Psychology at OISE/UT. He recently edited *The Pursuit of Excellence Through Education* and, with Larisa Shavinina, *Beyond Knowledge*. He is currently preparing a new volume on *Teaching for Wisdom.*

Sandra Folk's broad experience in education involves teaching students in preservice and graduate teacher education programs at OISE/UT. In her consulting work, she develops and implements large-scale programs to improve teachers' instructional strategies in mathematics. She also designs online learning programs to improve participants' written communication skills. Her work as an author includes journal articles and textbooks, and recently, she completed a college textbook on mathematics methodology.

Kathleen Gallagher is Associate Professor in the Department of Curriculum, Teaching and Learning at OISE/UT and newly appointed Canada Research Chair in Urban School Research in Pedagogy and Policy. Her book *Drama Education in the Lives of Girls: Imagining Possibilities* was honored as "most outstanding book in curriculum studies" by the American Education Research Association. Her most recent book is an edited collection entitled *How Theatre Educates: Convergences and Counterpoints With Artists, Scholars, and Advocates.* Her research and practice continue to focus on questions of youth, urban school contexts, and drama/theater education.

Ian Hundey taught in schools in Canada and England, in the Department of Curriculum, Teaching, and Learning at OISE/UT, and at universities in New Brunswick, Sweden, Pakistan, and Scotland. He was a school district curriculum consultant, was Manager of Education Outreach at the Library of Parliament in Ottawa, and has written or cowritten a dozen school texts. Currently he is a development editor for a textbook, writer, and educational consultant. With Mark Evans, he wrote "Instructional Approaches in Social Studies Education" in Alan Sears and Ian Wright (Eds.), *Challenges and Prospects for Canadian Social Studies Education.*

Clare Kosnik is an Associate Professor in the Department of Curriculum, Teaching and Learning at OISE/UT. She is currently on leave, serving as Executive Director of the Teachers for a New Era research and development project at Stanford University. She is a former Director of the elementary preservice program at OISE/UT. Her main areas of research and publication are teacher education and literacy education. Her books include *Primary Education* and *Spelling in a Balanced Literacy Program.*

Douglas E. McDougall is an Associate Professor and Associate Chair in the Department of Curriculum, Teaching and Learning at OISE/UT. His research interests are mathematics education, preservice education, and implementation of mathematics education in schools and school districts. Recent publications include *School Mathematics Improvement: Leadership Handbook* and *Teacher Training in New Technologies: The Case in Greece and Canada.*

Richard Messina is a teacher at the Institute of Child Study Laboratory School, OISE/UT.

Shawn Moore is a Senior Research Officer in the International Centre for Educational Change, Department of Theory and Policy Studies at OISE/UT. He is currently working on two projects: one on gender and principal succession and another on leadership practice and student achievement. His most recent publication is entitled, "Voice, Nostalgia and Teachers' Experiences of Change," with Andy Hargreaves and Ivor Goodson.

Richard Reeve is a teacher/researcher at the Institute of Child Study Laboratory School, OISE/UT.

Carol Rolheiser is Associate Dean, Teacher Education, at OISE/UT. Her work is reflected in a range of publications, including journal articles, book chapters, and books such as *Co-operative Learning: Where Heart Meets Mind, Self-Evaluation: Helping Students Get Better At It!, The Portfolio Organizer,* and *Beyond Monet: The Artful Science of Instructional Integration.*

John A. Ross is Professor of Curriculum, Teaching and Learning at OISE/UT and head of the Institute's research center in Peterborough, Ontario. His research interests are mathematics education, student assessment, and program evaluation. Recent publications include "A Survey Measuring Elementary Teachers' Implementation of Standards-based Mathematics Teaching" (with A. Hogaboam-Gray, D. McDougall, & A. Le Sage), "Student Self-Evaluation in Grade 5–6 Mathematics: Effects on Problem Solving Achievement" (with A. Hogaboam-Gray, & C. Rolheiser), and "Research on Reform in Mathematics Education, 1993–2000" (with D. McDougall, & A. Hogaboam-Gray).

Marlene Scardamalia is the University of Toronto's President's Chair in Education and Knowledge Technologies and the Director of the Institute for Knowledge Innovation and Technology, OISE/UT (http://ikit.org).

Preface

*T*eaching for Deep Understanding is the product of collaboration between a teachers federation (the Elementary Teachers' Federation of Ontario [ETFO]) and a university (Ontario Institute for Studies in Education of the University of Toronto [OISE/UT]). These organizations had collaborated before, but not often and not around such an ambitious set of purposes.

This publication attests to the value of collaboration among academic and practice communities. The synergies are obvious and fundamental. Teachers want to provide the best possible education for their students. In fact, a resolution at the 2002 ETFO Annual Meeting started this project. ETFO members identified a problem with the Ontario elementary curriculum and wanted further study to pinpoint the source and extent of the problem. ETFO approached faculty at OISE/UT, and our research partnership was formed.

The worlds of educational practice and of research, often working in isolation from one another, have been described as "two solitudes," and the distance between them often seems formidable. Not so in this project. And we believe the recommendations growing out of this collaborative effort are much more significant as a result. Educational policy makers, for example, typically consult with members of the teaching and research communities separately in the formation of their policies.

A significant challenge often arising from these parallel consultation processes is to reconcile differences in the advice received. School leaders, admonished to be "data driven" in their decision making, often find the "implications" of research obtuse or remote from the real-life solutions they need to their problems. Recommendations in *Teaching for Deep Understanding* represent the combined advice of both communities. While this eliminates the need to reconcile conflicting advice, it also reduces the sometimes politically attractive possibility of trading off one source of advice against another in the justification of policies supported by neither source. The practical nature of our recommendations should also be congenial to the actual world of teachers, administrators, and others offering leadership in their schools.

ACKNOWLEDGMENTS

Corwin Press gratefully acknowledges the contributions of the following individuals:

James Davis, Assistant Principal
Bethel Elementary
Concord, NC

William Ferriter
Senior Fellow, NBCT
Teacher Leaders Network
Cary, NC

Leslie Standerfer, Assistant Principal
Agua Fria High School
Avondale, AZ

Eliot W. Larson, Principal
Fugett Middle School
West Chester, PA

Kathy Grover, Director of Curriculum
Clever Public Schools
Clever, MO

PART I

The Significance and Meaning of "Deep Understanding"

Deep Understanding for All Students

The Overriding Goal for Schooling

Kenneth Leithwood

Pat McAdie

Nina Bascia

Anne Rodrigue

Shawn Moore

We root our case for deep understanding as the overarching goal of public schooling in six straightforward claims.

1. Many specific facts have a very short half-life.

2. You can have your cake and eat it too (or you don't need to trade off good test results).

3. The experience of deeply understanding something encourages further learning.

4. Most real-life tasks require serious, self-directed problem solving.

5. The broader context of our lives places a premium on deep understanding for survival.

6. The alternatives are not very compelling . . . If not deep understanding, then what?

OUR CASE FOR DEEP UNDERSTANDING

Schools now live in a policy world populated, for example, by the No Child Left Behind Act, which requires schools to meet annual yearly performance targets, weeks of time consumed by student testing, a narrow focus on literacy and numeracy, the constant threat of school reconstitution if external achievement standards are not met, and a host of other demands for greater public accountability. In this world, deep understanding, on the face of it, seems an unlikely focus for teaching and learning. Rather, the natural press would seem to be toward the achievement by students of ever more specific, explicit, and readily measured outcomes. This book is about why such a direction actually thwarts the aspirations most of us have for our children and what we can do about it. It aims to arm teachers, school and district administrators, teacher union staff, teacher educators, and parents with the knowledge needed to foster deep understanding among students on a large scale.

Our motivation for developing this research partnership was the conviction that deep understanding for all students ought to be—but is not currently—the overriding goal for public schooling. Deep understanding seems like such an obvious purpose for education that, at first blush, making a case for it, as we do in this book, may seem unnecessary. All teachers assume that students' understanding (depth aside) is the purpose of their instruction—certainly, none would claim to be teaching for misunderstanding or shallow understanding.

Whether assumed and obvious or not, there are overwhelming indications that, at all but the most advanced levels of education, deep understanding is rarely achieved by most students. Many of our own adult students, for example, have told us that until they became immersed in their doctoral research, formal education had simply expanded their superficial understanding of an increasing amount of codified knowledge in their chosen fields of study.

The North American Curriculum

It is often said that the purposes of schools are unclear and often contested, in spite of an official curriculum in most states and provinces literally teeming with things to be "covered." This only goes to illustrate, once again, the difficulty of seeing the forest when one is constantly required to focus on the trees.

The Canadian province of Ontario, the context in which we did this work, shares with many states and provinces a similar orientation to accountability. A key feature of this orientation is the proliferation of expectations or standards to be met by students. Their sheer number makes it extremely difficult either to discern the overall image of an educated person in any holistic way or to achieve deep understanding in relation to any one of them. "More is less" when deep understanding is the goal. Using the Ontario curriculum as a case in point, by the end of the eighth grade, elementary school students are intended to encounter, learn, or otherwise come to grips with a total of 3,993 specific expectations (we counted)! On average, there are about 500 specific expectations

> It is often said that the purposes for schools are unclear and often contested, in spite of an official curriculum literally teeming with things to be "covered."

for each grade until Grades 7 and 8, where specific expectations jump significantly (to 584 and 586 in Grades 7 and 8 respectively).[1]

If the school day averages five hours and the school year 190 days, students have about 950 hours to meet about 500 specific expectations, or about 1.9 hours for each expectation, at least theoretically. Of course, not all five hours of each day in an elementary school is focused on the curriculum.[2] So the real time per expectation is probably closer to 1.5 hours. From a teacher's perspective, this means 1.5 hours to ensure that all 25 to 35 students in one's class master each expectation, roughly 3 minutes per student. Seems a bit tight, doesn't it?

The curriculum for many North American school systems has often been described as "a mile wide and an inch deep." Small wonder.

In this book, we provide some perspective on the forest that is the North American curriculum. We describe what it feels like to be a teacher shepherding one's students through this forest. Suffice it to say, for the moment, that there is quite a lot of prickly and annoying underbrush to cut through to make much progress with one's charges. And before we dismiss such annoyance as trivial, we should remind ourselves of the central role that student welfare plays in the job satisfaction of our best teachers.[3] If teachers are annoyed and dissatisfied with the curriculum, we should be concerned about the value of that curriculum for our children.

THE CASE FOR DEEP UNDERSTANDING

Arguments about the purposes of schooling are often couched in either highly philosophical or ideological frameworks. We think that neither approach is actually very helpful for engaging a large proportion of either professional educators or policymakers, not to mention the public. So instead, we root our case for deep understanding as the overarching goal for public schooling in six straightforward claims.

Many Specific Facts Have a Very Short Half-Life

It's hardly news that what we hold to be true is always evolving, so we don't think this claim requires much defense. Regarding the physical world, for example, while what we observe directly may seem undeniably factual, our explanations for what we observe and how things got to be that way have gone through at least several paradigm shifts in the space of most of our lifetimes. In the medical world,

---

[1]The Ministry of Education is currently reviewing the curriculum. The Social Studies/History and Geography curriculum has been revised and is being implemented in 2005–06. However, the expectations have been reduced only slightly; some of the expectations have been combined; and many of the concerns expressed by elementary teachers were not incorporated into the revisions.

[2]There are, for example, snow suits to be contended with, voluntary activities such as Jump-Rope-for-Heart, bomb threats to be dealt with, upset students who require the immediate and full attention of the teacher, bus delays, and so on.

[3]See, for example, Desimone and Le Floch (2004).

recommended treatments for many illnesses change every decade at least in response to rapidly changing understandings about how the body works. As an example from the social sciences, dominant explanations for how people learn have shifted quite fundamentally as behavioristic, information processing, and social constructionist theories have gained and then waned in support among learning theorists; "brain research" has begun to dominate many people's beliefs about how learning occurs. Even our understanding of historical "facts" changes as we adopt different lenses on the past.

That said, some would argue that there is a corpus of facts and concepts that children should master if they are to participate in the human conversation. Advocates of this view, perhaps most notably Hirsch (1987), go so far as to list these facts and argue for their inclusion in the curriculum. Adopting deep understanding as an overriding goal for education does not come into conflict with this position as directly as might seem to be the case. After all, the recommended corpus of facts and concepts likely does dominate the conceptual starting points that many people share in order to unpack the meaning of their present experiences. Furthermore, the curriculum must have some subject matter to understand. But when deep understanding is the goal, subject matter is the stimulus for thought and exploration—not just the facts to be memorized.

You Can Have Your Cake and Eat It Too
(or You Don't Need to Trade Off Good Test Results)

For those attracted to a curriculum that emphasizes the mastery of predetermined knowledge and skills, adopting deep understanding as an overriding goal for schools should be particularly compelling. Growing evidence suggests that students benefit from a curriculum that fosters deep understanding; they perform at least as well as and sometimes better than students not so exposed on the tests typically used to assess student progress and hold schools accountable for student performance.

This claim has received support in several recent analyses—see, for example, Weglinsky's (2004) analysis of evidence from both the U.S. National Assessment of Educational Progress (NAEP) and the Third International Mathematics and Science Study (TIMSS). Both sets of data allow for the comparison of student performance on basic skills with performance on critical thinking, higher order thinking skills, and other outcomes associated with understanding. As well, both sets of data provide information about the forms of instruction used by teachers. Across most subjects, both sets of data associate better student performance with forms of instruction that emphasize deep understanding.

A review of evidence from TIMSS, as well as a half dozen other sources, came to a similar conclusion (Tighe, Seif, & Wiggins, 2004). And Ross and McDougall (see Chapter 5 of this volume) conclude from their review of a wide array of additional evidence about mathematics achievement:

> You would expect that students who were taught in traditional ways would do better on traditional objectives, but this is not the way it turns out. In most studies of this type, students who have been taught using the deep understanding approach do better on traditional tests than students who were taught using traditional methods. (p. 36)

The Experience of Deeply Understanding Something Encourages Further Learning

Indeed, with subject matter that is sequential, as in the case of mathematics and some of the sciences, failure to understand prior concepts dramatically reduces a student's ability to come to grips with more complex concepts, the understanding of which depends on those prior concepts.

We also know that one of the strongest motivations for further learning is a sense of success with prior learning. The sense of self-efficacy derived from the experience of success in one's prior learning tasks (e.g., Bandura, 1986) is a central source of motivation and commitment for further learning. Conversely, having only opportunities for superficial understanding robs the student of the satisfaction of insight, thereby diminishing commitment to continue learning.

Most Real-Life Tasks Require Serious, Self-Directed Problem Solving

Although this seems pretty self-evident, we offer a couple of examples to demonstrate the range of this claim. First, the case of Mom and Dad (M & D) and their 13-month-old baby, who is crying loudly at 3 a.m. Thirteen-month-olds don't tell you what's wrong with them. But if you are M & D, stopping the crying soon is definitely one of your short-term objectives. M & D define the problem as "some sort of physical or psychological distress that needs to be alleviated." Nonetheless, they do not have access to an effective and ready-made solution; they have to use what they know—or can find out pretty quickly—to create a solution. In this case, the relevant "domain" knowledge includes something about early childhood development, the signs of teething, possible lactate allergies, and the like. It also includes what they know about the causes of their son acting in this way in the past and their sensitivity to his emotional states. Out of this knowledge, they have to craft and try out a solution, which, if it doesn't work, will need revision and more trial. Dr. Spock's advice can come up short pretty fast in such cases.

The second case is the service adviser at your local car dealership. A customer drives in claiming that there is something wrong with the steering mechanism in her car. The adviser has choices. He could just write up the work order telling the mechanic to fix the steering mechanism, but he knows that 8 times out of 10, the symptoms described by the customer are caused by poor wheel alignment. If he writes up the work order focused on the steering mechanism, the mechanic and the shop will make more money because the customer will be charged for the time it takes, first, to rule out the steering mechanism and then to repair the wheel alignment. In this case, the service adviser walks out to the car and checks himself for uneven tire wear, a sure sign of misaligned wheels. This costs the customer nothing and points the mechanic at the real problem immediately.

Note that both of these example problems are common, require application of quite specific knowledge without which an effective solution is unlikely, and are to be found in both real-life personal and work contexts. Note, as well, that the second example—seemingly mundane and eminently practical—illustrates an ethical dimension to human problem solving. Finally, these cases demonstrate that deep understanding is not only about specific areas of knowledge but also about problem-solving processes themselves, including what is sometimes referred to as meta-cognition, an understanding of one's own thought processes.

The Broader Context of Our Lives Places a Premium on Deep Understanding for Survival

This claim is a direct extension of the previous one. Our daily lives routinely demand sophisticated problem solving, and our current point in social history places a premium on the possession of intellectual capital. We are constantly reminded that we now live in a knowledge society fueled by a global economy where intellectual capital is the competitive edge needed to survive and prosper. Furthermore—economics aside—most of us are confronted daily with personal and social challenges made increasingly complex by the increasingly diverse communities in which we live, the changing nature of family structures, and the sheer speed of social change, among many other things. Finding personal meaning in our lives depends on our ability to better understand this context and our preferred roles in it; being successful in doing this, on our own terms, depends on the habits of mind and other internal resources we have developed in part, at least, through our formal education. Deep understanding is crucial in meeting this challenge.

The Alternatives Are Not Very Compelling . . . If Not Deep Understanding, Then What?

If not deep understanding, then what? We know all too well the answer to this question, an answer foreshadowed in our previous claim. It is a superficial grasp of many themes, ideas, and topics, an outcome that serves our thinking and problem solving poorly. Consider the common experience of "cramming" these things into our brains before the big exam. Think about the residue left 24 hours later; perhaps something useful for subsequent games of Trivial Pursuit, but not a lot more.

> Our assertion that deep understanding ought to be the goal of education for all students is likely more controversial than the importance we attribute to deep understanding alone.

It is not too much of a stretch to argue that tripping across the top of many topics and ideas, as is fairly common in our schools, not only bores our students to death and deskills our teachers; it also is one of the most scandalous squanderings of scarce public resources we can think of. This feature of our curricula may be to blame for a large proportion of the overwhelming sense of boredom with school expressed by high school students (Olson, 2005).

Why All Students?

Our assertion that deep understanding ought to be the goal of education for all students is likely more controversial than the importance we attribute to deep understanding alone. At least until very recently, our culture implicitly reserved the intention of deep understanding as a goal for only the most academically inclined students.

However, a key explicit value for most North American school systems is equity, a value which suggests that if deep understanding is important for some students, it ought to be important for all. The most practical form of the question *Why all students?* is really *Why not?* What reasons are usually given for not achieving, or not trying to achieve, deep understanding for all students? Can these reasons be justified?

The two most common reasons are that (a) only some students are capable of developing deep understanding and (b) only some students actually need it. In response to the first of these reasons, we have a substantial body of evidence, some of it quite old (e.g., Bloom, 1981), demonstrating that a very high percentage of students are capable of mastering advanced levels of knowledge given suitable educational experiences; in this case, *suitable* means experiences designed in response to their interests, time required for learning, prior knowledge, and ways of processing new information. As to the second reason, the pervasive requirements for problem solving in both personal and work lives indicates, at least to us, that all students actually need deep understanding of a range of topics in the curriculum.

What Next?

In this chapter, we have argued the case for deep understanding among all children as the overriding goal for public schooling. We have also begun to demonstrate why some features of the typical North American curriculum are not helpful in realizing this goal for many children.

The remainder of the monograph

- Provides a rich and varied set of insights from theory and research about how to foster students' deep understanding in the classroom, both in and across the curriculum
- Describes what teaching for deep understanding looks like through illustrative examples, focusing on some subject areas and some cross-curricular teaching goals
- Reports new evidence from a large sample of elementary school teachers about their efforts to help their students develop deep understanding and the conditions that either contribute to or hinder such efforts
- Exposes many of the systemic obstacles that need to be addressed if this goal is to be more fully realized on a large scale
- Offers recommendations for better achieving this goal, recommendations aimed at everyone with a stake in our schools, from teachers, school and district administrators, and faculties of education through to policymakers

As the following chapters make clear, we know quite a lot about how children acquire deep understanding and what can be done to foster it. In one form or another, this has been a sustained focus of research for several decades. It is time we put that research to better use.

Many different people are in a position to help with this task—in fact, are necessary supports to ensure that teaching for deep understanding is a reality. This is why this book is intended for a wide audience—for teachers, principals, district administrators, teacher union staff, university-based teacher educators, and others. As a result, we know that readers will likely come to the book with a stronger knowledge and interest in some chapters than in others—but we encourage reading across the whole book to understand teaching for deep understanding in a *systemic* way. While some chapters may seem more conceptual than concrete, it is important for readers to sit with and try to absorb the concepts: This is exactly what deep understanding is all about.

Our Agenda

As this overview suggests, our longer term agenda is to prompt action at all levels of the school system. While we are critical of many features of the typical elementary school curriculum, both the intended and the delivered curricula are what concerns us. So responsibility for action, we argue, is widely distributed throughout the system.

State governments, for example, have the responsibility to reshape and align curricula and related policies to encourage a focus on deep understanding for all students. Parents are responsible for giving thoughtful consideration to the importance of deep understanding as a central educational goal, even when accomplishing that goal means engaging their children in educational experiences unlike those they experienced as students themselves. District and school administrators will need to revise and realign their management processes in support of teaching and learning that develops deep understanding among all students. And many teachers will need to invest in the further development of their own content knowledge and pedagogical skill. Unless these distributed responsibilities are assumed in significant degree, the chances of all of our children achieving deep understanding through their school experiences are much reduced.

Education is viewed as a top priority for reform across North America. But many reform initiatives hope to foster greater achievement through a focus on such issues as class and school size, school structure, organizational culture, educational governance, and funding. These are important features to address but only when they play supporting roles to more fundamental changes in the core technology of schools: teaching and learning. Furthermore, many currrent efforts aimed at fundamental changes in the core technology of schooling are highly prescriptive, one-size-fits-all solutions, such as the Comprehensive School Reform (CSR) models.

In spite of the widespread attention CSR models have attracted in districts and schools and the favor they enjoy in policy circles, empirical evidence of their success remains spotty at best from the perspective of all but the most committed advocates. Assisting schools to focus much more of their attention on teaching for deep understanding should be viewed as an alternative to adopting one of the CSR models, or, perhaps more productively, an initiative to be pursued in combination with implementing one or more of the CSR models.

2

Reflections
on Depth

Carl Bereiter

For Carl Bereiter, deep understanding means understanding deep things about subjects worthy of our students' attention. In this chapter, he sets the direction and tone for the chapters that follow.

1. How can teachers help students acquire a disposition for depth?

2. How can teachers identify deep things worthy of students' understanding?

3. How can teachers ensure students have intimate contact with those deep things?

4. How can elementary teachers, often responsible for all areas of the curriculum, develop a deep understanding within many disciplines?

Everyone is in favor of depth. We use the term with confidence, even though we cannot define it, and evaluating it is highly subjective. We speak of depth of understanding and depth of feeling. A book or an art work may be deep, and so may be our appreciation of it. In-depth analyses are always on offer. There can be depth of learning in any content area, any complex skill. There is depth in the treatment of concepts, issues, problems, and interpretations. In short, virtually all the more elevated educational objectives can be cast in terms of depth. Having so much educational weight resting on an undefined concept must give us pause, however.

The reason *depth* is so hard to define is that it has meaning only with respect to something specific. You cannot define depth in general terms, the way you can define honesty or fairness. Nevertheless, there may be general principles of teaching for depth. For one thing, it seems essential that students themselves value depth and pursue it through their individual and collective initiative. Although some degree of understanding can come about just through exposure, there is ample evidence from many different domains that difficult things are understood only with effort. The biologist E. O. Wilson said, "Natural selection built the brain to survive in the world and only incidentally to understand it at a depth greater than is necessary to survive" (1988, p. 61). In other words, the pursuit of deep understanding is not something that comes naturally as an expression of normal curiosity. It is an acquired disposition. Possibly deep appreciation can come about naturally in some cases; but educating people's sensibilities would seem to require getting them to pay attention to things they ordinarily overlook. And the right kind of attention probably requires a student who is trying to perceive more deeply.

DEPTH OF UNDERSTANDING

The two most common conceptions of understanding are one I call the *correspondence conception* and one that its advocates call the *performance perspective.* The correspondence conception has been most clearly set forth by Nickerson (1985) "One understands a concept (principle, process, or whatever) to the extent that what is in one's head regarding that concept corresponds to what is in the head of an expert in the relevant field" (p. 222).

The performance perspective, as advanced by David Perkins and his colleagues in Harvard's Project Zero, defines understanding as consisting of the performance capabilities and dispositions that would lead us to credit a person with understanding: ability to explain, to apply, to evaluate, and so on.

What would depth of understanding consist of in these two views? According to the correspondence view, deeper understanding would presumably consist of a closer match to the expert's knowledge. Depth, accordingly, is not an endless continuum but reaches its limit in a perfect match between what is in the head of the student and what is in the head of the designated expert. According to the performance perspective, depth would presumably be gauged by the quality of the performances. However, McTighe and Wiggins (1999) remind us that quality of performance can be influenced by a number of variables, only one of which is understanding. Thus evaluating depth of understanding requires inferences beyond the observed performance, and it is not clear how those inferences are to be made.

> ...the pursuit of deep understanding is not something that comes naturally as an expression of normal curiosity. It is an acquired disposition.

My own definition of depth of understanding is the following: Deep understanding means understanding deep things about the object in question.

When I offer this definition, people tend to shrug or snicker, for the definition sounds circular, avoiding an actual coming to grips with the meaning of depth. But the definition is not circular. Identifying the deep ideas in a discipline, the deeper meaning of a poem or story, the underlying causes of a historical event or a social condition, the deeper issues in a controversy—these are lively concerns of scholars and critics, curriculum committees, and professional associations. In any significant area, educators can get plenty of help in identifying the deep things worthy of students' attention and understanding. Teaching for depth means bringing students into intimate contact with those deep things.

Of course, what the deep things are may often be in dispute, and there is change over time. The deep things that scientists would agree need to be understood about genetics or the brain are quite different today from what they were 40 years ago. Every major literary work provokes different interpretations that point to different things to be experienced and understood. But these are signs of healthy disciplines. They should not deter us from doing the best we can to help students get to the depths of whatever they are studying.

DEPTH VERSUS BREADTH

Depth has two opposites: superficiality and breadth. Breadth is generally considered to be good and superficiality bad, yet educators know they go together. The realities of time and resources ensure that breadth is usually attained at the cost of superficiality. The survey course—Something-or-other 101—dramatizes the problem. If you get a group of experts in any field together to determine what is essential knowledge for a beginner, they will quickly generate a list too long to cover in any depth. To trim the list would be to imply that some of the scholars had been wasting their careers on matters of limited importance. And so superficiality is the inevitable consequence of too much to learn in the time available.

But there is value in wide-ranging superficial knowledge. The most comprehensive defense of this proposition is to be found in E. D. Hirsch's *Cultural Literacy* (1987). Anyone who is inclined to wax censorious about breadth should read with as open a mind as possible the first two chapters of that book. The part of the argument that connects breadth to depth shows that marginal understanding of a wide range of terms and facts, although of little value in itself, is essential for understanding the kinds of texts—books and quality magazines and newspapers—that do promote depth of understanding. Knowledge of this superficial kind is, curiously, called literacy—as in scientific literacy, historical literacy, and the like. Literacy, in this sense, does just mean a middling level of knowledge, sufficient for the intellectual needs of the educated nonspecialist. In advocating such literacies, we should keep in mind that we are in fact advocating breadth and tolerating superficiality.

Finally, it remains to be said that in some areas, most notably history, depth is impossible without breadth. Deep understanding of any particular topic in history— for instance, the French Revolution—requires understanding its broader contemporary context and also its relation to similar events—other revolutions—that may be distant from it in time and place. In general, we may say that the problems of depth/breadth become more acute the more saturated the field is with factual information. Thus, breadth is more important in history and social studies than it is in science, where a better case can be made for reducing breadth in the interests of depth.

> **IMPLICATIONS FOR TEACHING**
>
> Teaching for Depth = Internalization
> This happens when . . .
>
> - We encounter a powerful idea
> - We read a powerful book
> - We hear a powerful piece of music
>
> Teachers need to find ways to make this happen more often and in more powerful ways—starting by making contact with the deepest wellsprings of the learner's thought and feeling.

Breadth is generally considered to be good and superficiality bad, yet educators know they go together.

Uneasy compromise is the most available way of dealing with the competing demands of depth and breadth. In *How People Learn*, Bransford, Brown, and Cocking (2000) come out strongly for depth but then start to waffle:

Superficial coverage of all topics in a subject area must be replaced with in-depth coverage of fewer topics that allows key concepts in that discipline to be understood. The goal of coverage need not be abandoned entirely, of course. But there must be a sufficient number of cases of in-depth study to allow students to grasp the defining concepts in specific domains within a discipline.

Well-earned fame should await anyone who finds a coherent way of achieving breadth and depth through the same knowledge-seeking process, a way that does not relegate them to separate compartments of the educational program.

HIGHER ORDER THINKING SKILLS

Despite a certain semantic awkwardness about rising higher to go deeper, many educators feel comfortable equating higher order thinking with depth. Manifestly, deep understanding requires thinking of a high order. But it does not follow that the two kinds of educational objectives are interchangeable. Activities aimed at developing higher order thinking skills (HOTS) are typically of short duration, high in process, but short on content. The main emphases are on idea generation (e.g., brainstorming, lateral thinking) and critical analysis (e.g., logical inference, argumentation and debate, recognition of propaganda). Because there are many HOTS and many areas in which they may be applied, coverage tends to be superficial. Thus, although the objectives of HOTS are consistent with those of depth, the methods typically employed for pursuing them are antithetical. My own belief is that HOTS, multiple intelligences, and the like should be kept in mind in educational planning but should not be constituents of the curriculum (Bereiter, 2002, Chapter 10). Eliminating them will strike a blow for coherence and will free up precious time for the pursuit of depth.

Real Depth

Depth should not be confused with advanced study. An advanced course in physics may be just as superficial as a beginning course: It merely covers more advanced material. Advocates of scientific literacy and other such literacies are correct that nonspecialists do not need advanced courses, but this should not be taken to mean that they do not need greater depth of understanding. After students have learned the layout of the solar system and the movements of the planets; after they have overcome such misconceptions as that up and down are absolute directions and that seasonal change has to do with the distance of the Earth from the sun; after they have delivered all the relevant understanding

At the deepest levels, understanding of an important theory or work of art should change the way we perceive and experience the world.

performances of explaining, interpreting, and applying—what else is there if not more advanced study of astronomy?

In a word, what lies beyond is *internalization.* At the deepest levels, understanding of an important theory or work of art should change the way we perceive and experience the world. It should become part of our personality rather than only something we can bring to mind in appropriate contexts. If we have really internalized the Copernican model of the cosmos, then we should perceive the landscape visible out the window as part of a globe; we should not have to remind ourselves that that is what it is. (This does not preclude our dealing

> When applied to problems of understanding, idea improvement entails going deeper, using all the knowledge resources available.

with it as a flat surface or whatever most of the time.) If we have really internalized Shakespeare, it should change the way we respond to expressive language of all kinds.

Even the most in-depth of school studies tends to stop well short of internalization. The result is knowledge that may not be inert; it can serve practical and cognitive needs and provide a basis for further learning. But it does not in any fundamental way alter our outlook on the world. It does not make us better people. Every once in a while, something does break through. We encounter a powerful idea or read a powerful book or hear a powerful piece of music that changes us, that radiates through our whole person. Education for depth would find ways to make that happen more often and in more positive ways. Needless to say, such education would not be imposed on the learner. It would make contact with the deepest wellsprings of the learner's thought and feeling; natural processes would take it from there.

IMPLICATIONS FOR TEACHER EDUCATION

Teaching for depth presents a challenge for teacher education. All might agree that student teachers need to experience depth themselves if they are going to teach for it, but what should that amount to in practice? Regarding teacher education courses themselves, arguments for depth far outweigh arguments for breadth. There is very little indispensable content, although outside agencies may be imposing excessive coverage requirements, just as they do with the school curriculum. At the same time, there are big and often difficult ideas in education. Dewey's concept of experience and such modern concepts as self-organization are examples. These tend to be ignored or watered down in education textbooks on the apparent assumption that student teachers are ill disposed to wrestling with difficult ideas. However, if we are at all serious about promoting depth in school learning, we ought to have some confidence that teachers are capable of depth in their professional preparation.

In addition, a case can be made for depth of learning in the subjects future teachers will teach. What this entails has been well formulated by Bransford et al. (2000):

> Teachers must come to teaching with the experience of in-depth study of the subject area themselves. Before a teacher can develop powerful pedagogical tools, he or she must be familiar with the progress of inquiry and the terms of discourse in the discipline, as well as understand the relationship between information and the concepts that help organize that information in the

discipline. But equally important, the teacher must have a grasp of the growth and development of students' thinking about these concepts. The latter will be essential to developing teaching expertise, but not expertise in the discipline. It may therefore require courses, or course supplements, that are designed specifically for teachers. (p. 20)

The distinction I discussed earlier between depth and advanced courses is important here. Generally, university departments provide opportunities for more advanced courses but not deeper inquiry into basic subject matter. Accordingly, the result of requiring future teachers to gain better preparation in content areas is that they take courses dealing with content they will never teach. Courses going more deeply into such school subjects as arithmetic, the topics actually treated in school science and social studies, and the literary works actually studied in schools would meet an urgent need. In many universities, the number of teacher education students is large enough to justify such special courses (which would also be of value to other students seeking literacy in a field). It would also be a way of extending teacher education without adding time to the teacher education program per se.

Whether it is done in teacher education courses or in the going-deeper subject-matter courses discussed above, students ought to gain experience in the kinds of activity that actually produce depth. I have not elaborated on this matter here because it is a large and complex topic in its own right. The key, I believe, is knowledge building, understood as a social activity whose object is the creation and improvement of new knowledge and the solution of knowledge problems (Bereiter, 2002; Scardamalia, 2002). One of its cardinal principles, the one that most sharply distinguishes it from other constructivist approaches, is idea improvement. When applied to problems of understanding, idea improvement entails going deeper, using all the knowledge resources available. In a knowledge-building context, it also entails epistemic agency—personal and collective responsibility for advancing the state of knowledge in the community.

> Yet the pursuit of depth is—how else can we put it?—deeply rewarding.

Depth, we would all agree, cannot be imposed from the outside. But it also cannot be depended on to emerge naturally from ordinary activity, scholastic or otherwise. Yet the pursuit of depth is—how else can we put it?—deeply rewarding. One way or another, future teachers must experience its rewards and acquire a well-grounded faith that those rewards can be made available to their students.

3

The Starting Point

Constructivist Accounts of Learning

Clive Beck

Clare Kosnik

Clive Beck and Clare Kosnik discuss the constructivist approach, noting the importance of students' prior knowledge and values; the social, active nature of learning; and the need to avoid overly cognitive approaches. In this chapter, they outline nine constructivist principles for teachers who wish to teach for deep understanding.

1. How can teachers help students "go with them" as they teach for deep understanding?

2. How can elementary teachers help students identify topics and activities that are relevant to their lives within the current curriculum?

3. How can teachers ensure they have an understanding of students' prior knowledge? Are there constraints in the current structures and policies?

Teaching for deep understanding is usually described in terms of taking students further into a topic or discipline. In teaching about World War II, for example, teachers are encouraged to go beyond the dates, the combatants, and the ebb and flow of the war to questions such as causes of the war, social and economic dimensions, links to ideological movements, and so on. In mathematics, similarly, instead of just teaching how to add and multiply, teachers are urged to enhance students' understanding (and so their skills) by showing the close connections between these two processes. However, while extending the study of a topic or discipline in these ways is of great importance, teaching for understanding has other key dimensions as well.

> The complexity of teaching for deep understanding can be made clearer by an examination of constructivism, an approach to teaching and learning widely advocated today.

The complexity of teaching for deep understanding can be made clearer by an examination of constructivism, an approach to teaching and learning widely advocated today (Brophy, 2002; Fosnot, 1989, 1996; Hodson, 1998; Phillips, 1995; Richardson, 1997). According to constructivists, students acquire fuller understanding if they are personally involved in building their knowledge. It is not enough that teachers go further into a subject; students must go with them, and they will only do so if they are engaged intellectually, emotionally, and in other ways. In what follows, we will look at four strands in constructivism, each with important implications for teaching for deep understanding.

IMPLICATIONS FOR TEACHING

Nine constructivist principles to help you teach for deep understanding in your classroom . . .

Principle 1: In the classroom, extensive attention should be given to students' ideas, objections, and puzzlements.

Principle 2: Topics selected for study should be related, as far as possible, to students' past or present experience.

Principle 3: The relevance of knowledge to one's own and other people's values should be a major topic of exploration in classrooms.

Principle 4: The topics selected for study in the classroom should be, as far as possible, important for human well-being.

Principle 5: We should look for ways to ensure that the shared ideas in our classrooms are deepened.

Principle 6: We should work to ensure that individual students' ideas and experiences are made available to others in the class in an efficient manner.

Principle 7: We need to select topics that both build on and help build the class community.

Principle 8: We need to explore other dimensions of knowledge and life—not just the cognitive—in both the curriculum and the life of the classroom.

Principle 9: We need to select topics and activities that will engage students in a holistic way.

BUILDING ON STUDENTS' IDEAS AND EXPERIENCE

From a constructivist view, to gain deep understanding, students must link new learnings to the ideas they already have; otherwise, they will simply learn verbalizations. Even if their current ideas are later modified in light of the new learnings, these ideas are needed initially to give meaning to the new material. Students' minds are not blank slates on which we can write at will. As Dewey (1916) said, "No thought, no idea, can possibly be conveyed as an idea from one person to another" (p. 188). If we attempt merely to transfer ideas to students' minds without connecting to their ongoing thinking, we will likely "smother [their] intellectual interest and suppress [their] dawning effort at thought" (p. 188).

Constructivists do not suggest, however, that students' previous ideas will be unaffected by academic disciplines; on the contrary, discipline knowledge has a strong influence on them. As Wells (1994) says, "As the learner appropriates the knowledge and procedures encountered in interaction with others, he or she transforms them, constructing his or her own personal version. But in the process, he or she is also transformed" (p. 8). Moreover, the teacher's knowledge plays a key role by making relevant ideas available at appropriate points (Nuthall, 2002). Nevertheless, without links to students' current thinking, little impact from disciplines or the teacher will occur because students will be unable to make sense of the material presented.

Constructivism is sometimes seen as an enemy of systematic, discipline-based learning. It is assumed that the ideas developed by students will be idiosyncratic constructions that ignore or fly in the face of established knowledge. On our interpretation, however, students' constructed ideas typically will be a reasonable interpretation of concepts within the relevant discipline(s) and reflect students' genuine experience of the world. Rigor is required on both sides. The goal is that learners' knowledge should be deepened by discipline knowledge and discipline knowledge deepened by learners' constructions. This is in line with Dewey's (1938) position that, even within a child-centered, experience-based pedagogy, the goal is the progressive organization of knowledge: Disorganized knowledge is not an option.

> From a constructivist view, to gain deep understanding, students must link new learnings to the ideas they already have; otherwise, they will simply learn verbalizations.

How is it possible for students to deepen the knowledge of an established discipline? Is this not a fanciful notion? As writers such as Dewey (1938) and Schon (1983) have explained, the concepts and principles developed by academic disciplines are usually rather abstract, open to a variety of interpretations and applications. They require extensive specification and refinement at the level of practice and ordinary life. According to Dewey (1938),

> All principles by themselves are abstract. They become concrete only in the consequences which result from their application. . . . Everything depends upon the interpretation given them as they are put into practice in the school and the home. (p. 20)

Learning such principles, then, is not a matter of passively absorbing pre-set ideas but rather of giving meaning to them, in light of one's own ideas and experience; sometimes, indeed, it involves correcting the ideas, where academics have misunderstood certain aspects of the real world. This important deepening of understanding should take place continually as students grapple with disciplinary content in schools.

Of course, if students have not had experience relevant to a given idea, they may not be able to deepen its meaning. But then, perhaps, they should not be learning the idea because it may be of little interest to them, and

> On our interpretation, however, students' constructed ideas typically will be a reasonable interpretation of concepts within the relevant discipline(s) and reflect students' genuine experience of the world.

their learning will largely be verbal and superficial. We may hope that at some stage in the future, the students will understand the idea and find it useful, but this raises the issue of banking education. Freire (1972) argued that we should not treat students as bank accounts into which we deposit knowledge for later withdrawal and use. This parallels Dewey's point about the inappropriateness of conveying ideas directly to students' minds without their participation.

We believe that banking education does, in fact, have a place in schooling because often in later life, we are able to use key concepts that had little meaning when we first encountered them. However, such learning should be kept to a minimum because it exacts a heavy price. It often leads to the smothering of intellectual interest noted by Dewey. It gives rise to the phenomenon, only too common, of people learning a great deal at school or university but never again wanting to read a work of literature, do mathematics, or study science or history. Furthermore, it can result in an alienated class with little sense of ownership or community and a confrontational relationship with the teacher. Most important for the present discussion, it typically prevents students from using their own ideas and experience to deepen their understanding of what they are learning.

Implications for Teaching

Principle 1: In the classroom, extensive attention should be given to students' ideas, objections, and puzzlements. Instruction by the teacher is of key importance, but the relationship between teacher and students should be interactive and dialogical rather than top-down.

Principle 2: Topics selected for study should be related, as far as possible, to students' past or present experience. Such topics have the twofold value of being interesting to students and giving them an opportunity to critique and deepen discipline knowledge.

CONNECTING TO VALUES

So far, we have been discussing going further into academic disciplines, especially by forging links with students' ideas and experience, and our focus has been largely on factual knowledge. Another type of deep understanding, however, derives from approaching knowledge from a values perspective; that is, exploring its relevance for human well-being (ours and other people's). Sternberg (2003) stresses this aspect of students' expert knowledge:

> When schools teach for wisdom, they teach students that it is important not just what you know, but how you use what you know—whether you use it for good or bad ends. . . . Students learn to think wisely and understand things from diverse points of view. (pp. 7–8)

Once again, constructivism has been prominent in emphasizing this aspect of deep understanding. According to Piaget, a central figure in the constructivist movement, knowledge is instrumental in people's lives: "Learners construct ways to make sense of experiences, and will continue to use those constructions as long as they work" (Vadeboncoeur, 1997, p. 23). Ideas that work are ones that fit our needs (which may, in turn, relate to the needs of others) and so take us in appropriate directions. For example, students' concept of good literature should lead them to works they find interesting and enjoyable and can discuss with their friends. More sophisticated ideas about literature may eventually have a valuable impact on their lives, but at a particular stage, such ideas may be alienating and even discourage them from reading.

> Different individuals and subgroups have very different understandings of, for example, friendship, fashion, sexuality, and even knowledge itself, depending on their interests and circumstances. Factual knowledge, then, cannot be sharply separated from values.

Piaget claimed that the adaptive process affects the nature of our knowledge, not just how we apply it; and this insight has been elaborated by more recent thinkers such as Barthes, Foucault, and Derrida. Different individuals and subgroups have very different understandings of, for example, friendship, fashion, sexuality, and even knowledge itself, depending on their interests and circumstances. Factual knowledge, then, cannot be sharply separated from values. This means that in pursuing deep understanding, students must explore relevant interests and points of view. To take the earlier example of studying World War II, to achieve deep understanding of the war, students must be aware of resources that provide the perspectives of Germans and others, as well as the Allied Forces, not to mention their own present worldview as it relates to war. And returning to Sternberg's (2003) discussion of a wisdom-oriented approach to schooling, students of American history must learn

> that the same people that the European Americans called "settlers," some Native Americans called their equivalent of "invaders." The notion that Columbus "discovered" America makes sense in the context of a European American perspective, but not in the context of a Native American perspective. (p. 8)

The extent of the value dependence of knowledge varies across topics and disciplines. For example, the meaning of concepts in physics such as metal, heat, and expansion is more stable from one individual or community to another than political and psychosocial concepts such as democracy, friendship, and happiness. It is true that even in natural science fields, one's perspective and, to a degree, one's life needs can affect one's thinking. Kuhn (1970) has observed that scientists often cling stubbornly to their theories despite new findings (and as a result, science tends to advance funeral by funeral). However, there is a difference of degree. When we turn to disciplines such as history and literature, it is more apparent that students need to consider different values, interests, and perspectives to achieve deep understanding.

Implications for Teaching

Principle 3: The relevance of knowledge to one's own and other people's values should be a major topic of exploration in classrooms. This will increase students' interest in inquiry and also give them an opportunity to shape knowledge to their needs and circumstances and thus deepen it.

Principle 4: The topics selected for study in the classroom should, as far as possible, be important for human well-being. Because not everything can be covered in school, we should help students focus on the more important topics.

THE SOCIAL DIMENSION OF UNDERSTANDING

Constructivism today, often called social constructivism, tends to have a strong sociocultural emphasis, and this relates to a third aspect of teaching for deep understanding. Although Piaget stressed social factors in learning (e.g., Piaget, 1932),

Vygotsky and later constructivist writers developed this perspective further and in new ways. Whereas Piaget focused on peer relationships in learning, Vygotsky (1978) emphasized the importance of teacher-student dialogue. Vygotsky and others also explored the direct influence of language and culture on learners, an impact that often occurs without dialogue and outside learners' conscious control (Barthes, 1970/1982; Foucault, 1998; Vygotsky, 1978).

From a constructivist viewpoint, the social dimension is not just a frill added to make learning more enjoyable; it is fundamental to deep understanding. As Dewey said, "We never educate directly, but indirectly by means of the environment" (Dewey, 1916, p. 32); and "education is essentially a social process. This quality is realized in the degree in which individuals form a community group" (Dewey, 1938, p. 58). Even if they wished to do so, students could not isolate themselves from the class milieu; it continually impinges on their thoughts, emotions, and relationships, interpreting the messages they receive from teachers and other sources (Hodson, 1998). The classroom community is also important because it offers students firsthand experience of social phenomena and so deepens their social understanding.

> Even if they wished to do so, students could not isolate themselves from the class milieu; it continually impinges on their thoughts, emotions, and relationships, interpreting the messages they receive from teachers and other sources.

The impact of the class culture is often largely invisible to us; differences in student characteristics and opinions catch our attention more easily than similarities. Modern cultural theorists have shown that the divergence of individual thought in society is limited by commonalities of language, concepts, and forms of life. Added to this, in the classroom, is the intense desire of students to fit in and be accepted. During a recent visit to a seventh grade gifted class, we observed students making individual presentations on imaginary countries they had created, complete with population, natural environment, resources, industries, social and cultural life, and political institutions. Although the students had worked hard on their projects and were clearly intent on outdoing each other in originality and humor, we were struck by the underlying norms at work in determining what would count as an interesting, entertaining creation. In our view, however, rather than regretting or ignoring this kind of cohesiveness in our classroom, we need to work with it and try to ensure that the group insights achieved by our class are in the direction of deep and valuable understandings (Hodson, 1998).

Obviously, individual student development is also very important. But even students' individual understanding can be extended by interaction with peers in collaborative learning activities. As noted earlier, the knowledge students receive from academic disciplines is often quite abstract. In the process of making such knowledge meaningful and useful, students can benefit greatly from the countless qualifications, suggestions, and stories offered by peers, arising from their diverse perspectives and experiences. It is true that collaborative learning varies in its effectiveness, and this can be a source of frustration to students. However, we should not therefore retreat to noncommunal teaching approaches, but rather work to ensure that the wealth of insights available in the class (including our own) is used in a more systematic, effective manner.

An interactive relationship exists between collaboration and community. On the one hand, collaborative activity strengthens community because it ensures that students get to know each other better and helps them develop social interests and skills. But equally, collaborative learning is dependent on community: unless students know each other and get on well, their work together will be half-hearted, and they will lack the level of trust needed to share their views and take risks in developing new ideas. While fostering collaborative learning, then, we should also implement other measures to build community in our classroom.

Implications for Teaching

Principle 5: We should look for ways to ensure that the shared ideas in our classroom are deepened. To a large extent students develop their ideas together; much of our focus, therefore, must be on enriching class beliefs, attitudes, and behavior patterns, the culture of the classroom.

Principle 6: We should work to ensure that individual students' ideas and experiences are made available to others in the class in an efficient manner. The dubious reputation of collaborative learning is in part deserved. We need to enhance the effectiveness of the collaborative activities in our class. It is not sufficient that students are active and enjoy themselves, although this is important.

Principle 7: We need to select topics that both build on and help build the class community. As far as possible, topics studied should be relevant and interesting to the whole class and lend themselves to sharing.

CONNECTING TO A WAY OF LIFE

From a social constructivist perspective, deep understanding is dependent not only on exploring values and having social interaction, as discussed above, but on engaging all other aspects of the person as well, including attitudes, emotions, aesthetic experience, and behavior. The paradigm is strongly holistic. Dewey (1934/1980) argued continually against dualisms in thought and life, in particular the "opposition of flesh and spirit" (p. 20). Similarly, Barthes (1977), Foucault (1997, 1998), and Derrida (1967/1978) have stressed connections between knowledge, pleasure, ethics, aesthetics, the body, and human action. Although specialized academic disciplines are important, knowledge ultimately has meaning within a way of life. If students in school are to achieve deep understanding, they need opportunity and encouragement to develop a whole way of life and bring this to bear systematically on their academic learning, and vice versa.

> ...according to social constructivism, both academic knowledge and popular culture can have either a negative or positive impact, and both can be either superficial and peripheral or profound and central to life.

One aspect of this holistic perspective is recognition of the links between knowledge and popular culture. Schooling is sometimes seen as overcoming the negative influence of TV, movies, comic books, popular music, fashion, and so on; from an academic perspective, such interests are often viewed as superficial and peripheral. However, according to social constructivism, both academic knowledge and popular culture can have either a negative or positive impact, and both can be either superficial and peripheral or profound and central to life. Social constructivists try to reduce the separation between the academic and popular domains (Barthes,

1970/1982; Derrida, 1967/1978; Rorty, 1989). For education, this means supporting expression and discussion of popular culture in the classroom and critique of academic knowledge in light of popular culture, as well as the converse.

Too strong a discipline focus in school results in an overly cognitive orientation. This is why, in the 1960s, Goodlad (1966) expressed reservations about a widespread U.S. effort to deepen academic learning, objecting that "the structure of the disciplines stands at the center of curriculum planning and [determines] the very objectives, organizational patterns, and subject matter" (p. 114). While this was precisely what the reformers had in mind (as do many discipline-oriented curriculum developers today), Goodlad saw it as highly problematic. Dewey (1916) stressed that school is not just preparation for life (although it is that) but life itself. And Noddings (1992) argues that traditional liberal education, with its heavy cognitive emphasis, is not ideal for anyone, whether academically inclined or not. She maintains that a great many dimensions of life should be explored in the formal curriculum and experienced in the life of the classroom and school.

From this holistic point of view, pursuit of depth in education must eventually take us beyond understanding, while including it. This is why Bereiter (Chapter 2, this volume) suggests that we speak simply of teaching for depth—rather than depth of understanding—to allow for the range of elements (cognitive and noncognitive) that are involved. Whether one makes this move or just uses the term *understanding* in a broad sense is perhaps not crucial. What is essential is to recognize the need to explore a wide spectrum of aspects of life in the pursuit of depth of understanding and experience.

Implications for Teaching

Principle 8: We need to explore other dimensions of knowledge and life—not just the cognitive—in both the curriculum and the life of the classroom. This will deepen understanding in itself and also increase engagement, which in turn will further understanding because students will learn more.

Principle 9: We need to select topics and activities that will engage students in a holistic way. Some topics lend themselves more than others to being approached holistically.

CONCLUSION

Constructivist accounts of learning point to four requirements of teaching for deep understanding. First, students' current ideas and past and present experience must be engaged in developing disciplinary knowledge. Second, connections between knowledge and the values of students and others must be explored. Third, we must ensure that students have abundant opportunities to learn from each other and also grow in understanding as a class community. Fourth, we should avoid an overly cognitive approach to deep understanding, exploring for example the attitudinal, emotional, aesthetic, and behavioral dimensions of topics and encouraging these diverse types of expression in the classroom.

> Teachers are under pressure today to cover an enormous range of topics, regardless of their relative importance and interest to students. We must resist this pressure. . . .

A recurring theme in this chapter has been the importance of being selective about the topics studied in the classroom. As far as possible, we should choose topics that draw on students' ideas and experiences, that are important in their lives, that support and are illuminated by social interaction and engage students holistically. Teachers are under pressure today to cover an enormous range of topics, regardless of their relative importance and interest to students. We must resist this pressure and focus on topics that engage students and promote depth of understanding. Adopting such a stance is in the interests of both students and society generally.

4

Understanding *Understanding*

A Review of the Literature

Sandra Folk

Sandra Folk reviews the highlights of the education research literature to illustrate that understanding has many facets, including the following:

1. Understanding enables the transfer of knowledge from one situation to another
2. Understanding allows flexibility
3. Understanding promotes making
4. Understanding is a product and a process
5. Understanding can be conceptual, procedural, situational, or causal
6. Understanding is on a continuum from partial to more global understanding
   - How can teachers help elementary students draw on their prior experiences to deepen their understandings in a variety of areas?
   - How can teachers help students make connections across curriculum subjects?

Teaching for understanding is complex and challenging, as reflected in the education literature (J. Gallagher, 2000; Gardner, 1993; Newton, 2001a). Although Gardner (1993) tells us that "in practice, it is quite difficult" (p. 21), most teachers—myself included—believe that they do teach for understanding

(Byers & Herscovics, 1977; Cohen & Ball, 1990; Gardner, 1993). To fully understand and appreciate what it means to teach for understanding, it is necessary to look at the meaning of *understanding.*

Understanding is acknowledged as a worthwhile and valued goal in education (Gardner & Boix-Mansilla, 1994; Newton, 2001b). The definition of understanding varies in the literature. For example, in a discussion regarding what it means to understand in mathematics, Byers (1980) suggests that understanding will have different meanings depending on teachers' use. Some teachers, in speaking about the progress of their students, will say, "The student doesn't understand." What they really mean is, "The student does not comprehend the question" (Byers, 1980). Other teachers will use the term as a way of describing students' problem-solving ability. They will say that a student who is able to take a key step in solving a nonroutine problem, or who is able to grasp quickly the main idea of a piece of mathematics, understands. More specifically, Sierpinska (1994) explains that, in the context of mathematics, understanding may be used to talk more generally about understanding mathematics concepts and more specifically about understanding concepts such as number, quantity, volume, function, limit of sequence, or linear independence of vectors. She adds that other things such as patterns and phenomena are also objects of understanding.

> According to students, understanding meant being prepared to answer recall questions. For the researchers, it was a more complex and intellectually active process of conceptualization. The study also revealed that students' understandings of science in school did not fit with out-of-school usage of scientific knowledge.

A study exploring the nature of scientific understanding both inside and outside of schools noted that a discrepancy existed between researchers' and students' interpretation of the concept of understanding (Anderson & Roth, 1989). According to students, understanding meant being prepared to answer recall questions. For the researchers, it was a more complex and intellectually active process of conceptualization. The study also revealed that students' understandings of science in school did not fit with out-of-school usage of scientific knowledge.

My experience with children in classrooms in the area of mathematics is congruent with the findings of this science-based study. Like Anderson and Roth (1989), I have found that students' views of what it means to understand differ from mine. Many view understanding in mathematics as the ability to reduce knowledge to a list of facts to be memorized to complete a particular task. But for me, understanding is evident, for example, when students are asked to express different amounts such as $1.09 or $0.62 in fractional form to show their understanding of its part-whole relationship; some are unable to do so. They fail to understand that one dollar is the same as a hundred hundredths and that a part of a dollar can be expressed as a fraction out of one hundred.

For Newton (2001a), understanding is both a mental process and a mental product. As a mental process, understanding can be conceptualized as the ability to think and act flexibly with what one knows (Perkins, 1994). As a mental product, understanding can be described as a knowledge of the structure of the topic, the structure's purpose, and why it serves that purpose (Perkins, 1986). The product will vary according to the subject, and there can be various understandings in any one subject. The idea of making cognitive connections is central to theories of understanding. In their review of explanations posited in the literature, Fennema, Carpenter, and Peterson (1989) confirm that understanding involves establishing relationships between segments of knowledge. Good and Brophy (1991) counsel that, in order to achieve understanding, students must learn not only the individual elements in a network of related content but also the connections between them.

From a subject-specific perspective, Hiebert and Carpenter (1992) explain that understanding as making connections between ideas, facts, or procedures is a theme that runs through some of the classic works within the mathematics education literature. They further advise that many of those who study mathematics learning agree that understanding involves recognizing relationships between pieces of information.

Prawat (1989) also talks about the importance of connections—of developing networks of knowledge to develop understanding, particularly in science and mathematics. He compares these networks of knowledge to spiderwebs or Tinkertoys with nodes and connectors. Prawat suggests that connections can take many forms: reconciling formal knowledge with the informal knowledge students develop on their own; linking key concepts and principles in mathematics and science to physical representations, models, metaphors, and analogies; and demonstrating how separate concepts and rules are related.

> **IMPLICATIONS FOR TEACHING**
>
> Some teachers, in speaking about the progress of their students, will say, "The student doesn't understand." What they really mean is, "The student does not comprehend the question."
>
> If our goal is deep understanding...
>
> — We need to start by clarifying our goals
> — We need to understand what our students understand

Along with getting a "handle on things," Newton (2000) describes understanding as the ability to make connections between facts and ideas and to see relationships and patterns. Newton further explains that understanding, as opposed to memorization, is essential if children are to make sense of their world, if they are to learn by connecting new information to what they already know, if they are to remember what they have already learned, and if they are to solve problems (English, 2001).

Martin (1970) cautions that understanding is more than a matter of seeing connections. "One must . . . see the things to be connected as well as the connections between them, if one is to understand" (p. 167). Newton (2000) also proposes that there are several kinds of understanding in science: conceptual, procedural, situational, and causal. Conceptual understanding requires a learner to understand and relate fundamental concepts to prior knowledge and understanding. An understanding of ways of doing things, particularly in connection with practical work, is defined as procedural understanding. Situational understanding involves the exploration of a situation in which a learner is able to fully grasp and describe it. Causal understanding is described as a learner's ability to make sense of the cause-and-effect relationship of an event that involves some change in a situation (Newton, 2001b).

Some, such as Holt (1964) and Van Engen (1953), view understanding on a continuum, which allows for students' partial understanding of concepts and ideas. Holt's model of understanding is designed to help teachers come to grips with understanding and to learn what students really know as opposed to what they might give the appearance of knowing. He developed the following seven-point list for use in planning instruction and assessing learning.

I feel I understand something if and when I can do some, at least, of the following: (1) state it in my own words; (2) give examples of it; (3) recognize it in various guises and circumstances; (4) see connections between it and other facts or ideas; (5) make use of it in various ways; (6) foresee some of its consequences; (7) state its opposite or converse. (pp. 36–37)

According to Holt, this list is only a beginning in assessing students' understanding.

Van Engen (1953) describes understanding as a process of organizing and integrating knowledge according to a set of criteria: "Understanding is more nearly a process of integrating concepts, placing them in a certain knowledge [framework] according to a set of criteria. . . . Understanding is a process" (p. 76). He notes when a student says, "I know what you mean but I do not understand it," the student might know what to do but not why it should be done.

Gardner (1993) defines understanding as "having sufficient grasp of concepts, principles, or skills so that you can bring them to bear on new problems and situations" (p. 21). He explains that there are three kinds of understanding: the intuitive understanding of the young child, understanding where the learner is only able to apply knowledge in an explicit context, and genuine understanding, which constitutes expertise. He describes genuine understanding as "the capacity to use current knowledge, concepts, and skills to illuminate new problems or unanticipated issues" (Gardner & Boix-Mansilla, 1994, p. 200). It is suggested that "genuine understanding has been achieved if an individual proves able to apply knowledge in new situations, without applying such knowledge erroneously or inappropriately; if he or she can do so spontaneously, without specific instruction to do so" (Gardner & Boix-Mansilla, 1994, p. 200).

This performance perspective of understanding is at the core of an integrated curriculum project that Gardner (1993) and his colleagues designed to promote understanding within and beyond the disciplines. Perkins and Blythe (1994) pointed out that, from a performance perspective, understanding was "a matter of being able to do a variety of thought-demanding things with a topic—like explaining, finding evidence and examples, generalizing, applying concepts, analogizing and representing the topic in a new way" (p. 5). According to Perkins (1993b), the more thought-demanding the performance a student was able to display, the more apparent it was that the student understood.

This discussion makes clear that understanding is a complex concept with many facets. In some instances, a more global view of understanding is promoted, as in Gardner's (1993) Project Zero. For others, understanding is more subject-specific. Theories in the literature tell us that making cognitive connections is an important prerequisite to understanding. There are those (Perkins, 1993b) who talk about understanding in terms of performance—learners build up performances of understanding around a topic. Finally, J. Gallagher (2000) reminds us that understanding is never complete and can always be enriched and given new meaning. He suggests that this goal can be achieved through reflection, discussion, new modes of representation of ideas, and many other ways.

PART II

Teaching for Deep Understanding in the Disciplines

5

Mathematics

John A. Ross

Douglas E. McDougall

> In this chapter, John Ross and Douglas McDougall outline what deep understanding means from the student's point of view, describe how this approach differs from traditional mathematics instruction, and identify effects on student achievement. They highlight how districts can support teaching for deep understanding in math.
>
> 1. How can teachers gain confidence and their own deep understanding in math?
>
> 2. What changes need to occur in elementary mathematics classrooms to approach the kind of learning promoted here?

Teaching for deep understanding in mathematics has been starkly contrasted with traditional math teaching, as if teachers inalterably place themselves in one camp or the other. Such a view leads to "Math Wars," a closure of professional conversation that forfeits opportunities for improvements in teaching and learning. We see teaching for deep understanding and traditional math instruction as ends of a continuum rather than as dichotomous categories. Below, we briefly describe some of the formidable obstacles to the implementation of teaching for deep understanding and identify some facilitators of instructional change.

WHAT DOES TEACHING FOR DEEP UNDERSTANDING MEAN TO THE STUDENT?

Historically, students have experienced mathematics as a fixed body of abstract rules to be memorized by those cleverer than themselves. By this reasoning, only a few students are capable of doing mathematics, and they tend to work alone; eventually, mathematics becomes too hard for everyone.

Students in classrooms dedicated to the development of deep understanding have a very different experience of mathematics. They see it as something that all students can do. Mathematics consists of solving problems in real-life contexts, using concepts, procedures, and tools that are collaboratively developed or chosen by teacher and students. It means being a successful contributor to a mathematical community.

HOW CAN A TEACHER PROMOTE DEEP UNDERSTANDING?

Teaching for deep understanding can be described as "rich talk about rich tasks." We have used this slogan as the starting point for developing 10 dimensions of teaching for depth in mathematics classrooms (see Ross, McDougall, & Hogaboam-Gray, 2002). Based on observations and interviews with expert teachers, we created a rubric that describes four levels of teaching for each dimension (McDougall et al., 2000; Ross, Hogaboam-Gray, McDougall, & Bruce, 2001; Ross, Hogaboam-Gray, McDougall, & LeSage, 2003). The rubric is anchored at one end by traditional teaching (i.e., a focus on teaching students how to apply mathematical procedures) and at the other end by teaching for deep understanding (i.e., a focus on teaching students how to construct and use mathematical concepts). (A self-assessment is available at http://www.solidcs.net/mathtls.htm. It provides immediate anonymous feedback.)

> Students in classrooms dedicated to the development of deep understanding have a very different experience of mathematics. They see it as something that all students can do.

The teacher's role illustrates one dimension of the rubric, showing how the teacher's role changes as one moves toward the deep understanding end of the continuum (see Table 5.1). At the traditional end, the teacher, with the help of the textbook, is the fount of all knowledge. The teacher does the difficult cognitive work in mathematics class, for example, breaking complex problems into simple segments that can be easily answered by students with teacher prompting. The line between teacher and learner is sharply drawn. In contrast, at the deep understanding end, the boundary between teacher and learner is amorphous and porous. Talk about mathematical ideas provides the foundation for the development of a community of learners in which teachers and students share expertise and create knowledge together. The levels in between these poles are practices of Ontario teachers we have observed. Having intermediate steps is a helpful way of bridging the gap between the ends.

Teachers who are at the high end of the rubric are not there every moment of every math lesson. Anyone who tried to do that would have difficulty getting out of the first unit. Expert teachers flow between the two ends of the rubric, adjusting their

Table 5.1   The Teacher's Role

Dimension	Level 1 Procedural Focus	Level 2	Level 3	Level 4 Teaching for Deep Understanding
Teacher's Role	Teacher is the sole knowledge expert. Student roles focus on tasks which require minimal cognitive effort.	Although the teacher is the sole knowledge expert, some student expertise is acknowledged. Students are assigned roles with the teacher being central to the activities.	The teacher shares the knowledge expertise role with the students. More teacher-directed tasks are provided for students with lower abilities, and more student-centered activities are provided for higher ability students.	The teacher is a co-learner with the students. The teacher and the entire student body are responsible for building a math community. The teacher ensures that each student is an integral part of the learning process.

teaching strategies to meet the demands of the curriculum and students. What matters is a teacher's typical practice or the central tendency of a given teacher. It is unlikely that teachers will be at the same level on all the dimensions. Instead, a teacher will reach toward the deep understanding end on some dimensions while functioning toward the procedural end on others. Table 5.2 (adapted from Ross et al., 2001) summarizes each dimension, giving a short statement that describes what teaching for deep understanding is like in contrast with traditional mathematics teaching.

WHAT ARE THE EFFECTS OF TEACHING FOR DEEP UNDERSTANDING ON STUDENT ACHIEVEMENT?

There is consistent evidence from various kinds of studies that students learn more when they are in classrooms in which deep understanding is the focus of instruction (Ross et al., 2002). One body of evidence comes from "horse race" evaluations. In this type of study, the effects of teaching for deep understanding are compared to the effects of traditional math teaching. The finish line is student achievement. Some of these studies define achievement as student outcomes that matter to reformers, such as deep understanding of concepts, communication of mathematical ideas, problem solving, ability to represent mathematical ideas in multiple ways, and achievement in strands of mathematics that receive more attention in reform documents (e.g., Data Management & Probability). These studies have found that achievement is higher when teaching for deep understanding is in place. This is an important finding, as these outcomes are notoriously difficult to achieve, even for the most able students.

Other studies have defined achievement in more traditional ways: ability to apply mathematical procedures accurately, know math facts, and get the right answer on one-step problems. These are learning objectives that get less attention in deep

Table 5.2   Dimensions of Teaching for Deep Understanding in Mathematics

1. A broader program scope, teaching multiple math strands with increased attention to those less commonly taught such as Probability and Data Management, Patterning and Algebra, rather than an exclusive focus on Numeration and recall of algorithms.

2. All students have access to all forms of mathematics attempting complex problems. In traditional math programs, students attempt complex tasks only after they have mastered basic operations, a stage often not achieved by all students.

3. Teachers strive to raise student self-confidence in mathematics in a variety of ways (e.g., modeling positive attitudes, developing strategies to increase student success, and helping students recognize their mathematical ability). In the traditional math classroom, teachers build confidence by providing extrinsic rewards (e.g., praise) for achievement.

4. Student tasks are complex, open-ended problems embedded in real-life contexts; many of these problems do not afford a single solution. Students are expected to generate multiple ways of representing their ideas and select the most appropriate. In traditional mathematics, students work on routine applications of basic operations in single-solution problems often set in abstract contexts. Students are expected to use a single representation identified by the teacher.

5. Instruction focuses on the construction of mathematical ideas through student discovery. In traditional math, textbook knowledge is transmitted through recitation: presentation, practice, feedback, and remediation.

6. The teacher's role is that of a co-learner and co-creator of a mathematical community rather than sole knowledge expert.

7. Mathematical problems are undertaken with the aid of manipulatives and with ready access to mathematical tools (i.e., calculators and computers). Manipulatives are used to model mathematical ideas and to move from concrete to abstract conceptions. In traditional programs, the use of such tools is restricted to selected occasions.

8. The classroom is organized so that students work together to develop and share solutions. The teacher models and teaches cooperative learning skills, ways to communicate math ideas, and principles of shared leadership. In traditional math, students usually work independently.

9. Assessment is authentic (i.e., relevant to the lives of students), integrated with everyday instruction, and transparent; it taps multiple levels of performance. In contrast, assessment in traditional programs is characterized by end-of-unit tests; assessment criteria and procedures are developed by the teacher alone and are not made explicit to students.

10. The teacher's conception of mathematics is that of a dynamic subject that changes over time and that constitutes a network of integrated topics. In traditional programs, mathematics is a fixed body of knowledge consisting of rules and algorithms.

understanding classrooms than in traditional math programs. You would expect that students taught in traditional ways would do better on traditional objectives, but this is not the way it turns out. In most studies of this type, students who have been taught using the deep understanding approach do better on traditional tests than students who were taught using traditional methods. In some studies of this type, there is no difference between the two approaches on traditional measures. But there are no studies in which students in deep understanding classrooms do more poorly on traditional tests than students taught with traditional methods. The bottom line from horse-race evaluations is that teaching for deep understanding produces higher achievement on complex learning objectives with a good chance of higher (but not lower) success on computational objectives (for a summary of the evidence, see Ross et al., 2002).

> There is consistent evidence from various kinds of studies that students learn more when they are in classrooms in which deep understanding is the focus of instruction.

A very different type of research is the qualitative investigation. In this approach, a few classrooms are intensively examined, linking what students do to teachers' instructional strategies. These studies convincingly demonstrate that when teachers change their practice, students begin to think in different ways. For example, these studies have found that engaging students in sustained talk about their mathematical ideas has a positive effect on the quality of those ideas. By articulating what they are thinking, students become conscious of their thoughts and thus able to subject them to explicit examination. Talking makes errors and omissions visible. Sometimes students recognize these errors as they talk through their thinking and self-correct. Sometimes others recognize their learning needs and provide the support students need to get to the next level of understanding. Regardless of whether the talk is between teacher and students in a whole-class setting or among students in a small group, the evidence is clear: Teachers in these classrooms have a better understanding of what these students know and don't know about mathematics. The qualitative research explains why horse-race evaluations show that teaching for deep understanding is a winner.

IF TEACHING FOR DEEP UNDERSTANDING PRODUCES SUCH GREAT STUDENT LEARNING, WHY ISN'T EVERYBODY DOING IT?

Teaching for deep understanding is difficult. The main reason is that the current curricula ask teachers to teach in a way they have not themselves experienced as students. Teaching for deeper understanding is riskier—focusing on student understanding can take the lesson down unforeseen paths, perhaps to some mathematical ideas that the teacher is not really comfortable with or never really understood. Teaching for deep understanding may conflict with some deeply held beliefs about math (e.g., that it is a fixed body of knowledge), about how students learn (e.g., you have to master the basics before you can tackle complex problems), and about the teacher's role (e.g., the sole knowledge expert in the classroom).

IMPLICATIONS FOR TEACHING

Teaching for deep understanding in mathematics = Rich talk about rich tasks

1. There is a program scope.
2. Students have access to all forms of mathematics.
3. Teachers strive to raise student self-confidence.
4. Student tasks are complex, open-ended.
5. Instruction focuses on the construction of mathematical ideas through student discovery.
6. Teacher's role is that of a co-learner and co-creator.
7. Mathematical problems are undertaken with the aid of manipulatives.
8. The classroom is organized so that students work together to develop and share solutions.
9. Assessment is authentic.
10. Teacher's conception of mathematics is that of a dynamic subject.

New ways of teaching may conflict with parent and administrator expectations about what a math classroom should look like. Most important is time: It takes longer to work through math ideas—covering the curriculum appears to be faster. The huge number of individual expectations for each grade in the Ontario math curriculum accentuates the time problem.

At one time, the lack of suitable texts was an obstacle. Available textbooks were written for traditional math teaching, and teachers who wanted rich tasks had to create them on their own. The new text series (e.g., Quest 2000, Interactions) embody the deep understanding approach. When these texts became available, some teachers felt comfortable with the activities. They knew how to make the most of the resources and were able to supplement for deficiencies in the new texts (such as how to adapt complex problems to appropriately challenge all learners). For many teachers, the new texts were not helpful. What these teachers did was take the rich problems of the new text and transform them into traditional problems. The teacher did the heavy cognitive lifting—breaking the problem into a series of short steps that were parceled out as a series of short single-solution problems supported by highly detailed teacher prompts that often included telling students which algorithm to use (Ross et al., 2003).

> The qualitative research explains why horse-race evaluations show that teaching for deep understanding is a winner.

HOW CAN DISTRICTS SUPPORT TEACHING FOR DEEP UNDERSTANDING IN MATHEMATICS?

The key district task is to create teacher capacity for deep understanding. One method that has proved successful for many districts is to facilitate teacher access to quality inservice training. Implementation of teaching for deep understanding is more likely to occur with inservice that provides an ample supply of student learning materials, input from subject experts, collegial interaction to explore classroom applications, attention to beliefs about mathematics, and alignment with National Council of Teachers of Mathematics standards. For example, Ross and Bruce (in press) reported a case study of an elementary teacher who moved toward teaching for deep understanding through an inservice process that combined self-assessment with goal setting, peer observation, joint planning, "just in time" demonstrations of math teaching tied to the teacher's goals, and classroom observational data provided by external consultants.

Districts can create policies that contribute to teacher capacity in other ways. Especially important are policies that give teachers and principals greater control over instructional decisions. The effects are indirect. Teachers are more likely to try out instructional approaches that are risky and difficult, like teaching for deep understanding, if they expect to be successful in bringing about student learning. This expectation, called teacher efficacy, is an individual and a school characteristic ("I believe I can teach mathematics" and "I believe the teachers in this school constitute an effective instructional team"). Teachers with high expectations about the effects of their teaching set higher goals, try harder to reach them, persist through obstacles, and have higher student achievement (see the review in Ross, 1998). The role of the district comes into play when we look for school factors that influence teacher beliefs in their collective capacity. The key variables have to do with teacher ownership of school processes. Teachers have higher collective teacher efficacy when they work in schools that have a shared sense of purpose, where teachers work together on instructional tasks, where teachers believe that school plans fit the needs of students and staff, and where there is empowering school leadership (Ross, Hogaboam-Gray, & Gray, 2004). Districts can support the development of this sense of ownership by avoiding policies that overcentralize governance, finance, supervision, and curriculum development and by providing opportunities for schools to undertake school improvement activities of their own design.

> Teaching for deeper understanding is riskier—focusing on student understanding can take the lesson down unforeseen paths. . . .

Districts can also contribute to teacher capacity through their selection, training, and supervision of school leaders who encourage transformational leadership practices in schools. Transformational leadership is an approach in which principals encourage teacher development by engaging teachers in the creation of a school vision, providing intellectual stimulation and

> From the student's point of view, teaching for deep understanding provides a very different mathematical experience, one in which mathematics is a tool for solving authentic problems. It is a teaching approach that places more of the burden for learning on students' shoulders while providing the support they need to be successful.

support for individuals, modeling professional practices, setting high performance expectations, and sharing decision making. Ross and Gray (in press) found that principals who engaged in these practices increased teacher commitment to the school as a professional community, directly and indirectly, by increasing collective teacher efficacy. Teachers working in professional community schools are more likely to develop the capacity to teach for deep understanding.

A DIFFERENT MATHEMATICAL EXPERIENCE

From the student's point of view, teaching for deep understanding provides a very different mathematical experience, one in which mathematics is a tool for solving authentic problems. It is a teaching approach that places more of the burden for learning on students' shoulders while providing the support they need to be successful. From the teacher's point of view, teaching for understanding can be summarized as finding ways to stimulate rich talk about rich tasks. There are myriad ways of entering into the task and ample intermediate stations along the journey. Rubrics and self-assessment tools are available to guide professional growth trajectories.

There are formidable obstacles to changing how mathematics is taught. The key actor is the teacher. The district can provide support to teacher growth through provision of inservice opportunities and through policy making that contributes to school processes that build capacity. The research is conclusive: When the change to teaching for deep understanding happens, student achievement of traditional and nontraditional mathematics objectives improves significantly.

6

The Role of Literacy and Literature

David Booth

> In this chapter, David Booth outlines strategies and approaches to promoting literacy among today's students, giving special attention to those who are at risk of getting left behind.
>
> 1. How can elementary teachers nurture even the most reluctant readers?
>
> 2. How can teachers (and parents) balance allowing students to choose their own reading materials with ensuring they are exposed to literature sensitive to equity and gender issues?

Reading Journal Entry 4

I had never been a school person, and one of my weakest strengths would have to be reading. I was in a literacy class and was coming close to the end of the semester when I was told by my teacher that the class had to do a book report and had a month to work on it before the due date. I had no intention of reading. I was coming close to the due date for our book assignment and nothing had been read. I didn't even have a book.

Chris
Grade 12 Remedial Reading Class

Chris has been a student in our schools for 13 years, one of the many invisible students hiding in the classroom shadows, avoiding print texts at all costs (Tovani, 2004). The new emphasis on reading and writing has brought these challenging students sharply to our attention. As educators, we are now examining our programs to see how we can alter or augment our literacy instructional strategies in every curriculum area. Of course, for so many of us, how and what we read today is different from even the nearby past. We choose materials that can easily be handled in short bursts of time; we browse and sample newspapers, professional journals, magazines, Web sites—smaller snippets of text—and struggle to find time for longer items such as novels and biographies. Many selections are highly visual, filled with colored illustrations, detailed drawings, and photographs, with a variety of type fonts and sizes. Just notice how newspapers have changed their formats and styles for a public that reads differently from in the past.

PROMOTING STRATEGIES FOR LITERACY LEARNING

As readers, we need strategies for handling different types of texts. As we read, we continually glean new pieces of information from the text, which we add to our personal knowledge to construct new understandings. Piece by piece, we develop a more complete picture as new information merges with what we already know, and we begin to achieve new insights or change our perspective. Harvey and Goudvis (2000) say that reading involves putting together assorted parts to make a new whole. We synthesize the issues and ideas generated by our reading of a text in light of our own lives. We change what we thought we knew and expand our personal understanding. We move from recounting the new information into rethinking our own constructs of the world. We synthesize our new learning in order to consider the big ideas that affect our lives. Therefore, we want to develop readers who construct meaning by summarizing the content and responding personally to what they have read, by reflecting on their process of reading and assimilating these aspects of learning into a holistic understanding of being literate.

> We want to develop readers who construct meaning by summarizing the content and responding personally to what they have read, by reflecting on their process of reading and assimilating these aspects of learning into a holistic understanding of being literate.

We want students to weigh evidence from the text, to form their own opinions and judgments, and to combine textual information with their own background knowledge. They need to draw conclusions and apply logical thought to substantiate their interpretations. We want readers to make and to recognize informed opinions (Beers, 2003).

We want our students to work toward independence as readers of different texts; we want them to recognize that reading is the negotiated meaning between the author and the reader (Rosenblatt, 1978). How can we help students think carefully about the texts they read, to become aware of how literacy works?

There is a time and place for every kind of reading: reading for the big picture and reading for details. We need to see how the details fit together to form a whole and move toward sifting essential ideas and synthesizing our final thoughts. Allen

(2002) remarks that some students note details and main ideas, writing them down in notebooks and highlighting them in their textbooks, but are still unable to make meaning with the text. What strategies can we give them for determining what matters, which points will be significant, which details will affect their meaning making, and what connections they can determine?

Lists of predigested and impersonal comprehension questions are no longer part of my life or my classroom teaching. My questions should grow from conversations about the text, from the students' honest revelations of their own concerns as I try to guide them into deeper interpretations. I try to ask questions that are driven by their inquiring dialogue, as I would in a conversation with peers during a book club session, based on my listening to their interactions.

RESPONDING TO TEXT: DEEPENING AND EXTENDING COMPREHENSION

Students need opportunities to deepen and expand their understanding of complex texts in every curriculum area. When their reading experiences are extended and supported by their own and their classmates' written and artistic responses, they can move into interpretation and appreciation, understanding the negotiation that is required to participate in the act of reading what others have written. They are learning to consider the complexities involved in the relationship of text and reader. What we look for in responses to reading are instances where students

> There is a time and place for every kind of reading: reading for the big picture and reading for details.

- Challenge previous notions
- Gain new learning through interacting with others
- Discover a new way of viewing a character, a report, or an event
- See the text in a larger context
- Check the accuracy of their predictions
- Consider questions that were answered and others that were unanswered
- Review the main themes of the text
- Think about what they have read and link it to their existing knowledge
- Question, compare, evaluate, and draw conclusions from their reading
- Reflect on the experience of the text and incorporate it into their lives
- Represent their interpretations in a different mode, such as poetry

However, sometimes students spend more time on their responses to a text than on the act of reading. We need to support them while they are reading, for the accumulation of positive, meaningful reading experiences will drive them forward to become proficient readers and writers. Through carefully designed response activities, we can nudge them into different, divergent, and deeper levels of thinking, feeling, and learning.

TALKING OUR WAY INTO UNDERSTANDING

Some students develop a deeper understanding of a text when they can share personal meanings and responses. Such forums include talking with classmates and the teacher in literature circles, book clubs, and reading groups. By going public, students increase the connections they can make with those who are reading alongside them, where individual responses are both shared and altered by the contributions of others and by the support of the teacher. Literacy understanding can't be demanded, but it can be nurtured and supported.

Students need opportunities to deepen and expand their understanding of complex texts in every curriculum area. When their reading experiences are extended and supported by their own and their classmates' written and artistic responses, they can move into interpretation and appreciation…

We need to revise how we deal with students who don't find reading easy, enjoyable, or worthwhile. We can help them find reasons for reading rather than simply demanding that they read (although structured time and expectations that reading will occur are part of the solution).

> Independent reading time during school hours is necessary for enhancing reading abilities and encouraging a positive attitude toward books and reading. Providing suitable resources is the first hurdle; then, we need to support silent reading for these students, sitting nearby or chatting quietly at appropriate checkpoints to clarify what is happening in the story.
>
> Reluctant readers also need successful experiences with literature circles, where they focus on the big ideas as well as the words and structures. The groups should be of mixed ability, with the children selecting the books they want to read. Offering a wide range of suitable and appropriate books or anthologies is important so that we can accommodate the various stages of literacy development in our classrooms. Sometimes, we can allow those less able readers to listen to the book on tape, or have it read aloud to them by an older book buddy, so that they can enter a group discussion as full-fledged members.
>
> We need to model how we take part in literary discussions, encouraging participation through prompts and questions during the talk time, modeling appropriate behavior with our own responses, and inviting students into the conversation. When reluctant readers reveal that they, too, have ideas and thoughts about the text and its connections to the world we share, and when they begin to adopt main roles in the discussion, then we can see authentic evidence of their literacy growth.
>
> We need to help reluctant readers think about what they have read through a variety of activities. For example, as they connect their reading with their writing, they are strengthening their understanding of the text and making connections with their own meaning. As they participate in building graphic organizers in the form of webs and charts, they can often see the relationships between the characters in a story or the facts in an information text. (Booth, 2002, p. 44)

LITERACY AND LITERATURE

I have spent most of my life in schools as a language arts teacher, and the lens through which I have observed most learning has focused on books for young people. I have worked with children, teachers, and parents for decades, attempting to persuade them that a curriculum full of worthwhile books is one of hope for enriching young people's lives. But with the recent findings and information on the

I want each reader to be able to read whatever texts he or she wants to or has to read and to approach each text confidently, critically, and perhaps appreciatively.

new literacies (see Clifford & Friesen, 2004), I am changing my views on what matters most: I want each reader to be able to read whatever texts he or she wants to or has to read and to approach each text confidently, critically, and perhaps appreciatively. These thoughts are supported in the new Ontario Ministry of Education (2003) document *Think Literacy*.

We need to move toward supporting readers' decisions about the print resources they select—their newspapers, novels, and magazines, their work and organizational materials, and what they read for fun and games. As with films and television, appreciating literature is a lifelong process, dependent on many factors. It especially depends on the readers' attitudes toward texts, often determined by their school experiences. What we need to consider in our teaching is how to increase the options that print resources can offer and how to explore with students how different texts work—what to look for and what to expect—so that they can be informed about the choices they will make and select the resources that will give them the most satisfaction.

How can we support students who are reluctant readers to read what educators have labeled literature? As teachers, we have all experienced the disappointment that comes from a student revealing his or her boredom with what we had felt was a significant piece of literature. Finding appropriate and interesting books for our students is a complicated task, but it is at the center of our struggle to help them become appreciative readers, intent on extending their own knowing. Backgrounds and abilities differ widely in the students we meet, and yet, we need to help each of them to begin to consider their responses to different texts, to reflect on why they feel as they do, and to consider the author's role in determining how they responded to these ideas and words. Not surprisingly, teaching for deep understanding may hold the answers to many of the common problems teachers face in promoting literacy strategies with their students.

OWNING THE READING

We will need to discover the real reading interests of our students. They will need to sense ownership of their reading and writing selves by having opportunities to select some of the books they read, the topics they write about, and the projects they research. They will care more about activities they feel are their own, and they will want to invest their time and interest in them.

Many parents want their children to read the classics. Today, many readers still enjoy them, but as reading tastes and writing styles change, readers may make alternative choices. Students can find in the classics a different life from their own in terms of language, custom, place, time, or circumstance; for some, these differences can make the reading difficult. Independent readers may relish the depth of language and content that makes up classics; often, the media repopularize an old book, breathing new life into it, as we have seen with *Lord of the Rings*. On the whole, however, we should tread lightly in pushing these books, recognizing that our goal is literacy for students within the richest viable context we can create for them (see Booth & Barton, 2000).

The literacy canon for youngsters has not altered much over the last 30 or 40 years. The same novels are used throughout most school districts in North America, without much awareness of equity or gender issues or whether young people are being prepared for a literacy life. *Catcher in the Rye, To Kill a Mockingbird, Lord of the Flies,* and *A Separate Peace* appear on virtually every class book list. They are often read and analyzed chapter by chapter, with too little attention paid to the impact of choice and teaching strategy on the future literacy lives of the students. But reluctant readers tell us they want action, raw humor, familiarity, and complex illustrations; in contrast, teachers prefer elegance of story structure, sophistication of character development, complexity of description, irony, and references to other literature. How will we negotiate these differences in promoting literacy for deep understanding?

> We will need to discover the real reading interests of our students.

Young people are inundated with so many texts from television, cereal boxes, advertising, and computer games. How will a text medium full of long, uninterrupted print passages compete with the visual and aural sensations that beat on them and catch them in Jobe's (Jobe & Dayton-Sakari, 1999) "web of immediacy"? Can we use the range of powerful literature we have access to for motivating reluctant readers into exploring the ideas, the other worlds, the information, the surprises, the sense of imagination contained inside the very books they too often disdain? What if these readers could find themselves engaged in a powerful book they couldn't put down? What would change in their reading lives? Would they forget their reading difficulties and simply read? Why are some teachers and parents able to find the right books for those children who are at such a difficult stage in their reading lives? To develop a curriculum for supporting deeply structured literacy learning with today's students requires a careful rethinking of these questions.

THINKING DEEPLY AND WIDELY

Deep understanding requires an analytical approach involving a careful examination and consideration of the text, whether it is print or another form of media. We search for informed opinion, ideas that can take us beyond our own limitations and stretch and enrich us, so we bring more depth of understanding to what we have experienced. Wilhelm (2001) says we have to help students hear their own thinking about a text "out loud."

> ... the students led me in a different direction and opened up for me a new understanding of the book. This can only happen when we as teachers follow rather than lead the response to the text by those who were deeply involved.

In working with a Grade 6 class in a suburb of Toronto, I read to them *Ghost Train*, by Paul Yee (1996), about a young girl whose father left China for Canada in the 1870s to work in the gold fields. When his letters stopped, his daughter made her way to the new land to attempt to find him. A gifted artist, she sold her paintings to pay her way, only to discover that her father had died in a mining accident. However, he returned to her in a dream and asked her to paint the ghost train that carried the lost souls of those who had died without proper burial in China and to take the painting back home, burn it, and bury the ashes that represented the remains of the lost workers. For the students, the tension of the story lay in the girl's having to destroy her painting of the train. They felt that was all she had of the memory of her father's life after he had left her. Some were upset that she obeyed his wishes; others felt she had no choice. We then gathered in two groups representing the two views, and I asked each group to persuade the other to change their minds.

Their arguments revealed unusual depth of thought:

First student:	By burning the painting, the dust of the remnants of the painting will filter through the very air the descendants will breathe, and those men who died will live on forever.
Second student:	The painting is only a representation of the dream she had in the New Land. Her returning to China with the story is the actual burial. The truth is now known, just as when the dog tags of the U.S. soldiers were brought back from Vietnam. That is the returning of the souls to the homeland.
Third student:	She should sell the painting. The mission is complete. The souls are at last home. The money she receives from the sale will sponsor her career. That will be the return of her father's true spirit, giving her the strength to build her life as an artist.
Fourth student:	The train she saw was actually in her dream and was telling her to go home, to return to China. It was her own soul she had to save. Dreams are just symbols; you have to interpret them. (Booth, 2001, p. 38)

In my own reading of the book, I had not thought of the episode as a dream. I know how this author fuses folklore and history, and I had accepted this as a tale that he incorporated to illuminate the struggle of the immigrants. But the students led me in a different direction and opened up for me a new understanding of the book. This can only happen when we as teachers follow rather than lead the response to the text by those who were deeply involved. They listen to the story and observe the pictures, but they also experience the telling and the teller, as well as the force of the audience who is sharing in the experience. Why would they not have had a different experience from me? We can discover with our students what they think they saw and heard and felt, helping them to come to grips with their own and others' perceptions. I change as they change. The story text, the conversation text, and the drama text wrap us, as readers, in layers of new meanings.

LITERACY AND THE PLUGGED-IN GENERATION

As parents and educators, we need to be aware of the power and popularity of technology both in and outside of the classroom. We can no longer view the texts we use during literacy teaching as primarily written or linguistic—texts are made up of images, of sounds, of movement. The texts that students read and enjoy at home are print and electronic. Our choice of texts in the classroom needs to reflect the multimodality seen on the Web and in CD-ROMs to appeal to students' reading behaviors. Yet, computer use can be balanced by programs involving print resources that connect the students to the worlds they inhabit while at the same time stretching their abilities and interests; we can include novels, biographies, poems, columns, and articles that represent the best writers we can find who will enrich the lives of our students. Resources that touch the emotions and the intellect have a much greater opportunity for moving readers into deeper frames of understanding. Aesthetic knowledge lets us see further and to sense the "as if," the hallmark of thoughtful, mindful citizens (Greene, 1995).

> We want to encourage students to become more critical in their use of all media, including the Internet; therefore, we need to teach them to be active and critical readers who can make the most connections possible.

We want to encourage students to become more critical in their use of all media, including the Internet; therefore, we need to teach them to be active and critical readers who can make the most connections possible. This will be best achieved through teachers who are committed to reaching their students, to providing resources that are accessible and relevant and that move students beyond where they began (Lyons & Pinnell, 2001).

Mary Jo is one of these teachers. We met her student, Chris, at the beginning of this article. Mary Jo revels in the challenges her students bring and recognizes that we cannot lose even one opportunity to offer a student a chance at growth through literature experiences. Her letter reveals her determination to move this boy along the path, to nudge him into deeper learning than he thought he could manage. And like all good teachers, she rose to the challenges. As you will see from his next journal entry, Chris did indeed drink from a deeper well (see Booth, Green, & Booth, 2004).

Dear David,

Chris informed me that there was no way that he could read a novel and that now of course he was going to fail and it was surely my fault. I suggested "Monster" by Walter Dean Meyers.

"No, I told you I can't read."

"What if I get you the tape? We could go to the library right now."

He agreed. In the library there are NO TAPES. Nobody can find them. I offered Chris some other suggestions, i.e., Stephen King. I got the book. The bell rang! Chris heads for the door—no book, no tapes, no plan, and no hope? In desperation I called out to him that I would be back in the library at 1:00 P.M. if he wanted to try again.

At 12:50 P.M. I am back in the library searching for the damn tapes. The librarian had put them away for me. At 1:00 P.M., who comes strolling through the door but Chris, reeking of smoke?

"Glad to see you. Found the tapes. What do you think? Do you want to give them a try?"

Chris still isn't sure he wants to play the game but finally says, "Yeah, sure." The librarian asks for Chris's card but of course he doesn't have one. I announce that I am signing the tapes out for Chris because he really wants to read this book. Now the policy has to be explained about teachers not signing materials out for students. I assure her that I know what I am doing and this is Chris and he came back to the library just to pick up these tapes so he could read the book tonight.

Wednesday morning. 8:10 warning bell. Chris comes striding down the hall—right up to me . . . and the words are tumbling out . . .

"Miss . . . you know the court room, like I could see it in my mind and . . . I knew just knew what he meant . . . I am not finished yet but I could see it just like he said. I will finish it tonight. I really like the way . . . "

I will never forget the excitement in his voice and the sparkle in his eye.

Mary Jo

Reading Journal Entry 5

Before even opening the book, I thought that I might be able to relate to it, but the only problem was that I am a very slow reader and I only had four days to complete my report on "Monster." I had talked to Mrs. O'Brien and asked if there was a tape of "Monster" that I might be able to listen to because I did not have any faith that I would be able to finish this book on time if I did it independently and she was nice enough to take me to our school library and get the tape for me. I knew I would be able to finish the book in time if I had someone read it to me as I just followed along. I brought the tape home and played it while following along, while writing my report step by step on what I had learned so far from the book.

What interested me about the book was that Steven was a lot like me because he too got caught up with the wrong crowd and committed crimes that could have been avoided. Steve was intimidated by bullies, too, and got charged with a crime that he truly had no part in . . .

My feelings on the book at the point where I was halfway done in my project were amazing and I say this because I don't like reading, but I found something that I could relate to and that made the project worthwhile. I knew what it was like when handcuffs get placed on you and you are read your rights for the first time, and the only way I could describe my feeling at that time to someone that has never experienced that before, is you feel like you are so alone and there is no one to help.

I have almost graduated from my school and am pleased to say that I will never be returning to that life style again. "Monster" helped me realize that I can do anything I put my mind to and if it wasn't for my teacher helping push me to work hard, I would never have finished my report and passed that class. I have been told time and time again that life is too short to be messing around, and I would have to say that everyone is right.

7

Imagine . . .

An Enlightening and Empowering Science and Technology Education

Larry Bencze

Larry Bencze challenges us to imagine a better science and technology education that is more enlightening and empowering for all students. He suggests that we need to "do more with less," identifying eight principles to help classroom teachers promote science literacy.

1. How can elementary teachers expose students to diverse ideas and beliefs in science?

2. What changes would need to occur in elementary science classrooms to approach the kind of learning promoted here?

I magine a school system organized and equipped to educate all children to their potential. As John Lennon said, "You may say I'm a dreamer." However, if we don't dream about—and, more important, take action toward—a better science and technology education, we will be allowing many of our children to continue experiencing grave injustices. It is my belief, and that of others who study science education in schools, that school science is overall elitist, conformist, and disempowering. It seems to be geared toward serving the interests of the most powerful members of society. Although it is relatively easy to imagine improved science and technology education, it will not be easy to bring it about because of the power that elite groups have over schooling. Nevertheless, we must not abandon efforts to strive for an enlightening and empowering education for all.

Given the diversity of needs, interests, perspectives, and abilities, along with the situational nature of every teaching and learning event, it is absurd to suggest that there can be a perfect education for all children. There can be only some broad principles to be applied by caring and skilled teachers. Based on considerable support from educational research reports, I would like to suggest that the following principles, if implemented, would provide most, if not all, students with opportunities to become enlightened and empowered in matters relating to science and technology.

EIGHT PRINCIPLES TO CONSIDER

Do More With Less

Perhaps the greatest barrier to effective teaching and learning in science and technology is the sheer mass of content that students are expected to learn in a relatively short time period. Science and technology have long histories and many, many achievements. The list of what could be taught is seemingly endless; there are many well-developed laws and theories and inventions in physics, chemistry, biology, geology, environmental sciences, and space sciences.

There are a few important general domains of learning, including to learn "science" (i.e., achievements, such as laws, theories, and inventions), "about science" (i.e., characteristics of scientists, including, for example, human bias and relationships among sciences, technologies, societies, and environments), and learning to "do science" (i.e., developing expertise for solving problems using appropriate selections of methods of science and technology in unique contexts) (Hodson, 1998). Students also should develop strong ethical positions regarding relationships among sciences, technologies, individuals, societies, and environments. In short, because of the sheer mass of expectations for learning "science," students' learning opportunities in most other domains often are compromised.

> Identifying just what is essential for science literacy for each jurisdiction (such as Ontario) might be needed.

- Excessive content loading (expectations for learning science) also causes teachers to cover concepts too rapidly, giving students few opportunities to apply their learning in meaningful problem-solving contexts, so that most students end up only memorizing (and later forgetting) what they could be learning well. In a sense, the curriculum is "a mile wide and an inch thick." As recommended several years ago, school systems need to "do more with less"; that is, "schools do not need to be asked to teach more and more content, but rather to focus on what is essential to science [and technology] literacy and to teach it more effectively" (American Association for the Advancement of Science [AAAS], 1989). Toward that end, for example, the AAAS identified four themes for science literacy: systems, models, constancy and change, and scale. Identifying just what is essential for science literacy for each jurisdiction might be needed. Progress in that direction has been made by the Peel District School Board (2001) with the recent publication of the document *Enduring Understandings, Learning About the World Around Us.* Once essential outcomes for science and technology literacy have been agreed on, teachers will be able to allow more time for students to consolidate their understanding of each of the concepts, skills, and so on—for example, through using them in science project work. Without determining these essential learnings, the following recommendations (and other possibilities for school science) will be much more difficult. Some useful Web resources along these lines are:

http://www.project2061.org/tools/sfaaol/Intro.htm

http://www.nuffieldcurriculumcentre.org/

Plan for Representative Literacy

Curriculum content in science and technology education tends to prioritize teaching and learning from a white Western male perspective. For example, "around the world, . . . science students are expected to construct scientific concepts meaningfully even when those concepts conflict with indigenous norms, values, beliefs, expectations, and conventional actions of students' life-worlds" (Aikenhead & Jegede, 1999, p. 270). What to know and how one might come to know it needs to represent—as much as possible—the diversity that exists in the world.

> Teachers need to be proactive in ensuring that students gain access to the scientific and technological ideas and skills developed by other cultures.

Much of this diversity will surface from students themselves, depending on the diversity in the classroom—particularly if teachers encourage students to express and explore their preinstructional ideas. That will not likely be enough, however. Teachers need to be proactive in ensuring that students gain access to the scientific and technological ideas and skills developed by other cultures. This is a complex matter, however. Because each teacher is a member of particular subculture, for example, it may be difficult for him or her to fairly represent diverse other subcultures. Also, although students from various subcultures need access to dominating Western scientific knowledge in order to participate in decision making on matters relating to science (e.g., regarding policies on genetically modified foods), they do not necessarily have to change their fundamental belief systems. The concept of border crossing into the subculture of Western science (and back to one's own subculture) has great potential to create more culturally accommodating curricula. It allows people to develop understandings of scientific concepts without becoming committed to them (Aikenhead & Jegede, 1999). Some useful Web links along these lines are:

http://www.upei.ca/~xliu/multi-culture/home.htm

http://capes.usask.ca/ccstu/welcome.html

Choose Practical Curriculum Content

Too often, curricula in science and technology prioritize professionals' knowledge and practices—often leaving students questioning the relevance of what they learn. Although much about professional achievements and ways of working may be important to students—and may become more so in the future—in many ways, their relevance is, indeed, questionable. In particular doubt, for example, is the usefulness of abstract, theoretical scientific knowledge—such as particle theory or theories about magnetism. The decontextualized nature of these subjects tends to discriminate against students who are relatively deficient in cultural capital (Bourdieu, 1983); that is, a richness of thought and action that comes from advantaged life experiences, including encouragement to read and to discuss matters in the abstract. Moreover, despite its high status over a long history, abstract theoretical knowledge is, in many cases, not directly useful for the development of technological innovations or inventions (Layton, 1993). Consequently, despite myths that it is appropriate only for "less able, concrete thinkers" (Fensham & Gardner, 1994, p. 168), many are calling for a science and technology education that emphasizes practical applications familiar to students (e.g., Cajas, 1999; Hurd, 1998). Further support for this recommendation comes from research that indicates that students are more naturally interested in practical applications than in theoretical abstractions (Schauble, Klopfer, & Raghavan, 1991). While more concrete suggestions about the sorts of activities teachers can use in their programs are provided below, some relevant information can be found here:

http://www.scpub.org/home/index.asp

http://www.christineterry.com/mt/

Personalize Teaching and Learning

Teaching and learning in science and technology tends to begin from the perspective of adults' methods and conclusions, as if students' minds were blank slates on which to write. Students tend to begin lessons, however, already possessing ideas and skills relating to what teachers intend to teach. Often, these preinstructional conceptions are different from those in the curricula. Moreover, these ideas tend to be entrenched in students' minds and are more difficult to change as students get older. Claxton (1991) reported, for example, that elementary age children often believe the following from their everyday experiences: weeds are not plants because plants have to be nurtured; steam turns into air once it disappears into the air; light beams travel farther at night than during the day; objects can only move if there is a force on them; cold water freezes faster than hot water; the sun revolves around the Earth, thus explaining sunrise and sunset. Students from different cultures also will have different conceptions of Nature (and how to go about investigating it). All of these ideas and skills need to be honored, despite the extent to which they may differ from conclusions of Western science. Telling students their preinstructional ideas are useless, naïve, or wrong can damage their self-esteem. As well, it is possible that students' ideas, skills, and so on may be better than those of Western science or, as often is the case, more useful for students' particular interests.

Although students tend to hold such preinstructional views, they often are unaware of them—because many of these are subconscious. Accordingly, teachers need to use activities that will help students to make their preinstructional conceptions conscious. Teachers intending to teach students about photosynthesis (chemical reactions in plant cells that convert simple chemicals like carbon dioxide and water

> Further support for this recommendation comes from research indicating that students are more naturally interested in practical applications than in theoretical abstractions.

into sugar and oxygen) could, for example, simply ask students to make observations about seedlings at different stages of growth and explain what they observe. Students also could be asked to predict and explain what would happen to the plants under different circumstances; for example, with more or less light or water. To help students (and the teacher) organize and keep track of these preinstructional ideas, students could be taught to use various visual organizers such as concept maps, mind maps, fish bones, KWL charts, and so on. Some useful Web links along these lines are:

http://www.eduplace.com/graphicorganizer/

http://www.graphic.org/goindex.html

Having become more aware of their preinstructional conceptions, students may reconsider them when presented with alternatives and make these the subject of more personalized scientific investigations or invention projects.

> ...elementary age children often believe the following from their everyday experiences: weeds are not plants because plants have to be nurtured; steam turns into air once it disappears into the air; light beams travel farther at night than during the day....

Avoid Discriminatory Discovery Activities

A widespread and deeply entrenched educational myth is that students should be engaged in doing science to learn science. Discovery learning or inquiry-based learning has a long history and continues to be promoted. These strategies are fine if teachers intend to allow students to discover laws, theories, and inventions that become apparent to them through their inquiries. However, they are highly problematic if teachers expect students to discover ideas that may have taken teams of scientists and engineers many years to develop. Unless students already have conceptions similar to those they are supposed to be discovering, they are unlikely to discover them. Generally, the students who do not have these conceptions in their heads tend to be the ones from disadvantaged backgrounds—who tend to lack the cultural capital (as described above) through which they are likely to acquire these ideas. Such activities, therefore, discriminate against less advantaged students. Invariably, when students do not discover what the lab activities are

> Discovery learning or inquiry-based learning has a long history and continues to be promoted. These strategies are fine if teachers intend to allow students to discover laws, theories, and inventions that become apparent to them through their inquiries. However, they are highly problematic if teachers expect students to discover ideas that often may have taken teams of scientists and engineers many years to develop.

designed to indicate, teachers may, and often do, guide students or tell them what they should have discovered. Such guidance tends to compromise students' self-esteem and their understanding of the nature of scientific knowledge building.

Accordingly, teachers need to use more direct teaching approaches to ensure all students have access to ideas and skills in the curriculum. Before mentioning what kinds of direct approaches to use, however, it is worth noting that these should be used in concert with activities in which students have opportunities to apply the taught concepts, skills, and so on. Teachers could engage students in an interactive (with questions and answers) demonstration of, for example, a particular kind of chemical reaction (e.g., displacement of hydrogen from an acid by a metal). Students could then be engaged in a somewhat less teacher-directed activity intended to enable students to experience these sorts of reactions and, in addition, explore effects on them of various factors (e.g., concentration of acid, type of metal, temperature, etc.). Similarly, teachers could show students a film, video, or multimedia presentation on the Internet and then have them use the ideas or skills demonstrated through these sources in practical activities in class. Some useful Web links along these lines are:

http://www.mhhe.com/socscience/education/methods/resources.html

http://www.crlt.umich.edu/tstrategies/teachings.html

Portray Professional Science and Technology as Realistically as Possible

Often, professional science and technology are cast in the most positive light possible—often obscuring some of their more problematic traits. Students need to learn negative as well as positive aspects. This will enable them, as future participants in democratic processes, to make decisions about public and private matters relating to science and technology. Students can, to some extent, learn about the nature of science and technology by participating in authentic scientific problem-solving activities. They may, for example, design and conduct their own experiments and attempt to develop—like scientists—scientific knowledge from these activities. Their knowledge can be further developed by asking them to reflect on what they did, how it worked out, and how they might improve their investigative activities. However, again, it will be difficult for students to discover many aspects through such implicit activities (a kind of learning by osmosis). They may not, for example, consider negative relationships among science, technologies, individuals, societies, and environments. So, again, teachers need to explicitly (directly) teach some of these ideas and concepts. One successful approach is the use of case studies of science and technology in action. Students can read historical accounts, participate in role-playing activities, and debate various issues surrounding approaches to and effects of science. Some useful Web links along these lines are:

http://www.nuffieldcurriculumcentre.org/

http://www.science.ca/

http://tortoise.oise.utoronto.ca/~lbencze/NoSTedRes.html

http://ublib.buffalo.edu/libraries/projects/cases/ubcase.htm

Enable Students to Construct Their Own Knowledge About Nature

Paradoxically, students seldom get to do science (and technology) in school science. Almost ubiquitously, students are placed in the role of knowledge consumers rather than knowledge producers. Such an education can be indoctrinating, steering learners toward thought and action that serve the interests of those controlling curriculum and instruction. Although students need access to the intellectual riches of their forebears, in a democracy, they also deserve opportunities and expertise to self-determine their thoughts and actions—within safety and resource limits (e.g., space, equipment, and supplies). In other words, students must be given opportunities to be engaged in scientific investigation and invention projects for which they decide the goals, methods, results, conclusions, and ways of reporting. Students might choose, for example, to determine effects on bacterial growth of changes in pH of media (and explanations for this); approaches to protecting public statues from erosion by acid precipitation; effects of various amounts of electromagnetism on time-keeping accuracy of clocks (and possible explanations for apparent effects). Through such projects, students can become much more skilled in and confident with problem solving in science and technology, they can learn some things about the nature of science and technology, and they can develop knowledge and skills unique to their needs, interests, perspectives (for example, cultural and gender), and abilities.

Students asked to sink or swim when conducting their own science projects may often sink, however. Frequently, they lack expertise enabling them to conduct projects independently. Consequently, it is necessary for teachers to provide students with an apprenticeship (Bencze, 2000). Teachers can, for example, model certain techniques—such as how to develop cause-result questions, how to design controlled experiments, how to construct appropriate graphs, how to critique their own methods, how to carefully draw conclusions, or how to debate conclusions with peers. After such modeling, teachers can give students more independence with similar activities. Teachers can act as guides, mentors, or facilitators in these situations. These activities may be partly teacher- and partly student-directed. However, they should still be open-ended, so that they mimic what happens in professional science, where appropriate conclusions are not known ahead of time. Teachers could, for example, give students some materials and equipment—say, yeast, sugar, water, a heat source—and then ask them to design and conduct their own experiments using variables of interest to them (e.g., changes in sources of sugar as they affect yeast carbon dioxide production). Once students gain sufficient expertise and confidence, they can be encouraged to conduct student-directed, open-ended science and invention projects. Some useful Web links along these lines are:

http://www.scientificmethod.com/b_body.html

http://www.dur.ac.uk/richard.gott/Evidence/cofev.htm

http://www.primarydandt.org/home/index.asp

http://njnie.dl.stevens-tech.edu/curriculum/boilproj/index.html

http://tortoise.oise.utoronto.ca/%7Elbencze/InquiryDesignEd.html

http://www.letsdoprojects.ca

Promote Stewardship

Often, science and technology are portrayed as neutral with respect to their relationships among individuals, societies, and environments. There are, for example, many negative effects of technological development and industrialization on ecological environments, and these may receive scant treatment in government curricula,

> . . . students must be given opportunities to be engaged in scientific investigation and invention projects for which they decide the goals, methods, results, conclusions, and ways of reporting.

textbooks, and instructional contexts. Many people are calling, therefore, for a science and technology education that promotes moral reasoning and action on issues involving relationships among sciences, technologies, individuals, societies, and environments (e.g., Pedretti, 2004). Often, these involve engaging students in such issues, enabling them to gain access to related attitudes, skills, and knowledge, and then encouraging them to take action in morally defensible ways. For some resources along these lines, consider these sources:

http://www.projectwild.org/

http://www.urbanoptions.org/SustainEdHandbook/

http://ceres.ca.gov/tcsf/seg/

http://www.secondnature.org/

http://www.earthday.net/footprint/index.asp

REALIZING AN ENLIGHTENING AND EMPOWERING SCIENCE AND TECHNOLOGY EDUCATION

A science and technology education with the characteristics recommended above is likely, unfortunately, to be met with formidable opposition. There is considerable evidence that society is under immense pressure from large businesses to assist them in their efforts to successfully compete in increasingly globalized economic markets (Dobbin, 1998). In dramatic and forthright criticism of the effects of such economization on education, John McMurtry (2003), a well-known philosopher and political commentator, said such market-based education systems aim to employ

> a many-sided corporate plan to convert public and higher education to its permanent and guaranteed profitable exploitation, with the unstated terminus ad quem of this process the reproduction of all present and future students as [enthusiastic and unquestioning] consumers and employees whose desires for commodities and willingness to compete for corporate functions are imprinted reliably into neuronal processes from the moment they enter school to their graduation. (p. 7)

> There are . . . many negative effects of technological development and industrialization. . . . Many are calling, therefore, for a science and technology education that promotes moral reasoning and action regarding issues involving relationships among sciences, technologies, individuals, societies, and environments.

The sort of science and technology education that would exist based on the recommendations above is, in many ways, antithetical to this economic ethic. Through the ideal education described above, more citizens would think and act independently, questioning powerful groups' claims to knowledge, knowledge-building practices, and possible negative effects on individuals, societies, and environments. Clearly, however, in a democracy, all citizens deserve such rights.

To enable a more enlightening and empowering science and technology education to be realized will, therefore, require a monumental paradigm shift in how people view society in general and science education in particular. Various stakeholders—including corporate and government leaders, educators, parents, and others—will need to realize that there is a crisis and that alternative perspectives and practices, such as those briefly outlined above, have been imagined.

8

Understanding Technology

Carl Bereiter

When people talk about technology these days, they often refer only to recent, mainly digital, technology. But our lives are surrounded by technology, some of it very old, and much of it unnoticed. In this chapter, Carl Bereiter outlines an approach to understanding technology that will help equip students for full participation in a knowledge society.

1. Many think of technology as tools. How can teachers help students understand how these tools work?

2. How can teachers encourage their students to see that technology is a result of human thought?

If Benjamin Franklin were to reemerge on the street in a modern city, many things would of course amaze him. He would be puzzled by the number of people who appear to be carrying on conversations with little gadgets held up to their ears, and he would wonder about the vehicles that apparently move under their own power. But he would probably be most fascinated by technology he could understand, for instance, the varied means of people-powered locomotion—bicycles, Rollerblades, and skateboards. Any of these could have been produced in his own day, but he would quickly perceive that they all depend on other technology, such as the technologies that produce smooth sidewalks and streets, which make such conveyances practical. He would marvel at the tall buildings and would wonder how they were constructed, but, like most of us, he would be little aware of the vast amount of technology required to make such structures livable—the heating and air conditioning, the plumbing, the elevators, all of which needed to be specially devised to accommodate buildings of great height.

There are four aspects to an understanding of technology. One is technical: understanding how things work, understanding the engineering and design principles and the bodies of scientific knowledge underlying them. The second is understanding the big picture in its historical and social scientific aspects: understanding technology's development over time and its social effects. The third, and probably the most challenging, is understanding technological thinking and developing the ability to practice it. The fourth aspect is critical and evaluative: understanding the intended and unintended consequences of technology and weighing alternatives. All are important. Although these aspects are interrelated, a sequential dependency needs to be honored: The first kind of understanding facilitates the second, the first two facilitate the third, and the first three kinds of understanding are an important basis for the fourth. Indeed, one of the challenges for technology education is to overcome the kind of sophomoric criticism that reflects ignorance of the technology being criticized, a narrow and ahistorical perspective, and a stereotyped conception of technological thinking.

We now briefly consider ends and means with respect to the four aspects of understanding.

UNDERSTANDING HOW THINGS WORK

There was a time when mechanically inclined people could acquire a fairly deep understanding of the workings of their automobiles and could extend their knowledge by tinkering. That is no longer the case. Like many other common devices, automobiles have become forbiddingly complex in their inner workings, and tinkering is liable to produce unfortunate results. It is not only working devices that have become too complex for nonspecialists to understand but also materials and processes. With no possibility of developing an understanding of all the technology that surrounds their students, educators must decide what, if anything, is worth studying in depth.

Priorities for understanding, it should be noted, are different from priorities for practical knowledge. The most important practical knowledge of technology is that which will help students get along better in their daily lives. The most important technological understandings, we suggest, are those that have maximum potential for demystifying the built environment. Accordingly, the design of a curriculum for technological understanding ought to be grounded in research on what students actually find most mystifying in the technology surrounding them. However, identifying the maximally demystifying concepts is a step beyond, one that cannot be derived directly from such research. Students may wonder how cell phones work, but a direct explanation is likely to leave unexplained how radio transmissions spreading out into the atmosphere get captured

> The most important technological understandings, we suggest, are those that have maximum potential for demystifying the built environment.

and converted back into intelligible signals. Understanding that will serve to demystify not only cell phones but radios, television transmission, and wireless Internet connections.

Other technology principles that have widespread explanatory power are:

- *Error-nulling feedback,* as involved in everything from the centrifugal speed governor on a steam engine to the servomotors on a robot arm
- *Data (digital and analog),* basic to understanding varied types of information technology
- *Switches,* as represented in everything from the common light switch to the transistor
- *Properties of materials*—not a single principle but a range of ways in which natural and manufactured materials meet various needs; for instance, how plastics can be made harder than steel

Many other principles could serve, depending on what research shows to be most mystifying to students of various ages.

UNDERSTANDING THE BIG PICTURE

Historical study should lay to rest the idea that technology is something of recent origin and mainly the product of large American corporations. During the Middle Ages in Europe, when science and mathematics were stagnating, technology was moving ahead, largely through the creative efforts of artisans. During the same period, China was experiencing a veritable golden age of technological creativity. We do not suggest, however, that the history of technology should be taught as a separate subject or branch of history. Instead, it is best understood in the broader context of cultural history. Students will see how Late Stone Age technology gave rise to both intertribal trade and intertribal warfare. They will see how agricultural technology yielded food exports that made cities possible and the revolutionary cultural changes that followed from that. And they will see how steam power and mechanization made possible the growth of modern industries and, by reducing the need for farm labor, provided the workers such industries required. In all these cases, furthermore, the social changes interacted with technological changes, each spurring the other.

An advantage of historical study is that the older technologies are easier for students to understand, thus contributing to demystification. The origins of ancient technologies are usually unknown and open to speculation (there have, for instance, been a number of theories about the invention of the wheel). But from an educational viewpoint, this speculative character can be an asset: Students can play the game, too, and thus engage in what we discuss next as technological thinking.

IMPLICATIONS FOR TEACHING

Understanding technology is advanced by . . .

1. Understanding how things work
2. Understanding the big picture
3. Understanding technological thinking
4. Critical understanding of technology

Historical study should lay to rest the idea that technology is something of recent origin and mainly the product of large American corporations.

Technology's social effects have sometimes been profound yet remarkably unpredictable. Did anyone predict the drastic social changes brought about by the automobile? Or television? Has the computer had effects of comparable magnitude—or will it? Investigating questions like these should bring students to an informed consideration of social aspects of technology. Other questions can broaden their understanding. Why do some technologies catch on and others fail to do so? Are the young always the most ready to take up new technology? What does this imply for an aging population? How justified is the belief that technological barriers will always eventually be overcome?

UNDERSTANDING TECHNOLOGICAL THINKING

Scientific thinking and technological thinking are both characterized by systematic, sustained efforts at idea improvement. Scientific thinking, however, has been extensively examined by philosophers and behavioral scientists, whereas technological thinking has received much less attention. Given that there is little agreement on whether such a thing as scientific method actually exists, it would be presumptuous to suggest that there is a teachable technological method. Students could, however, profit from investigating the stories of major technological achievements, how they came about, and the individual and collective thinking that went into them. Fascinating stories that have much to teach beyond the bare technological bones are those of Watt and the steam engine, the Wright brothers versus Santos-Dumont as contenders for first credit in heavier-than-air flight, Canada's Avro Arrow, and the Macintosh computer.

Besides studying how others thought their way to technological innovations, students should themselves engage in the essential activity of sustained idea improvement. Suggesting how some device or computer application could be improved is a common exercise in creative thinking, but students need to appreciate that this is only a first step, and often the easiest step in technological thinking. They need to work on design improvements that can be carried forward through research that identifies possibilities and obstacles and through further thinking that builds on this knowledge.

> Besides studying how others thought their way to technological innovations, students should themselves engage in the essential activity of sustained idea improvement.

At least some of their work should involve actual construction, testing, and further improvement of technology, using design challenges such as those coming out of the Learning Science by Design project (http://www.cc.gatech.edu/edutech/projects/lbdview.html).

CRITICAL UNDERSTANDING OF TECHNOLOGY

Students are bombarded with advertising aimed at creating uncritical acceptance and an urgent demand for the latest technology. Little wonder that some students react with equally uncritical rejection, amounting to a general cynicism about technological progress. It is true that technological solutions to problems frequently create new and unforeseen problems, which are sometimes worse than the

> By demystifying technology, we free students of the ignorance that treats technology as magic and the fearfulness that often seems to lie behind the more sweeping condemnations of technology.

original problems. Critical understanding starts with the recognition that this is true of action of all kinds, not just technologically based action, and is typically true of inaction as well.

Probably the best protection against both gullibility and cynicism is a solid grounding in the first three aspects of understanding. By demystifying technology, we free students of the ignorance that treats technology as magic and the fearfulness that often seems to lie behind the more sweeping condemnations of technology. A global historical view will impress students that many of humanity's greatest achievements have been technological, but it will also impress them with the importance of social progress and the magnitude of problems that technology has not solved. And, of course, the issues raised in connection with the social science of technology lead directly into critical analysis of innovations. Perhaps the biggest gain, however, will come from the students' developing a feeling for and some competence in technological thinking. In this way, they will see technology as a result of human thought— thought of which they themselves are capable and thought which, like all human thought, is susceptible to error and always open to improvement. They will also be less likely to be led astray by the demonizing of technology developers and by such epithets as technical rationality. By gaining a fuller understanding of such difficult issues as genetic modification and control of greenhouse gases, students will be better able to exercise the kind of judgment required for full participation in a knowledge society.

9

Deepening Understanding and Competence in Social Studies Teaching

Mark Evans

Ian Hundey

Mark Evans and Ian Hundey consider the factors that guide teachers' instructional choices and highlight four instructional frameworks that provide a basis for deepening knowledge and competence in social studies teaching.

1. In your social studies teaching, do you use any of these frameworks for guiding your instruction?

2. How could you apply aspects of these frameworks into social studies instruction and instruction in other areas of the curriculum?

3. Do classroom teachers need additional resources to employ these frameworks?

A number of recent studies illustrate that "teacher expertise is one of the most important factors in determining student achievement . . . that is, teachers who know a lot about teaching and learning and who work in environments that allow them to know students are the critical elements of successful learning" (Darling-Hammond, 1998, p. 6). A critical element of teacher expertise is an understanding of and skill in instruction. Proficiency in this critical element allows both for the teaching of social studies in depth and also for student learning of the deep structures in social studies.

When we completed our teacher education methods courses in the 1960s and 1970s, we were introduced to a rather limited repertoire of instructional practices. In contrast, university methods courses in social studies today typically aim at the development of a broad instructional repertoire—what Bennett and Rolheiser (2001) refer to as instructional intelligence, as an understanding of instruction that involves not only technical competence but also an understanding of the theoretical and research underpinnings. This aim is further supported through foundational components of teacher education programs, which provide a deepened understanding of the overlapping factors affecting teaching and learning (Shulman, 1986; Turner-Bisset, 2001).

Attention to this aim is also reflected in an increasing range of professional learning opportunities offered to practicing teachers by faculties of education, professional associations, and school districts. Indeed, in recent years, there has been growing attention to thinking about teaching and learning in social studies in schools. Reforms in curricula across Canada, as well as initiatives on the part of social studies teachers, have sparked new instructional approaches such as case-based learning, public issues research projects, cooperative learning structures, community-based learning activities, youth forums, and Internet-based inquiries and linkages. An examination of these practices reveals a range of sophisticated learning strategies that attend to deepened conceptual understanding, critical judgment and communication, and building of capacity for personal and interpersonal understanding and involvement, among other objectives (see Evans & Hundey, 2000).

> Official curriculum goals—and ways to achieve those goals—can sometimes be at odds with what we know about effective instruction from both research and practice.

INSTRUCTIONAL INFLUENCES/ INSTRUCTIONAL CHOICES

Teachers' instructional choices relate to a range of factors that underscore not only the complexity of instructional influences but also the difficulty teachers face in making instructional choices.

Approaches to Curriculum

Teachers who follow a discipline-specific curriculum (separate history, geography, politics, and sociology) will make different instructional choices from those who favor an integrated social studies curriculum that blends elements of these disciplines. Some teachers follow the traditional sequence of curriculum planning steps: objectives or outcomes or expectations; teaching and learning strategies; student activities; resources; assessment and evaluation; transition to the next topic; and program review and modification. Others practice backward design, starting with the desired goals or standards in mind in the form of a culminating assessment task or performance, "and then derive the curriculum from the evidence of learning (performances) called for by the standard and the teaching needed to equip students to perform" (Wiggins & McTighe, 1998, p. 8). Whether working through an integrated or subject-based curriculum—using either forward or backward planning—teachers make instructional choices based on their approach to curriculum.

Understandings of Subject Matter

A teacher's understanding of subject matter (e.g., facts and concepts and/or the ways and means by which knowledge is generated and established) influences instructional decisions. Consider the potentially different approaches to the teaching of history. A teacher believing that "the main purpose of history teaching at practically every level below graduate instruction is to teach [knowledge] content" (Bliss, 2002) might emphasize key concepts, events, and turning points, choosing instructional approaches such as a lecture, a lecture linked to cooperative learning structures, or a concept-attainment activity. On the other hand, a teacher believing that history must "deal with multiple causes, conflicting belief systems, and historical actors' differing perspectives" (Seixas, 2002) might emphasize the analysis of primary documents for bias, objectivity, and conflicting interpretations, using constructivist-oriented instructional strategies such as creative controversy.

Understandings of Teaching and Learning

Teachers' understandings of teaching and learning also influence what instructional practices are used in the classroom. Some believe that students arrive at school with certain abilities that continue to develop as they mature and learn. Others believe that experience is the basis of learning. Still others think that students learn through constructing their own knowledge based on personal and collaborative inquiries. Teachers also have varying understandings of specific types of teaching and what is achieved through their use. To take one example, consider the range of teachers' familiarity and expertise with the models of teaching developed by Joyce and Weil with Calhoun (2000). The level of familiarity with these models greatly influences teaching for depth, especially in complex and multifaceted social studies areas such as informed decision making, critical thinking, and ethical reasoning.

Student Characteristics

Student characteristics such as prior knowledge and ability, age and developmental factors, motivation,

FOUR INSTRUCTIONAL FRAMEWORKS

Dimensions of Learning Framework
Positive attitudes about learning + knowledge acquisition and integration + knowledge extension and refinement + meaningful use of knowledge + productive habits of mind

Critical Thinking Framework
Community of thinkers + critical challenges + intellectual tools + assessment of critical thinking

Story-Model Framework
Drawing on the power of the story form/Using that power in teaching

Productive Pedagogies Framework
Intellectual quality + relevance + supportive learning environment + recognition of difference

self-esteem, gender, cultural background, and socioeconomic status may influence a teachers' choice of instructional strategies. Teachers have become increasingly attentive to student diversity and inclusion, especially as they have come to understand how fully traditional instructional approaches serve a dominant or mainstream culture and only a portion of the learners. Choosing culturally responsive instructional approaches is not, however, simply a matter of assessing the cultural mix in a classroom. Significant reform, as Blair and Jones (1998) suggest, "does not involve a simple matching of instruction to cultural features but it is also a matter of adjusting and adapting instruction to meet the needs of all students. It requires a departure from familiar patterns of instruction and a willingness to utilize newer patterns" (p. 9).

Learning Context

Choosing effective instructional practices can also be influenced by the many contextual factors within both the school and community/communities. According to Turner-Bisset (2001), the "socioeconomic level of the catchment area, the type and size of school, the class size, the amount and quality of support teachers and other colleagues give to each other, the feedback teachers receive on their performance, the quality of relationships in the school, and the expectations and attitudes of the head teacher" (p. 17) are just some of the influential factors. Across the community of a school district or a province, curriculum context is an important factor. In recent years, the social studies curriculum has been revised to become more descriptive and more prescriptive in terms of student outcomes. Clearly defined curriculum goals and intentions allow for specificity of instructional focus across the community. Yet, official curriculum goals—and ways to achieve those goals—can sometimes be at odds with what we know about effective instruction from both research and practice. Also, in some jurisdictions, the sheer number of outcomes creates a curriculum overload that gets in the way of wise instructional choices.

All of these factors draw attention to the complexity of instructional influences and the difficulty teachers face in making instructional choices. One way to deal with this difficulty is to make use of instructional frameworks that allow teaching for depth and that also provide mechanisms for reflection, discussion, and further learning about instruction.

FOUR INSTRUCTIONAL FRAMEWORKS

Characteristics of the Four Frameworks

- Applicable across topics
- Set high standards
- Unique features
- Research based

What follows is a brief overview of four instructional design frameworks that respond to a complex and integrated understanding of instruction. These overarching frameworks include not only a whole array of instructional and assessment approaches, but also perspectives from which to analyze instructional practices. In writing this next section, we were very aware that there are many models and frameworks from which to choose. We chose to introduce you to these particular four because they are widely applicable across all social studies disciplines and topics; they have pedagogical integrity in terms of setting high standards for social studies learning; each has at least one unique feature that advances instructional sophistication; and they are the products of disciplined and grounded inquiry.

1. Dimensions of Learning Framework

The Dimensions of Learning (Marzano, 1992b) Framework is an extension of Marzano's (1988) work on cognition and learning described in *Dimensions of Thinking: A Framework for Curriculum and Instruction*. The framework infuses a variety of evidence-informed instructional approaches with the primary intent to improve the quality of teaching and learning. The framework forefronts five key dimensions (Marzano et al., 1997):

Dimension 1—Positive attitudes and perceptions about learning. This dimension acknowledges the importance of using instructional strategies that foster both self-esteem and efficacy and nurture a safe and positive classroom climate.

Dimension 2—Acquiring and integrating knowledge. This dimension refers to the use of instructional strategies that encourage knowledge acquisition: acquiring new knowledge, achieving knowledge retention, and integrating it (scaffolding) with the learner's prior knowledge in ways that help students make sense of the new phenomena in light of their existing beliefs and thought patterns rather than the accumulation of facts.

Dimension 3—Extending and refining knowledge. This dimension focuses on that dimension of learning that encourages students to think more critically and creatively about a social studies theme and/or issue. Instructional strategies that encourage various types of thinking are encouraged:

Comparing

Classifying

Abstracting

Inductive reasoning

Deductive reasoning

Constructing support

Analyzing errors

Analyzing perspectives

Dimension 4—Using knowledge meaningfully. This dimension refers to the dimension of learning that encourages students to use and demonstrate their knowledge in meaningful ways. Instructional strategies highlight ways in which students might demonstrate their capacity to investigate issues and/or problems that stand out in the social studies curricula and/or are of personal interest:

Decision making

Problem solving

Invention

Experimental inquiry

Investigation

Systems analysis

Dimension 5—Productive habits of mind. This dimension is concerned with one's personal approach to learning. Instructional strategies nurture habits viewed as important to various forms of thinking, in particular critical thinking, creative thinking, and self-regulated thinking.

Critical thinking habits (e.g., be accurate and seek accuracy, maintain an open mind, take a position when the situation warrants it)

Creative thinking habits (e.g., generate new ways of viewing a situation, generate trust, and maintain your own standards of evaluation)

Self-regulated thinking habits (e.g., monitor your own thinking, plan appropriately, identify and use necessary resources)

Marzano (1992a, p. 15) stresses that "the five dimensions of learning are not independent of one another" and ought to be used "in complex ways, not in any one set pattern." Learning "is a highly complex set of interactive processes that differ from person to person and from context to context." Instructional strategies offered within this framework keep each of these dimensions in mind.

2. Critical Thinking Framework

The term *critical thinking* has different meanings for different social studies teachers. For some, it has meant the encouragement of healthy skepticism or academic rigor—often in regard to particular issues-based topics. For others, critical thinking has been viewed as a skills area developed through strategies such as problem solving or decision making. These perspectives have resulted in a limited view of critical thinking, relegating it to episodes in the curriculum and heightening tensions between teachers' concerns for covering the core content and their interest in critical inquiries. In recent years, more comprehensive approaches to critical thinking have suggested that it is a fundamental element—the core—for a social studies curriculum.

One recent approach promoting critical thinking as the core of the curriculum is based on the proposition that "critical thinking is in some sense good thinking. It is the quality of the thinking, not the process of thinking, which distinguishes critical from uncritical thinking" (Bailin, Case, Coombs, & Daniels, 1999, p. 288). This approach has been developed within the Critical Thinking Consortium, a nonprofit society consisting of 21 school districts, three universities, and several provincial associations in British Columbia. The consortium's materials define critical thinking as "the thinking through of a problematic situation about what to believe or how to act where the thinker makes reasoned judgments that embody the qualities of a competent thinker" (Case & Daniels, 2003, p. i).

This definition of critical thinking leads to a four-pronged approach to help students improve as critical thinkers (Case & Daniels, 2003):

- Building a community of thinkers within the school and classroom—so that students frequently experience learning opportunities requiring critical thinking, engage in critical and cooperative dialogue with others in the community, critically examine their own work and that of their peers, and see their teachers as models who themselves practice critical thinking and collegiality in learning.

- Infusing critical challenges throughout the curriculum—so that students are deliberately presented with problematic situations that require a critical thinking response. Four questions guide the choice of critical challenges: Does the task require judgment? Is the challenge meaningful to students? Does it reflect key subject components of the curriculum? Do students have the tools to address the challenge, or can they be taught them in addressing it?

- Developing the intellectual tools for critical thinking—so that students have the knowledge, skills, and dispositions to respond to the critical challenges: background knowledge; criteria for judgment; critical thinking vocabulary; thinking strategies; and habits of mind.

- Assessing students' competence in using the tools—so that there is coherence between what is taught in promoting critical thinking and what is assessed and evaluated. The intellectual tools are the basis of the criteria for assessing students' work.

Educators in the Critical Thinking Consortium have been using this critical thinking/critical challenges approach for several years, and an ambitious program of resource publication is under way. Sample social studies activities based on this four-pronged model may be viewed on the Web at https://public.sd38.bc.ca/RTR Web/ProductsPage. You may best appreciate the value and potential of this approach by choosing a social studies topic and working through the framework yourself. Start by developing a question that embodies a critical challenge; for example, Which three factors best explain why settlers moved West in the years 1880–1914?

3. Story-Model Framework

Social studies teachers use stories to help students conceptualize big pictures. They use the stories of interesting people, decisive actions, natural phenomena, and political breakthroughs to illustrate topics within their social studies curricula. Teachers do so because they know that the elements of story—friction, drama, heroism, disaster, triumph, emotion, imagination, and commonalities among peoples—appeal to students' imagination and that they provide powerful tools for learning. Some educators have gone beyond the practice of using stories as part of their instruction to using stories as the basis for planning curriculum and organizing instruction. They see story-based planning as an authentic way to link student thinking to real-world stories and as a means of developing integrated or holistic curriculum. Two educators, in particular, have explored the possibilities of story-models as a basis for curriculum and instruction.

Susan Drake has proposed two approaches. The Journey of the Hero is the basis for many stories throughout time and across cultures. The hero is called to adventure; he or she leaves the kingdom in search of this adventure. Ahead are the demons to be confronted, the dragons to slay (struggle). Finally, the hero slays the dragon, receives a reward, and returns to the kingdom, where he or she must share the lessons of the journey (Drake, 1993). You might see this journey-story as the basis for studying exploration or settlement or the exploits of a human rights reformer. More widely applicable to social studies and more familiar to social studies teachers is Drake's (1992) story model for developing integrated curriculum. This model asks students to look at the present story, examine its roots, speculate about the future story, create a new story, and find personal meaning in the story.

The other educator associated with a story model is Kieran Egan. Egan provides an alternative approach to outcomes-based planning and a counterview to the assumption that teaching must proceed from the concrete to the abstract. His Story Form Model proposes a framework that "draws on the power of the story form and uses that power in teaching" (Egan, 1986, p. 2). His Story Form Model considers the following elements:

1. *Identifying importance:* What is important about this topic? What is affectively engaging about it?

2. *Finding binary opposites:* What binary concepts best capture the affective importance of the topic? (For example, the concept "powerful versus powerless" helps students learn about the rise of unions or the women's movement.)

3. *Organizing the content into a story form:*

   First teaching event: What content most dramatically embodies the binary concepts, in order to provide access to the topic? What image best captures that content and its dramatic contrast?

   Structuring the body of the lesson or unit: What content best articulates the topic into a clear story form?

4. *Conclusion:* What is the best way of resolving the conflict inherent in the binary concepts? What degree of mediation is it appropriate to seek? How far is it appropriate to make the structuring binary concepts explicit?

5. *Evaluation:* How can one know whether the topic has been understood, its importance grasped, and the content learned?

4. Productive Pedagogies Framework

The Productive Pedagogies framework, developed in Australia by the Queensland School Reform Longitudinal Study (SRLS) Group, highlights four broad dimensions: intellectual quality, relevance, supportive classroom environment, and recognition of difference. Productive Pedagogies responds to two central questions: What classroom practices contribute to increased student learning for all students? and What classroom practices contribute to more equitable student learning? The framework requires teachers to think more deliberately about what and how they are teaching, the learning styles and backgrounds of their students, and the contexts in which they are teaching. Various educators and researchers in schools in

Queensland and New South Wales, Australia, have been involved in aspects of its implementation, assorted research studies, and the development of a number of classroom resources and high-quality instructional approaches (New South Wales Department of Education and Training, 2003, p. 4).

The following is an overview of the Productive Pedagogies framework:

Dimension 1—Intellectual quality. This dimension focuses on knowledge acquisition and knowledge-in-use. Instructional approaches are encouraged that require students to demonstrate deepened understandings and perform tasks that reflect higher order thinking, problem solving, and constructivist forms of thinking rather than a simple transmission of information (New South Wales Department of Education and Training, 2003, p. 2).

Higher-order thinking

Deep knowledge

Deep understanding

Substantive conversation

Knowledge as problematic

Meta-language

Dimension 2—Relevance. This dimension emphasizes the need to ensure that the focus of learning is relevant to students and to themes and/or issues of significance outside the classroom. Instructional approaches are encouraged that help students examine real issues and real-world problems and make connections to their past experiences and background knowledge and the world beyond the classroom.

Knowledge integration

Background knowledge

Connectedness to the world

Problem-based curriculum

Dimension 3—Supportive classroom environment. This dimension focuses on the importance of creating an inclusive learning environment that is respectful and attentive to the diverse learning needs of all students, particularly students from disadvantaged backgrounds. Instructional approaches that provide social support for students' achievement, academic engagement, and a high degree of self-regulation and direction are encouraged.

Student direction

Social support

Academic engagement

Explicit quality performance criteria

Self-regulation

Dimension 4—Recognition of difference. This element, often silent in other instructional approaches, focuses on the importance of valuing individual and cultural difference, in particular nondominant cultural knowledges. Instructional approaches that attend to the "recognition of differences" and "encompass inclusivity of non-dominant groups" are stressed.

> Cultural knowledges
>
> Inclusivity
>
> Narrative
>
> Group identity
>
> Active citizenship

This framework assumes that the four broad dimensions of learning are being infused throughout the particular social studies course and that instructional activities and strategies being used are congruent with the focus of learning. As with the Dimensions of Learning framework, an aspect of one dimension may be infused into a particular lesson or unit or aspects of various dimensions may be integrated into a lesson or unit to achieve more sophisticated learning outcomes.

CONCLUSION

Teachers use different kinds of knowledge in various combinations when making choices about instruction. What teachers think affects what they do. Highly competent teachers build up a complex instructional repertoire that incorporates and integrates understandings of the curriculum, subject matter, processes of teaching and learning, characteristics of learners, and the learning context(s). Attempting to build this instructional repertoire in the form of a thick cookbook of accumulated strategies can be a daunting exercise and may lead to instructional chaos.

The four instructional design frameworks provided in this article offer contexts for thinking about instruction in deeper, more holistic, and integrated ways rather than seeing it as simply a collection of all known strategies. These frameworks, all the products of disciplined and grounded inquiry, attempt to respond to deepened understandings of instruction by providing navigational aids as you think and act as a social studies teacher. They provide varying perspectives within which ongoing professional learning might be stimulated and thoughtful instructional choices might be made to advance theoretical sophistication, technical know-how, and student learning in the development of effective social studies instruction.

10

Imagining Drama/Theater and the Arts

Kathleen Gallagher

In this chapter, Kathleen Gallagher illustrates what it might mean to teach for deep understanding through the arts, and in drama classrooms especially, while imagining that the demanding work of curriculum development for a new era be placed firmly and confidently in the hands of teachers.

1. How can elementary teachers use this perspective on the importance of drama across the curriculum?

2. How can we ensure that drama and other aspects of the arts curriculum are valued in achieving our goal of teaching for deep understanding for all students?

In our education system, theatre and drama must preserve their urgency and become a place where self-creation, imagination, and dialogue are still possible; where the engagement of people in productive conflict and thought can be generated.

(Gilbert, 2003, p. 113)

S chools, in most parts of the world, are recognized as the primary instrument for improving the lives of children and youth, while the arts in education are frequently seen as one important route to academic and social success for young people, particularly those students perceived to be most "at risk" of failure. The arts increase possibilities for collaboration across social divides and academic differences and help us to better understand the complex pedagogical and social relations particular to classrooms. Among school subjects, drama/theater is unique. It is both about itself and about the world we inhabit. In its finest curricular and pedagogical capacities, theater/drama education has a powerful role to play in the globalized environment of Ontario schools. Drama, in many Ontario classrooms, illuminates the intersections of youth's personal and cultural lives with their school lives in the formation of their social and academic identities. Teaching for deep understanding through drama and the arts is, therefore, both essential and difficult work.

Drama provokes a curriculum and pedagogy that draws from young people's experiential, cultural, and "home" knowledges. It asks teachers to work not from textbooks but from the very substance of their students' lives. As students shift into role-play in drama classrooms, they are aware of their position in the class relative both to their peers and to the role they are inhabiting; the device of becoming somebody else through moving into a role introduces a range of choices perhaps otherwise unavailable to these students. But to what extent are their choices bounded by concerns for how they will be viewed by their classmates or teacher? What strategies should teachers consider when asking students to engage in improvised performances and collaborative projects?

> For teaching to result in discerning curriculum understanding, we must forestall the compulsion to evaluate, in often perfunctory ways, every step of learning.

In our research, we have observed that without certain aesthetic and pedagogical footholds, students' social concerns—saving face, hiding their vulnerability—will wash away the first tentative steps they take toward the wider world of their potential and mire them in what one of my research assistants has aptly observed as "an everyday cycle of gains and losses."

The principles put forward in the following pages come from both my experience of teaching drama and my current research project, which examines the experiences of youth in urban drama classrooms (two in Toronto and two in New York City).[1]

---

[1]This research project, "Drama Education, Youth and Social Cohesion: (Re)constructing Identities in Urban Contexts," examines the experiences of youth in urban drama classrooms in order to develop a theoretical and empirically grounded account of the dynamic social forces of inclusion and exclusion experienced by adolescents within their unique contexts of urban North American schooling. The ethnography of four urban sites (two in Toronto, two in New York City) is concerned with investigating the extent to which drama education in classrooms illuminates the intersections of youth's personal and cultural lives with their school lives in the formation of their social, artistic, and academic identities. We are interested in observing how the social (everyday) performances in classrooms inform, influence, or interfere with aesthetic and academic processes. We suggest a theoretical approach for researchers that might open onto pragmatic actions for classroom teachers who need, often in the moment, to address behaviors that limit students' capacities to fully participate in, and learn from, their classroom activities and one another.

FIVE PRINCIPLES TO CONSIDER

The Process of Learning Through Drama Takes Time

For teaching to result in discerning curriculum understanding, we must forestall the compulsion to evaluate, in often perfunctory ways, every step of learning. Teaching for deep understanding means appreciating that the quality of the process will have a direct impact on the quality of the product. Doing drama is a process, as I have argued elsewhere (K. Gallagher, 2000), often simultaneously involving a loss and a discovery of realities as students respond to abstractions or fictional worlds, both their own and the inventions of their peers. Too often in education, we have given curriculum over to its "intended" or quantifiable outcomes without allowing the time and space for the process of working to evolve, take shape, and challenge old ideas. If drama is meant to engage the imaginative, cognitive, and affective elements of learning, then time must be taken for the reflective and pre-evaluative moments of curricular engagement. In drama, this might mean written or oral reflections within the drama work or postdrama reflections that help students to begin to make meaning from the kinesthetic and embodied experiences of the drama work.

The skill of improvisation is key to drama learning, whether this takes the form of students performing in scripted theater pieces or devising their own plays and characters. Improvisation is difficult to evaluate precisely because the outcomes are often not known or difficult to predict. Drama in schools must work toward resisting the immediate, often stereotypical improvisations and caricatures—examples of which are legion in television culture—that force young imaginations into stereotypical and narrow notions of creating. While these activities might be playful, even enjoyable, drama in schools must lay claim to the wider range of improvisational activities—in writing, character development, play making, movement—that carefully layer in more complex ways of creating and understanding.

The temptation to evaluate every stage of development must be challenged by teachers of drama who, perhaps unlike teachers in any other subject, have the capacity to immerse students in extended and integrative experiences; students might otherwise experience school as a set of insular and unconnected disciplines. The method, therefore, of teaching through drama allows for the integration of different kinds of subject knowledge. These cross-disciplinary discoveries can then be reconciled with the cultural and experiential forms of knowledge that young people bring to their learning experiences every day.

Drama Is a Dialogic Art Form Productively Powered by Conflict and Tied to the Social Health of the Classroom

As education has, over the last 20 years, moved toward more cooperative modes of learning, research on the complex and often conflictual nature of group learning has not kept pace. The arts, and drama particularly, rely heavily on a group's ability to work cooperatively toward shared goals. Even the more traditional cognitive disciplines have recently favored group strategies for content learning. In other words, as Jenny Simons (1997) puts it: "What we know can be partly retrieved from working with our fellow drama students" (p. 199). Simultaneously, school systems have begun to pay greater attention to conflict as it arises in both classrooms

IMPLICATIONS FOR TEACHING

Five principles to consider when teaching for depth in drama classrooms:

1. The process of learning through drama takes time.

2. Drama is a dialogic art form productively powered by conflict and tied to the social health of the classroom.

3. Planning, in drama teaching, is not a lock-step activity that unequivocally dictates the actions of a classroom.

4. The drama classroom connects with the community and makes central the student's world.

5. The projects of theater and the arts are the projects of life.

Controversial education policies such as Zero Tolerance and Ontario's Safe Schools Act represent attempts made by administrators of education to combat what seems to be growing evidence of violence in our schools.

and school communities. Controversial education policies such as Zero Tolerance and Ontario's Safe Schools Act represent attempts made by administrators of education to combat what seems to be growing evidence of violence in our schools. These policies and other attempts to manage conflict have not always understood conflict between young people as well as they might. I would suggest that part of the problem is that these policies operate as though violence is the natural outcome of conflict. As a drama educator, however, my perspective on conflict, and its potentially rich relationship to the curriculum, is rather different.

The productive exploration of conflict, rather than its management, does not repress or pathologize one's often-healthy desire to differentiate oneself from others. Instead, it demystifies those issues that seem to stand between students, often preventing them from engaging in collaborative work. The drama curriculum itself hinges on conflict between ideas, rather than between people. Characters, therefore, often represent positions that are at odds with one another, but these are situated characters within the drama, and they signify particular interests and investments. When students have the opportunity to examine conflict in the context of the drama world, they often begin to better understand what is at stake for self/other in their actual working relationships in the classroom. It is this analogous way of working in drama that helps students bring important "real life" understanding to their experiences of conflict, both within the school and beyond.

The intersubjective experience of making drama stands apart from other disciplines. In exploring this shared experience of making drama, different perspectives on assumed agreement can be productively generated. The eruption of conflict often signals a clash of structures of relevancy between students. The possibility, then, in the arts is to challenge and enlarge the "relevant worlds" of differently situated young people. Thinking about arts processes, Deborah Britzman (2001) makes this key observation: "We might also come to know something of our own complexity through encountering the complexity of others" (p. 18).

In my previous study of adolescent girls and drama (K. Gallagher, 2000), I discovered that, at a developmental stage often marked by contradiction and conflict, young girls were beginning to better understand themselves and others within larger social groupings by engaging in the dialogic art form that is drama. Creating with others leads us toward a deeper and more differentiated understanding of ourselves. The aesthetic impulse to contemplate and frame the detailed workings of dramatic action makes the small loom large. Harvesting self-contradiction through role-play and encouraging a multiperspective view of life promotes both questioning and self-questioning. Avoiding clichés, searching for fresh expression, allowing for new ways to look at old subjects—all of these support more complex views of human beings. And this kind of complexity is greatly needed in schools. Rosa, a Grade 10 student in my study, put it this way:

> I learned that in every situation everyone views their own story as the truth, builds up their own truth. And through acting out different points of view we understood why everyone wanted their story to be the truth. (K. Gallagher, 2000, p. 135)

In my current study of schools in Toronto and New York, I was interviewing a teacher, attempting to understand her idea of success in her drama teaching. I asked her to share three anecdotes from the semester that she would identify as artistically or academically successful moments in her classroom. What became immediately apparent is that this teacher identified moments of success that were also clearly moments of community in her classroom, moments where the social health of the classroom was in evidence. The students, too, readily identified the impact of group dynamics and classroom social health on the quality of their learning in drama.

In richly diverse classrooms, we clearly need to understand more about each other to break down the obvious barriers that get erected between students. The importance of the social health of the classroom cannot be overemphasized. Rather than managing conflict when it arises in classrooms, teachers and students need to work toward understanding the complexities of group dynamics. Putting students into groups and calling the activity cooperative can have devastatingly negative effects on student learning. In drama especially, trust is required, but the idea of trust must be understood by teachers as a performative act. Trust is negotiated moment by moment; trust is not a state that can be achieved for all time. The negotiation of trust among peers has something to do with making the classroom, the school, and by extension, the world a safer and more humane place. If any progress is to be made, if we intend for students' engagement with subject matter to be strengthened, we must prioritize the health of the classroom environment and pay careful attention to the inevitable conflicts that will ultimately improve students' understanding of one another.

> In richly diverse classrooms, we clearly need to understand more about each other to break down the obvious barriers that get erected between students. The importance of the social health of the classroom cannot be overemphasized.

Planning, in Drama Teaching, Is Not a Lockstep Activity That Unequivocally Dictates the Actions of a Classroom

Pedagogically, drama is a fascinating discipline. In its freedom to replay, rehearse, and repeat activities, deeper understanding is always possible. Planning, in drama teaching, is not a lockstep activity that unequivocally dictates the actions of a classroom. Planning means learning to be clear about expectations for students and anticipating how our actions—as teachers and facilitators—will be received by them. Quantz (1992) argues that "culture should always be understood to refer to both the structured patterns of a group and the meanings members give those patterns" (p. 486). Knowing our classroom contexts, in all their idiosyncrasies, is an important first step in the pedagogical planning process. What meaning structures might students bring to the drama scenarios we prepare for exploration?

Anticipating what students may think or feel is a common planning technique of teachers. Drama teaching should always build in the opportunity to revisit and reconsider ideas and pedagogical choices and espouse a belief in what I have called "survivable failure." We afford students the possibility of "trying again"; we must afford ourselves the same flexibility. In the classroom, we must all be able to revise our stories of who we are and what we know. I can think of few things that will extend and deepen the teaching and learning enterprise more effectively.

> Part of what powers teachers in the classroom is what they receive from their students. We ignore this essential part of the equation at our peril.

I have observed before (K. Gallagher, 2000) that teachers of drama are, at once, both inside and outside the curriculum. In the fictional play of drama, teachers are both "senders" and "receivers" in and out of role:

> Drama teachers as part of their craft must know how to "give up" power in role, to direct the drama from various registers within the context of the group. Drama teachers must often "feel" when to move in and when to move out. (p. 114)

Curriculum theorist Madeleine Grumet (2000) suggests that recently, we have been "too far 'outside' the work, concerned about skill acquisition and process, losing the texture and specificity of substance" and that "in the old days we were only inside the work, curled in its phrases, circling its history and structures" (p. xi). And so she agrees that the brilliance of good pedagogy is found in this mutable and shifting movement the teacher makes between the inside and the outside of the students' connection to the world of the curriculum.

The Drama Classroom Connects With the Community and Makes Central the Student's World

Pioneering drama practitioner Dorothy Heathcote once explained in an interview that she was not at all sure how to teach teachers, but she did think it had something to do with teaching teachers how to receive. She was referring, I believe, to that aspect of pedagogy that is given much less attention in faculties of education and professional development workshops. Part of what powers teachers in the classroom is what they receive from their students. We ignore this essential part of the equation at our peril. There are many unanticipated reactions and responses to the curricular work we structure for our students' learning. If we truly think about drama as a dialogic art, then our pedagogy must take serious account of the responses we plan for, as well as those that we least expect, from our students.

In an interesting analogy, Rebecca Martusewicz (2001) has compared the idea of pedagogy to that of a choreographed skater's performance. In this appealing metaphor, she imagines that the choreographer of the skater's routine structures the moves and gestures that the skater must execute. It is not the simple execution of the dance that is most important, however, but what happens between the choreographer and skater that is most exciting. She recounts:

> For while I may have had a specific idea in mind and worked hard to define that idea within the set of gestures and moves, the very relation between my idea and Erin's enactment of it vibrates with the power of difference. (p. 45)

There is, therefore, variance in form with each new performance and among different performers. Although we may understand this philosophically, as teachers, it is nonetheless difficult to stay the course in an age of standards and exemplars. Add to this the very real concerns of increased class sizes, greater disparities in academic abilities among learners, and the host of other social and academic concerns teachers bring to their classroom and the attractive dance metaphor can easily lose its appeal and relevance.

These challenges often explain why we find new teachers searching for recipes, searching for ways to easily translate the curriculum goals into generalizable formulations that can be universally applied to specific contexts. Hannah Arendt's (1958) thinking about the human condition is particularly useful here. She argues that *action,* unlike *behavior,* means taking initiative or setting something in motion. She observes that the character of "startling unexpectedness" is inherent in all beginnings. That is, in the classroom, the dialogue, the tensions between the particular and the general, the collaborations and conflicts fuel the pedagogical movement and must not be seen as either insignificant to, or a distraction from, the main event. Scholar and arts advocate Maxine Greene (2001) likes to help teachers think about moving from the predictable to the possible. The predictable, as she describes it, is what is seen and measured from the outside; the possible is what is seen from the vantage point of the actor, the one with a sense of agency, the beginner. The actor metaphor here works very well. Drama pedagogy asks both teacher and learners to enter together into a shared and negotiated experience to explore the endless possibilities of the fictional, and by extension the actual world.

With our earlier dance metaphor, the choreographer might be striving to find the most beautiful expression of movement. With a pedagogy for the arts, the teacher, too, must decide what this is all in the service of. And the answers to this question vary enormously from teacher to teacher and may significantly shift and change emphasis within one teacher at different stages of her or his career. But having in mind why we teach the way we do is an important piece of developing one's own pedagogical philosophy. Teaching for deep learning requires, I would suggest, that teachers continue to struggle with the broad and philosophical ideas about why we teach the way we do. Some may decide that creating healthy citizens and environments—helping students to think about problems of social justice, for instance—is at the core of their teaching actions. Others may want to inspire their students' passion for a particular discipline or may see it as their primary job to teach students how to learn. However varied the motivations behind our teaching actions, reflecting thoroughly about why we do what we do is central to our growth as artful practitioners.

The Projects of Theater and the Arts Are the Projects of Life

The drama curriculum should be both about what is of utmost interest to students and what may be just beyond their current understandings of the world. It is this push and pull between the experiential knowledge of the learners and the ways in which those understandings can be cast into new and ever-widening realms of understanding that is central to the drama curriculum. The drama curriculum in schools has often aimed to strike the difficult balance between understanding its connection to a great tradition of dramatic literature and providing space in the school where an emergent and creative curriculum can be collaboratively constructed—between teacher and students and among students themselves—based on their interests and their experiential learning, in the Deweyan sense.

For young people, the movie and television frame of reference is powerful. I would propose that deep learning often happens through drama when popular culture is brought into the classroom for creative and critical examination. I have suggested before that television stereotypes have a powerful stranglehold on the imaginations of young people. Rather than banish these aspects of popular culture from school, the drama curriculum has the possibility of (and perhaps even the responsibility for) bringing these images into the classroom for careful and playful examination. It has been my experience, in drama teaching, that students' work becomes riddled with stereotypes when they feel insecure about how to create. Like all of us, they fall back on what is familiar and comfortable. But popular culture consumed uncritically can impoverish the imagination. The drama curriculum, then, is better poised than most disciplines to critically and creatively examine those aspects of popular culture that often compete for students' attention and interest.

The aims of the drama curriculum must be broad and meaningful. Drama will hone theater skills and also afford students the time and space to work through issues that vie for their attention. The curriculum can, therefore, be responsive to the needs of young people in a way that is embedded in the "hard" skills of theater but also attentive to the ongoing popular preoccupations of the young learner.

Ultimately, the arts are about human activity. The projects of theater and the arts are the projects of life. Renowned author and actor Ann-Marie MacDonald (2003) put it this way:

> It is interesting because both those areas—theatre and education—are very, very forgiving at one level, but they are the most rigorous at another. Yet there is also something very humane about both pursuits. The fact that they can tolerate a multitude of ineptitude doesn't take away from the fact that they are driven by excellence, like anything else. It is human activity with a very, very wide embrace. (p. 249)

The how of learning in drama, and the arts more generally, is often privileged over the what. Dramatic learning is hinged on structure, not content, on how action is put together and shaped. In this regard, drama promotes a postmodern curriculum, one in which ideas are pieced together as in a collage of interconnected and sometimes contradictory ideas. Understanding relationships, forging ahead, shaping aesthetic understanding, practicing creative intelligence and problem solving, developing a tolerance for ambiguity, these are the real skills or "outcomes" of the drama curriculum. Drama and the arts are, therefore, good antidotes to some of the more competitive and exclusionary practices of schools. They can provide safe haven for learners through their implicit values of collaboration and shared leadership. The arts accomplish this by robustly respecting the idea that the learning that can be expected for one individual may be very different than for another. Even those with similar backgrounds or experiences, or similar academic abilities, will find their most significant moments in different aspects of this shared experience of the drama curriculum.

It is this push and pull between the experiential knowledge of the learners and the ways in which those understandings can be cast into new and ever-widening realms of understanding that is central to the drama curriculum.

Teaching for deep understanding means both deep understanding of the art forms and media within which we work and deep understanding of the complex world in which we live and create. Again, Maxine Greene (2001) helps us to better understand the role that imagination must play in our encounters of teaching and learning. Aesthetic education, for Greene as for many arts educators, speaks to our efforts to look at things as if

> Drama and the arts are, therefore, good antidotes to some of the more competitive and exclusionary practices of schools. They can provide safe haven for learners through their implicit values of collaboration and shared leadership.

they were otherwise, to imagine a more just, a more generous, a more artful world. In classrooms, we are engaged in this work daily. Greene calls on Herbert Marcuse to support this expansive view of the arts. Marcuse said that the arts do not change the world, but they can change the living beings who might change the world (cited in Greene, 2001). Much is made of this idea of transformation in education. One thing the arts might contribute to this vast area of study and reflection is the importance of invention in our lives. We reinvent ourselves with each new understanding we come to as we imagine ways toward a better social order, toward alternative realities. When we think about the arts in schools, we cannot help but think about the branch of philosophy called aesthetics, which is concerned with questions of perception and imagination and how these things relate to our understanding of the world. This is a rich heritage to which arts educators might lay claim. When the arts become purely functional or mechanistic, as they can in schools, we lose this proximity to important philosophical questions about how we come to know others, the world, and ourselves.

Drama education produces a particular kind of aesthetic awareness because students learn to signify and give meaning to their perceptions, experiences, and ideas through the embodiment of characters in alternative worlds; it is a self-consciously aesthetic response to the curriculum prompt. Maxine Greene (2001) talks about learners who "lend works of art their lives." Others use clay, paint, or song to structure their sensual experiences. The arts curriculum, then, as both methodology and content—or "learning through" and "learning about"— offers spaces in a school where traditional lines that

> I think teaching for deep understanding begins with the learner, who, in the case of drama, uses the medium of language, gesture, and movement in space to give form to tacit understandings.

divide disciplines can be productively blurred and students can imagine themselves and their ideas into the world differently.

To close, can I suggest that an adequate curriculum in the arts is one in which the arts disciplines produce, unapologetically, both works of art and workings of art. That is to say, in the creation and execution of curriculum, teachers must be deeply concerned with both what is made and how it is made, with the products of the arts and the range of richly intersubjective educational processes we invite students into in their art making. No longer can we support the arts as "frill," as appetizer to the main course. The arts are integral to the development of young learners, their intellectual, affective, perceptual, and imaginative development, in short, the crucial sense of themselves as social actors in their world.

PART III

Teaching for Deep Understanding Across the Curriculum

11

Multiliteracies Pedagogy and the Role of Identity Texts

Jim Cummins

In this chapter, Jim Cummins introduces a way to teach for deep understanding in classrooms where linguistic and cultural diversity is the norm and where students are engaged in many forms of literacy practice outside the school. This approach—multiliteracies pedagogy—is supported by research on how people learn.

1. What resources can teachers draw on in their communities to support children from a variety of backgrounds?

2. What multicultural projects would make sense in your classroom? Different languages? Different media? How could these projects be shared with families and the community?

Author's Note: I would like to acknowledge all members of the OISE/UT Multiliteracies Project team and partner teachers in the York Region District School Board and the Peel District School Board who have contributed to the ideas in this paper. In particular, I would like to thank Sameena Eidoo, who assisted in conducting the interviews with students involved with the Shakespearean Festival. The research reported in this chapter was carried out with funding (2002–2005) from the Social Sciences and Humanities Research Council of Canada. To view student and teacher work as well as relevant research, visit www.multiliteracies.ca.

Discussions of topics such as teaching for deep understanding almost inevitably assume a "motherhood" quality. As with motherhood, it is hard to imagine anybody opposing the goal of teaching for deep understanding. No academic has yet made his or her reputation by championing the cause of teaching for shallow understanding. And yet few educators would dispute the fact that despite pious policy statements, good intentions, and often intense commitment on the part of teachers, much of the interaction between teachers and students generates superficial rather than profound understanding of issues and topics.

We have been working collaboratively with educators in the Greater Toronto Area as part of a Canada-wide project (Early, Cummins, & Willinsky, 2002) to explore how to engage students from diverse backgrounds in the kinds of interactions that will result in deep understanding. This chapter sketches the *multiliteracies pedagogy* that is emerging from some of this work, in particular, as it shows the power of what we term *identity texts* in fueling sustained learning for deep understanding.

Several core ideas that form the context of this emerging pedagogical framework are discussed below. These include

- Multiliteracies
- Pedagogical orientations including transmission, social constructivist, and transformative approaches
- Research consensus on how people learn

These constructs set the stage for the description of a framework for the development of academic expertise (Cummins, 2001). The framework differs from many others that have been proposed in that it postulates identity investment as a central component of learning for deep understanding and views the negotiation of identities as a primary determinant of whether or not students will engage cognitively in the learning process.

THE CORE IDEAS

1. Multiliteracies

The essence of a multiliteracies approach is that schools in the 21st century need to focus on a broader range of literacies than simply traditional reading and writing skills.

The term *multiliteracies* was introduced by the New London Group (1996) to highlight the relevance of new forms of literacy associated with information, communication, and multimedia technologies and, equally important, the wide variety of culturally specific forms of literacy evident in complex pluralistic societies. From the perspective of multiliteracies, the exclusive focus within schools on linear text-based literacy in the dominant language of the society represents a very limited conception that fails to address the realities of a globalized, technologically sophisticated knowledge-based society. In urban contexts across North America and Europe, the student population is multilingual, and students are exposed to and engage in many different literacy practices outside

> The essence of a multiliteracies approach is that schools in the 21st century need to focus on a broader range of literacies than simply traditional reading and writing skills.

the school (Pahl & Rowsell, in press). Within schools, however, the teaching of literacy is narrowly focused on literacy in the dominant language and typically fails to acknowledge or build on the multilingual literacies or the technologically mediated literacies that form a significant part of students' cultural and linguistic capital.

The New London Group proposed a pedagogical framework that highlighted the importance of situated practice, overt instruction, critical framing, and transformed practice. The essence of this framework is that students should be given opportunities to engage in meaningful experience and practice within a learning community, and the development of concepts and understanding should be supported by explicit instruction as required. Students should also have opportunities to step back from what they have learned and examine concepts and ideas critically in relation to their social relevance. Finally, students should be given opportunities to take the knowledge they have gained further—to put it into play in the world of ideas and come to understand how their insights can exert an impact on people and issues in the real world.

2. Pedagogical Orientations

The themes articulated in the New London Group's (1996) multiliteracies pedagogical framework can also be viewed in the context of three pedagogical orientations, variations of which have been discussed by many authors (e.g., Skourtou, Kourtis Kazoullis, & Cummins, 2006). As illustrated in Figure 11.1, the three pedagogical orientations are nested within each other rather than being distinct and isolated from each other. These orientations are labeled *transmission, social constructivist*, and *transformative*:

- **Transmission**—Transmission-oriented pedagogy is represented in the inner circle with the narrowest focus. The goal is to transmit information and skills articulated in the curriculum directly to students.
- **Social constructivist**—Social constructivist pedagogy, occupying the middle pedagogical space, incorporates the curriculum focus of transmission approaches but broadens it to include the development among students of higher-order thinking abilities based on teachers and students co-constructing knowledge and understanding.
- **Transformative**—Transformative approaches to pedagogy broaden the focus still further by emphasizing the relevance not only of transmitting the curriculum and constructing knowledge but also of enabling students to gain insight into how knowledge intersects with power. The goal is to promote critical literacy among students to encourage them to read between the lines of societal discourses rather than to skim along their surface. In other words, the goal is deep understanding.

The development of critical literacy is particularly relevant in an era of global propaganda, where skillfully crafted multimedia messages broadcast by privately owned media conglomerates dramatically influence public perceptions and attitudes. Witness the fact that more than 40 percent of the U.S. population continues to believe that Saddam Hussein was instrumental in the 9/11 attacks despite the universal acknowledgment, even grudgingly by the Bush administration, that this was not the case. Thus, there is an urgent necessity to teach for deep understanding and

Figure 11.1

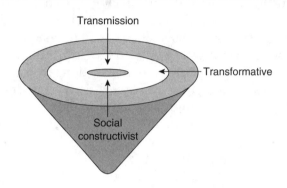

critical literacy, not so much because the economy demands it but because the survival of democratic institutions in our societies may depend on it.

It is clear that these pedagogical orientations intersect with the themes articulated in the New London Group's multiliteracies framework. In both cases, a legitimate role is assigned to overt instruction (transmission pedagogy) but only as one component of a more inclusive and comprehensive framework for learning. In a similar way, the cognitive psychology research on learning reviewed in the next section highlights the limitations of teacher-student transmission of information and skills. This research suggests that cognitive engagement and deep understanding are more likely to be generated in contexts where instruction builds on students' prior knowledge and where learning is supported by active collaboration within a community of learners.

3. How People Learn

Research data relating to *how people learn* was recently synthesized in a volume with that title published by the National Research Council in the United States (Bransford, Brown, & Cocking, 2000). This volume represents a significant consensus among cognitive psychologists in relation to how learning occurs and the optimal conditions to foster learning. The authors emphasize the following conditions for effective learning:

- **Learning With Deep Understanding**

Knowledge is more than just the ability to remember; deeper levels of understanding are required to transfer knowledge from one context to another. This implies that instruction for deep understanding involves the development of critical literacy (reading between the lines) rather than simply literal comprehension of text.

- **Building on Preexisting Knowledge**

Prior knowledge, skills, beliefs, and concepts significantly influence what learners notice about their environment and how they organize and interpret it. This principle implies that in classrooms with students from linguistically diverse backgrounds, instruction must explicitly activate students' prior knowledge and build relevant background knowledge as necessary. The implied acknowledgment and affirmation of students' language and cultural backgrounds is not sociopolitically neutral. Rather it explicitly challenges the omission and subordination of students' culture and language within typical transmission-oriented classrooms.

- **Promoting Active Learning**

Learners should be supported in taking control of and self-regulating their own learning. When students take ownership of the learning process and invest their identities in the outcomes of learning, the resulting understanding will be deeper than when learning is passive.

- **Support Within the Community of Learners**

Learning takes place in a social context, and a supportive learning community encourages dialogue, apprenticeship, and mentoring. Learning is not simply a cognitive process that takes place inside the heads of individual students; it also involves socialization into particular communities of practice. Within these learning communities, or what Gee (2001) terms *affinity groups,* novices are enabled to participate in the practices of the community from the very beginning of their involvement. Lave and Wenger (1991) describe this process as legitimate peripheral participation. The learning community can include the classroom, the school, the family and broader community, and virtual communities enabled through electronic communication.

This account specifies some minimal requirements for effective learning. It also brings into immediate focus the lack of scientific credibility of approaches that rely on simple transmission of knowledge and skills from teachers to learners. Exclusive reliance on transmission pedagogy is likely to entail memorization rather than learning for deep understanding, minimal activation of students' prior knowledge, and passive rather than active learning. Because active and creative use of language by students is typically regarded as "off-task" within a transmission approach, there is no community of learners.

> **IMPLICATIONS FOR TEACHING**
>
> Multiliteracies pedagogy = Effective pedagogy
>
> Conditions for effective learning
>
> — Learning with understanding
> — Building on preexisting knowledge
> — Promoting active learning
> — Support within the community of learners

Transmission approaches typically entail one-size-fits-all learning objectives and sometimes scripted instruction. These approaches are unable to accommodate the diversity of language and cultures that represents the new mainstream in North American urban schools. For example, within a transmission approach, it is virtually impossible to enable recently arrived second-language learners to participate effectively in the life of the classroom when their knowledge of the language of instruction is initially minimal. By contrast, a multiliteracies approach, which attempts to incorporate students' language and culture into the curriculum, is much more capable of including all students productively within the learning community. Recently arrived students can express their intelligence, imagination, and literary/artistic talents through writing in their home language and then working with peers to create bilingual identity texts (Chow & Cummins, 2003; Leoni & Cohen, 2004). The theoretical constructs that underlie this type of pedagogical approach have been articulated in the Academic Expertise framework.

THE ACADEMIC EXPERTISE FRAMEWORK

This framework incorporates the same emphasis on critical literacy, active learning, deep understanding, and building on students' prior knowledge articulated in the pedagogical approaches discussed above. However, it also argues for the centrality of identity negotiation and identity investment in any conception of teaching for deep understanding. Teacher-student interactions and other interactions within the learning community create an interpersonal space within which knowledge is generated and identities are negotiated. Learning will be optimized when these interactions maximize both cognitive engagement and identity investment (Cummins, 2001).

> The framework attempts to express in a very concrete way the kinds of instructional emphases and language interactions required to build students' academic expertise.

The framework attempts to express in a very concrete way the kinds of instructional emphases and language interactions required to build students' academic expertise. Optimal instruction will include a focus on meaning, a focus on language, and a focus on use. The focus on meaning entails the development of critical literacy rather than surface-level processing of text. The focus on language involves promoting not just explicit knowledge of how the linguistic code operates but also critical awareness of how language operates within society. If students are to participate effectively within a democratic society, they should be able to "read" how language is used to achieve social goals: to elucidate issues, to persuade, to deceive, to include, to exclude, and so on. The focus-on-use component parallels the New London Group's transformed practice but expresses in much more concrete ways what this might look like within the classroom context. It argues that optimal instruction will enable students to generate knowledge, create literature and art, and act on social realities.

The Academic Expertise framework also makes explicit the fact that classroom instruction always positions students in particular ways that reflect the implicit (or sometimes explicit) image of the student in the teacher's mind. How students are positioned either expands or constricts their opportunities for identity investment and cognitive engagement. The nested pedagogical orientations in Figure 11.1 represent a continuum ranging from relatively constricted to more expanded opportunities for identity investment and cognitive engagement.

Although the construct of identity investment has not received much attention in the cognitive psychology or educational reform research literature, it has emerged as a significant explanatory construct in the educational anthropology and second-language learning literature (e.g., Fordham, 1990; Norton, 2000). In the sections that follow, we illustrate the role of identity texts in developing academic expertise.

IDENTITY TEXTS

The relevance of what we are calling identity texts can be appreciated by visiting the Dual Language Showcase site created by educators at Thornwood Elementary School in the Peel School District (http://thornwood.peelschools.org/Dual/). First- and second-grade students from culturally and linguistically diverse backgrounds created stories initially in English (the language of school instruction); they illustrated these stories and then worked with various resource people (parents, older students literate in the home language, some teachers who spoke a variety of students' languages) to translate these stories into their home languages. The stories and illustrations were then entered into the computer through word processing and scanning. The Dual Language Web site was created to enable students' bilingual stories to be shared with parents, relatives, or friends in both Canada and students' countries of origin who had Internet access (Chow & Cummins, 2003).

The Academic Expertise framework proposes that optimal academic development within the interpersonal space of the learning community occurs only when there is both maximum cognitive engagement and maximum identity investment on the part of students. The products of students' creative work or performances carried out within this pedagogical space are termed identity texts insofar as students invest their identities in these texts (written, spoken, visual, musical, dramatic, or combinations in multimodal form), which then hold a mirror up to students in which their identities are reflected back in a positive light. When students share identity texts with multiple audiences (peers, teachers, parents, grandparents, sister classes, the media, etc.), they are likely to receive positive feedback and affirmation of self in interaction with these audiences. Although not always an essential component, technology acts as an amplifier to enhance the process of identity investment and affirmation. It facilitates the production of these texts, makes them look more accomplished, and expands the audiences and potential for affirmative feedback.

In our work in various highly diverse classrooms where students have worked collaboratively to write and publish bilingual/multilingual identity texts, we have found evidence for the following claims:

1. Students' home-language knowledge is an educationally significant component of their cultural capital.

2. Even in an English-medium instructional context, teachers can create an environment that acknowledges, communicates respect for, and promotes students' linguistic and cultural capital.

3. Newly arrived students whose knowledge of English is minimal are enabled to express their artistic and linguistic talents, intelligence, and imagination through the creation of identity texts written initially in their home language. In this way, they quickly join the classroom and school learning community as valued members rather than remaining at the periphery for an extended period.

4. Students' attitude toward and use of their home language changes positively in supportive classroom contexts.

5. Parent-student communication and collaboration increase when dual-language literacy projects such as book authoring are initiated.

6. Technology can increase the audience for students' books and provide reinforcement for students' literacy practices.

7. Dual-language initiatives can serve to normalize linguistic diversity within the school and result in more coherent and effective school policies with respect to (a) affirmation of students' linguistic and cultural identities, (b) parental involvement, and (c) technology use within the school.

These claims become relevant for policy and pedagogy because the normalized "default options" in most schools are very different. Specifically, the following assumptions and practices have become normalized in ways that constrict both the identity options for culturally diverse students and their cognitive and academic engagement:

- Literacy is assumed to equal English literacy.
- There is minimal acknowledgment or promotion of students' cultural/ linguistic/imaginative capital.

- The involvement of culturally and linguistically diverse parents is limited and passive.
- Technology use is sporadic and unconnected to coherent pedagogical philosophies and practices.

MULTILITERACIES PEDAGOGY REVISITED

A radically different image of the child is implied in the classrooms we have observed compared with more typical transmission-oriented classrooms. Within the framework of multiliteracies pedagogy, broadly defined, educators expand the opportunities for children to express themselves—their intelligence, imagination, and linguistic and artistic talents. When this kind of expression is enabled, children come to see themselves as intelligent, imaginative, and talented. In some cases, identity texts will involve children's home languages; in other cases, English may be the medium. Similarly, technology has the power to amplify and enhance the "peak experience" (Maslow, 1968/1999) that the identity text represents, but it is not always an essential component.

The emergence and appreciation of self in the context of identity texts was expressed very powerfully by Grade 8 students in Markham Gateway School, who acted in and helped produce three Shakespearean plays (directed by teacher Shyrna Gilbert) during the latter part of the school year. Comments such as the following illustrate the power of identity texts to transform students' sense of self and their orientation to literacy. Students' identities are affirmed and expanded through the reactions of significant others (e.g., teachers, parents, and siblings) to the identity text:

- Ms. Gilbert thought that we would have the most challenging part. I think she thinks that we did a phenomenal job.
- We had so much fun—one month of the best Grade 8. This was probably the best thing I have ever done in school.
- My parents were thrilled. They never knew I can act. They never knew. This was the first time they'd seen me act. They were like, "Whoa! Pretty good." (Focus Group A)
- My parents were really impressed.
- My mom didn't speak English. She watched the acting. She said I was good. (Focus Group D)
- I have never read so much in my life. . . . Now I feel like a movie star. . . . We feel so professional. (Focus Group E)
- Now I'm more brave. I liked drama before. I improved on my drama skills too. . . . You look back and say, "Grade 8 was one of my best years because I had Shakespeare." I got to learn more things that will help me.
- It [auditioning for parts] was like *American Idol*. It was like a competition. That's the interesting part of it, the competition for that role. When we showed it to our parents it was like professionals. It's like a real theatre with lighting and all that stuff . . . My parents were happy, but when I was practicing my lines at home they thought I was weird.
- My brother came to the play. He was pretty impressed. He never had Shakespeare in Grade 8 and he was like, "I wish I had it. You're really lucky."

He told me that in high school, it's going to be pretty hard. Shakespeare comes up a lot. He was really impressed. He really liked it.

- My mom couldn't make it that night because my dad was out of the country. She had to go to work and everything. But when my brother told my mom, she really felt bad that she didn't come, that she missed something that big. She didn't think it was big at first. Afterwards, she felt that it was pretty big. (Focus Group F)

On the basis of the collaboration with educators in the project schools, we can articulate in a very concrete way five central components of a multiliteracies pedagogy that prioritize the role of identity investment in learning for deep understanding:

- Multiliteracies pedagogy constructs an image of the child as intelligent, imaginative, and linguistically talented; individual differences in these traits do not diminish the potential of each child to shine in specific ways.
- Multiliteracies pedagogy acknowledges and builds on the cultural and linguistic capital (prior knowledge) of students and communities.
- Multiliteracies pedagogy aims explicitly to promote cognitive engagement and identity investment on the part of students.
- Multiliteracies pedagogy enables students to construct knowledge, create literature and art, and act on social realities through dialogue and critical inquiry.
- Multiliteracies pedagogy employs a variety of technological tools to support students' construction of knowledge, literature, and art and their presentation of this intellectual work to multiple audiences through the creation of identity texts.

As sketched above, multiliteracies pedagogy draws on transmission, social constructivist, and transformative orientations to teaching and learning. Although entirely consistent with the empirical research on how people learn, it represents a radical departure from the normalized assumptions that characterize many Canadian classrooms serving culturally and linguistically diverse students. The funds of knowledge (Moll, Amanti, Neff, & González, 1992) represented in the community form the foundation for knowledge building within the school. Instruction is oriented explicitly to enable students to express and expand their linguistic and cultural capital. By contrast, the normalized approach that ignores students' cultural and linguistic capital fails to acknowledge students' preexisting knowledge and is thus significantly less capable of teaching for deep understanding.

12

Teaching Wisdom Through Deep Critical Thinking and Development of Character

Michel Ferrari

> Students need to be prepared not just to become experts in disciplinary knowledge but also to become wise. In this chapter, Michel Ferrari discusses theories of wisdom and its development and how wisdom can be taught in schools. The relationship between wisdom and deep understanding is addressed.
>
> 1. How can elementary teachers help young children to become wise?
>
> 2. Do some subjects lend themselves more than others to including the seeds of wisdom?

Public schools have as their primary task to prepare students to become full participants in our society. Part of this task requires teaching students to master basic skills (such as reading, math, or computer skills) and disciplinary knowledge (such as English, history, or science). However, North American society, and in particular urban schools, are becoming increasingly multicultural, leading to potential conflicts both between individuals and between ethnic communities within these schools. Resolving such conflicts within and outside of school requires wisdom. For this reason, students need to be prepared not just to become experts in disciplinary knowledge but also to become wise.

WHAT DOES IT MEAN TO PREPARE STUDENTS TO BECOME WISE?

Despite its rich world history, wisdom is not easy to define scientifically—a problem already noted by Hall (1922), one of the first to try. Historically, wisdom has been discussed in philosophy and religious studies, but recently, several empirical sciences have begun to study wisdom, including cultural anthropology, political science, psychology, and education (Baltes & Staudinger, 2000; Sternberg, 2001a, 2001b, 2004, 2005). Among the most widely known cognitive psychologists to propose a problem-solving or pragmatic expertise approach to fostering wisdom are Paul Baltes and Robert Sternberg. Baltes and Staudinger (2000) found several common characteristics of wisdom in the cultural-historical and philosophical literatures. Wisdom addresses how to live a meaningful life and how to deal with difficult life problems through superior judgment and critical thinking. Wisdom also allows people to give advice based on knowledge that shows exceptional scope, depth, measure, and balance, while admitting the limits of any knowledge in an uncertain world. Wisdom, Baltes and Staudinger believe, requires a synergy of mind and character to establish personal well-being and the well-being of others.

The study of wisdom can help optimize personal development across the life span (Baltes & Staudinger, 2000). Studies by Baltes show evidence of wisdom by seeing how people answer questions about universal life problems faced by fictional characters. Here is an example: "Someone receives a telephone call from a good friend who says that he or she cannot go on like this and has decided to commit suicide. What might one/the person take into consideration and do in such a situation?" Baltes and his colleagues have collected a lot of empirical data supporting their view of wisdom as expertise about the fundamental pragmatics of life (Baltes & Staudinger, 2000). For example, older individuals nominated for their wisdom performed as well as did clinical psychologists on wisdom-related tasks. In addition, measures of intelligence and personality only partially overlap measures of wisdom in their research. In recent work, Baltes and his colleagues have begun to consider the seeds of wisdom in adolescence (Pasupathi, Staudinger, & Baltes, 2001); however, they have not tried to specifically teach students in ways that foster wisdom. The best example of teaching for wisdom in public schools is the work of Robert Sternberg.

According to Sternberg (2001a, 2001b, 2005), the essence of wisdom is balance or equity, or a view that he calls his "balance theory of wisdom." Wisdom is here defined as applying knowledge, tacitly and explicitly, toward achieving a common good. For Sternberg, this always implies common values needed to determine the

> The best example of teaching for wisdom in public schools is the work of Robert Sternberg . . . the essence of wisdom is balance or equity, or what he calls his "balance theory of wisdom."

IMPLICATIONS FOR TEACHING

Seven Ways to Teach for Wisdom...

1. Provide problems that require wise thinking to solve

2. Help students think in terms of a common good

3. Help students think in ways that balance the interests of all stakeholders

4. Provide past examples of wise thinking and analyze them

5. Role-model wise thinking for students (a tall order)

6. Help students think dialectically— essentially, show that problems do not have right and wrong solutions but better and worse ones, which vary according to sociocultural context

7. Show students you value wise information processing and wise solutions (Sternberg, 2004)

best balance between personal, community, and outside interests over both the short term and long term, as one adapts to, shapes, and selects particular situations and circumstances. In other words, to be wise, people must balance understanding produced by critical thinking and act to account for competing interests, immediate and lasting consequences of those interests, and the situation in which they occur. All of this is done in the service of attaining a common good, understood within a system of values, the most important of which perhaps is equity. As we will see, this has important implications for how specific subjects like history are taught in school.

The main point for Sternberg and Baltes is that people adopt a pragmatic, case-based approach in which the wisest decisions are made in light of critical thinking about particular circumstances as informed by values—a very old idea (Jonson & Toulmin, 1990). Like the philosopher Charles Taylor (1995), Sternberg avoids moral relativism by saying that, ultimately, foundational values are those that can be denied only by self-contradiction. For example, one cannot deny the value of free speech without also denying the right of one's own speech to be heard.

Wisdom, in this sense, seems inherently bound up with judgments of excellence relevant to particular groups of people in one's own circle or community. These standards of excellence and the criteria they imply are mentally constructed, not found in the world; thus, they are limited only by the human imagination, although some imaginings will be easier than others, given our common evolutionary history. These ideas about excellence toward which wisdom strives do not stand alone but are organized into conceptual systems—especially into theories or canonical narratives (Bruner, 2002). Although categories may change, category systems do not change as easily. This is why we largely continue to recognize Homer's Odysseus as a hero even though so much has changed between the time when the character was created and now—including our theories about god(s) and the way the world works. The category system that allows us to categorize people as wise or as heroes has not changed (Amsterdam & Bruner, 2000).

The implications for teaching children (or adults) to become wise then boils down to getting them to think more thoroughly and more clearly about their decisions.

For many people, cognitive development is crucial to this knowledge-centered view of wisdom, and early adolescence is perhaps the earliest time when students can think abstractly enough to arrive at a balanced understanding of a situation that transcends the interests of particular actors (Habermas & Bluck, 2000). In the neo-Piagetian tradition, some say that children should not be capable of such (postformal) abstractions before, at least, their late teens. Hence, although the seeds of wisdom may be fostered in children, true wisdom would be impossible before university at the earliest (e.g., Alexander & Langer, 1990; Granott & Parziale, 2002; Mascolo, Li, Fink, & Fischer,

2002; Pasupathi et al., 2001). Whether this is true is an empirical question that is now being investigated.

> In effect, we are journalists or historians of our own lives and those of people we care about. . . .

The implications for teaching children (or adults) to become wise then boils down to getting them to think more thoroughly and more clearly about their decisions. However, personally, I doubt that any purely intellectual methods can reach students on such a deep level as to foster wisdom, just by improving their critical thinking. It is one thing to know what to do and another to have the will to do it at a personal cost (to achieve balance and not be self-centered). Consider saving money by keeping a strict budget of everything you spend and then cutting out frivolous and luxury items. Some will fail miserably at such a challenge, and others will manage to accumulate a lot of money by sheer determined effort. Whatever the difference is between those who succeed and those who don't, I suspect that it lies deeper than any critical thinking about their current budget. It is common wisdom that to save money you need to spend within your means or find ways to raise new money—but not everyone manages to implement these goals. Success depends in part on character.

WISDOM AS THE EXPRESSION OF CHARACTER

An alternative approach to deep understanding is to believe that children have an innocence that is the essence of wisdom. Wisdom, then, is the authentic expression of a certain way of engaging life—an expression of character—and involves narrative understanding. Unlike the expertise view, where people deepen their understanding by thinking critically about typical and atypical cases, narrative understanding depends on the perceived likelihood of how a story will turn out (Bruner, 2002). Wisdom as expertise relies on increasingly sophisticated knowledge of some problem area, whereas wisdom as narrative relies on understanding character and is essentially tied to self-knowledge. What is more, whereas expertise and critical thinking emphasize objective intellectual understanding, character expresses emotional, subjective understanding (Oatley, in press). Narrative allows us to acquire and express wisdom about the depths of human nature and our relation to others and the world (Shen, 2001).[1]

Understanding character is often associated with the literary analysis of novels and hence with fiction. But Oatley (1999, 2003, in press) argues that just as thought experiments can generate new truths in science (Kuhn, 1964/1981), fiction can generate new truths about psychology for the same reason: Both involve realistic imaginative simulations of possible events (albeit perhaps rare or difficult to observe) to provide new information about the world. The importance of narrative understanding of character is not necessarily tied to fiction or simulation; "new journalism" is increasingly adopting literary techniques developed in novels to render true stories more vivid and meaningful (Oatley, 2003; Wolfe, 1975), and narrative is critical to the understanding of legal decisions that govern our lives (Amsterdam & Bruner, 2000).

---

[1]Also see Kathleen Gallagher's treatment of the role of drama (Chapter 10)—Editors' note.

Characters are situated within narratives, and these are organized into genres. Some narrative genres (like hero tales or saints) have certain stock features that allow them to be exemplary tales (Amsterdam & Bruner, 2000; Bruner, 2002). A wonderful illustration of this is in Leonard Cohen's *Beautiful Losers,* in which he reinterprets the story of Kateri (Catherine) Tekakwitha, a Native American girl who was canonized by Pope John Paul II in 1980, by contrasting her ideal religious image to what is known of Tekakwitha through historical documents from the 17th century. The narrator originally falls in love with (and wants to make love to) her idealized religious image and is shocked to discover that the historical Tekakwitha was scarred by smallpox and unattractive. This sometimes jarring juxtaposition of images is effective precisely because it violates the canonical form for this sort of story.[2]

WISDOM AND CHARACTER DEVELOPMENT

Understanding of character has also developed, historically, through at least four levels (Oatley, 2003, in press):

- In *Level 1,* character is simply a behavioral disposition. In the oldest narratives available to us, such as the Epic of Gilgamesh or the Bible, we know nothing about the inner life of the protagonists and understand them only through their actions and reactions.
- In *Level 2,* character becomes the emotional source for action; for example, in ancient Greek tragedy, the emotion of hubris is responsible for the actions of the main character that result in tragedy. It is this deeper understanding of the source of action that leads us to have compassion for the protagonist.
- In *Level 3,* characters are recognizable as individuals; this is not seen before the Renaissance, when the idea emerges that people create themselves by making emotionally significant choices and by reflecting on those choices—what Taylor (1995) calls "strong-evaluation."
- Finally, in *Level 4,* the modern literary conception of character emerges. In these works, character involves an agent's sustained inward emotions and the goals that these emotions engender, amplifying choices. At this level, character is typified through emblematic actions and is understood to possess ever-deeper layers that are revealed through people's actions in the world.

Evidence also shows that the historical development of the literary portrayal of character does parallel both historical and personal development of individuals' understanding of themselves as having a particular identity or character (Ferrari, 2003; Habermas & Bluck, 2000). This is not surprising if we believe, with Daniel Dennett (2003), that our subjective understanding of self—although it is essential to living a meaningful human life—is no different a construction than that which goes into a novelist's creating a fictional character. In effect, we are journalists or historians of our own lives and those of people we care about (Dennett, 2003). Furthermore, for Dennett, human nature is a symbiosis of biology and culture, a view that has

---

[2]Thanks to Lora Pallota for pointing out this example.

profound importance for the study of wisdom. This is important because it suggests that although wisdom may have certain universal aspects that are biologically predisposed, it necessarily involves developmentally, historically, and culturally specific understandings of people and of what constitutes a good life, all of which are expressed though narrative.

Wisdom, in this view, relates to work by Erikson and his followers, who equate wisdom with generativity and deep personal gains, especially in adulthood (Erikson, 1968; McAdams & de St. Aubin, 1998). It also has an affinity to the Buddhist view of the middle way, which suggests that wisdom emerges out of a critical insight into our own nature. For Varela (1992/1999), we have to practice to remove habits that mask a natural wisdom that issues spontaneously from our total experience. This sort of deep understanding, or ethical expertise, is not developed through moral rules (even if codified in such rules). In fact, "unless such rules . . . are informed by the wisdom that enables them to be dissolved in the demands of responsivity to the particularity and immediacy of lived situations, the rules will become sterile, scholastic hindrances to compassionate action rather than conduits for its manifestation" (Varela, 1992/1999, p. 74). Yet, despite the emotional basis of this response, it becomes increasingly expert and appropriate precisely because of the deep intuitive understanding of human experience that generates it. Ironically, such wisdom involves understanding that we have no fixed character and that our nature is to be spontaneous and endlessly creative (Varela, 1992/1999), what Amsterdam and Bruner (2000) see as critical to metacognition:

> Seeing the obvious as strange requires metacognition, a clumsy word for making one's own thoughts the object of one's own thinking. . . . Disturbers of the canonical peace [e.g., artists, philosophers, agitators, dissidents] may be disapproved of by those in charge of the banal and obvious. But they are always left some room to do their thing. This is to lure us into metacognition, into the imaginative space where mind can envision other possible worlds. Each culture maintains its distinctive imaginative space, teeming with alternatives to the actual.

Exceptionally wise thinkers proceed metacognitively by planning, monitoring, and evaluating their reasoning and their intuitions. Perhaps more to the point, such thinkers also seem to have exceptional versions of what Flavell (Pinard, 1992) calls "metacognitive experiences." Metacognitive experiences are the emotional concomitants to metacognition; they guide one's intuition about what problems are worth pursuing.

TEACHING FOR WISDOM THROUGH KNOWLEDGE BUILDING

All that I have said so far is a bit abstract, I admit. But it is a necessary foundation for the practical advice it suggests for teachers in public schools. Schools are designed to prepare individuals for society. Educational systems are highly institutionalized and embody their own values. As with all institutions, they also invent ways to distribute skills, attitudes, and ways of thinking and of

At least ideally, education aims to teach people to use a culture's toolkit to become better architects and builders, according to the standards set by their culture (the starting point for what Sternberg calls "the common good").

perpetuating particular practices. At least ideally, education aims to teach people to use a culture's toolkit to become better architects and builders, according to the standards set by their culture (the starting point for what Sternberg calls "the common good"). Teachers are transmitted the best knowledge that has been developed by culture and seek to train students not only to be critical thinkers who establish ever higher standards of excellence but also to become wise.

What are the implications for education of teaching not just for critical thinking but especially for wisdom? To begin to address this question, let us first consider the role of schooling generally.

THE ROLE OF SCHOOLING

Schools have a variety of aims that sometimes come into conflict and need wisdom to balance. Egan (1997) suggests at least three principal aims for schooling:[3]

1. To teach truths about the world that are not immediately apparent (e.g., that the Earth is a sphere circling the sun and not a flat surface that the sun goes around, as one might initially suppose)

2. To prepare individuals for the workplace or for their adult life in society (e.g., reading and math skills, computer literacy, and other general skills, as well as forming good character)

3. Individual flourishing (i.e., to live the fullest life possible that expresses one's unique combination of intellectual and personal potential)

Although all three aims are important, ultimately, I believe that fostering deep understanding is best achieved through wisely balancing critical thinking about objective truths with encouraging individuals to flourish within society.

TEACHING FOR WISDOM

Unlike creativity and critical thinking, which focus on knowledge, wisdom concerns ideals both for human understanding and for action—whether our own or (through the advice we give) that of others. How to educate students to foster wisdom is a deep and abiding concern. As Sternberg (2004) reminds us, truly exceptional gifts at discerning the import of delicate social situations are not measured by current intelligence tests or by tests of giftedness. Indeed, no one cares about the IQ of Martin Luther King, Jr., or Gandhi. Wisdom is not captured by broader theories of intelligence such as Sternberg's triarchic theory or Gardner's theory of multiple intelligences, not even by measures of social or emotional intelligence. Rather, wisdom is attributed to individuals who judge rightly or show discernment in complex cultural fields of endeavor. Sternberg argues that educators need to promote giftedness that fosters or expresses wisdom, and he suggests that failure to do this is part of the reason why—although IQ has risen markedly over the past generations—wisdom

---

[3]For Egan (1997), education toward these aims will be best accomplished differently at different ages, as children learn to appreciate first myth, then romance, logic, and finally irony.

(or lack or it) remains very much a constant companion of humankind. I agree with Sternberg (2004), who proposes seven ways to teach wisdom:

1. Provide problems that require wise thinking to solve.

2. Help students think in terms of a common good.

3. Help students think in ways that balance the interests of all stakeholders.

4. Provide past examples of wise thinking and analyze them.

5. Role-model wise thinking for students (a tall order).

6. Help students think dialectically—essentially, show that problems have not right and wrong solutions but better and worse ones, which vary according to sociocultural context.[4]

7. Show students you value wise information processing and wise solutions.

In my view, however, developing wisdom along these lines is greatly helped by innovative educational practices which scaffold[5] individuals' efforts to continuously improve on their knowledge. Although the type of learning Sternberg (2001b) proposes can occur in regular classrooms, Scardamalia (Chapter 13, this volume) proposes that knowledge building is most likely to occur—or at least to occur most quickly—only when students experience dynamic scaffolding. This sort of scaffolding is best supplied by instructional software such as Knowledge Forum®,[6] as supported by collaborative classroom environments (Bereiter, 2002; Scardamalia, 2003b; Scardamalia & Bereiter, 1999). The effectiveness of Knowledge Forum® in promoting deep understanding has been shown in classrooms from the elementary level to university and in professional workplace settings.

> ... truly exceptional gifts at discerning the import of delicate social situations are not measured by current intelligence tests, or by tests of giftedness. . . .

Other transformative learning environments exist, for example, in innovative programs such as the late Ann Brown's (1997) program to foster communities of learners. Another possibility is to use computer simulations and games such as Court Square (1995–1997) or Capitalism (1996), which allow students actively to construct practical knowledge about how to excel in business, and similar games that exist for tacit learning about science. These simulations

---

[4]Of course, we can still judge the merits of different cultural solutions ad hominum in light of perspicuous contrasts, even if we must do so within the horizon of our own understandings (Taylor, 1995).

[5]Scaffolding simply means providing necessary support to children, which allows them to succeed at tasks that they might not otherwise be able to do. After providing such help initially, scaffolds can be removed as children become able to complete all aspects of the task independently (and hopefully can themselves go on to scaffold others who are just learning).

[6]Marlene Scardamalia, Director of the Institute for Knowledge Innovation and Technology, along with Carl Bereiter and a team of others, created CSILE (Computer Supported Intentional Learning Environments), one of the first networked collaborative learning environments for schools. This environment allows members of a learning community to read and comment on each other's ideas (whether text or graphics) and to track how ideas and comments are interrelated. It is now a second-generation commercial product called Knowledge Forum® (http://www.knowledgeforum.com/) and is used by more than 150 organizations in 19 countries, including schools, health care and community organizations, and businesses.

involve both expert knowledge and narrative. How one plays Capitalism, for example, says as much about what sort of person one is as it does about one's understanding of economics, although knowledge of economics is critical to being successful at the game. By engaging in simulated activities with detailed and targeted feedback about how to be successful at them, such activities offer real potential to transform students in profound and not merely superficial ways. Although these ideas are not new, there are increasing efforts to help teachers incorporate the transformative educational power of these activities into their classrooms (Ferrari, Taylor, & van Lehn, 1999).

Even within the regular curriculum, the implication of all this for teaching is clear: Teachers should use news and fictional stories to get children to think imaginatively and critically about difficult choices in complex settings. The discussions and thinking this activity generates will help them become wiser, even at a young age. But perhaps as children grow older, they can begin to consider characters and themselves and ask what matters most to them and how significant choices influence their own lives and those of others—something that may improve even into adulthood. But teachers must also encourage children to trust in their deep intuitions about situations and to feel free to act as needed and not according to some artificially constructed character.

All such classrooms will be more conducive to teaching for wisdom, regardless of whether the emphasis is on developing ethical expertise or an understanding of character. And wisdom, I believe, is necessary for true depth of understanding in education.

13

Technology for Understanding

Marlene Scardamalia

In this chapter, Marlene Scardamalia discusses determinants of understanding–prior knowledge, discourse, and effort to understand–and how information and communication technologies address these factors. She points out that technology is seldom used to promote deep understanding, but it could, and should be.

1. Is the technology used in your school appropriate for teaching for deep understanding?

2. How does your current use of technology enhance or detract from teaching for understanding?

The learning sciences are a relatively new field, located at the intersection of learning research and technology development. Problems of understanding have been a focus of research in the learning sciences over the past quarter-century. Much of this research has dealt with problems of understanding in particular subject areas, but learning science research has also yielded general findings relevant to achieving understanding in all areas. The following three factors deserve special attention because they are often neglected in both traditional and constructivist approaches to teaching for understanding:

1. Prior knowledge—Prior knowledge is a major determinant—frequently the major determinant—of what will be understood and also of how it will be understood. Prior knowledge provides the framework, schema, or mental model within which new information is interpreted (Anderson & Pearson, 1984). Misconceptions typically arise when prior knowledge differs in a fundamental way from the intended knowledge.

2. Discourse—Experiments, observations, reading, and various kinds of first-hand experience yield information. The converting of such information into knowledge does not take place automatically. It requires reflection, which in turn depends preeminently on discourse (Brown & Campione, 1996). Discourse that is limited to the sharing of information and opinions does not serve this reflective purpose.

3. Effort to understand—Activities such as experimentation and use of manipulatives frequently fail in many students to produce the desired understanding. Further investigation shows that those who achieved it were actively trying to understand whereas those who failed to grasp the intended principles focused only on the activity itself (Bereiter & Scardamalia, 1989).

Information and communication technology (ICT) approaches to teaching for understanding differ considerably in the ways they deal with or fail to deal with these three factors.

ICT DESIGNED TO PROMOTE UNDERSTANDING

Three distinct lines of ICT development have implications for increasing depth of understanding:

1. **Computer-assisted instruction (CAI)**. The teaching of concepts and principles has been a major interest of instructional scientists working in this field. Designers of CAI aim to optimize presentation sequences for information, thus enabling students to master designated concepts.

2. **Simulations, games, laboratory tools, and other hands-on resources**. ICT has considerably expanded the possibilities of "learning by doing" in the classroom.

3. **Supports for explanation, argument, and knowledge building dialogue**. These range from the ubiquitous threaded discussion forums to software environments expressly designed for sustained work with ideas.

> The most commonly used ICT in schools ... is productivity software ... but ... there are growing complaints that it encourages attention to presentation style rather than content, thus militating against pursuit of understanding.

The most commonly used ICT in schools, however, is not any of these. It is productivity software—word processors, presentation software, spread sheets, facilities for producing Web pages, and so forth—designed for business use. An international survey showed this to be the case worldwide, even in schools identified as innovative (Kozma, 2003). Although there are special versions of productivity software for schools, they are generally simplifications designed for ease of use but otherwise similar to the business applications. One might expect such technology to be neutral as regards learning with understanding, but in fact, there are growing complaints that it encourages attention to presentational style rather than content, thus militating against pursuit of understanding. (Such complaints are arising even in the business literature: Executives are accused of lavishing too much effort on flashy presentations and not enough on the quality of information and ideas.)

Another widely used type of ICT that is ostensibly neutral with regard to understanding is course delivery systems. Developed for higher education but now making their way into schools, course delivery systems are essentially tools for putting conventional courses online. Hence, they provide for electronic reading lists; online lectures, readings, and other instructional "objects"; and electronic submission of course assignments, quizzes, discussions, and e-mail communication between instructor and students. As in conventional courses, teaching for understanding is the responsibility of the instructor or course leader and depends on the kind of information delivered and the kinds of

> Most of the CAI used in schools is of the drill-and-practice variety, which makes no pretense of teaching for understanding.

activity promoted. Far from being neutral with regard to pedagogy, course delivery systems transfer traditional courses to an online format, along with their bias toward information transmission rather than constructivist educational approaches.

The remainder of this chapter concerns itself with the three ICT approaches that are directly aimed at teaching for deeper understanding. In all of these cases, it is difficult to make general evaluative statements because quality ranges from low to high. Also, there is so much diversity within each type that it is difficult to say what constitutes quality. We can, however, point out some of the less obvious strengths and weaknesses of each type of resource and offer suggestions about how ICT may be used in efforts to foster deep understanding.

COMPUTER-ASSISTED INSTRUCTION

The oldest of the three approaches, CAI, varies from simple drill-and-practice software to sophisticated applications that use artificial intelligence to gauge the state of the learner's knowledge and to select strategic moves to enhance it. Most of the CAI used in schools is of the drill-and-practice variety, which makes no pretense of teaching for understanding. This is true even of most programs that purport to teach reading comprehension or mathematical problem solving. In effect, they merely provide drill and practice on comprehension or problem-solving test items. Nevertheless, instructional design theory, the scientific discipline underlying CAI, has been much concerned with teaching for understanding, and there are CAI programs in science,

IMPLICATIONS FOR TEACHING

To serve purposes of deepening understanding, schools should be using technologies that provide students with ...

1. Simulations that allow for deeper exploration
2. Discourse that supports sustained inquiry and idea improvement
3. Web search tools that zero in on explanatory rather than merely topical information
4. Knowledge building environments that provide a coherent framework for pursuit of understanding

Such technologies exist but are underused.

mathematics, language, and social studies that teach concepts and principles (Reigeluth, 1999).

With regard to the three learning science principles of teaching for understanding, CAI typically pays little attention to students' prior knowledge or misconceptions. However, CAI designers usually employ some form of task analysis to identify prerequisite knowledge, and they try to ensure that the prerequisites are in place before a next step in learning is introduced. As regards effort, CAI tends to focus students' efforts on getting correct answers rather than on understanding. To the extent that getting the right answer is an indicator of understanding (and in well-constructed CAI programs this is the case), the program may be said to enlist students' efforts in ways that promote understanding. Still, this is not the same as getting students to try to understand or to adopt understanding as a goal. The weakest aspect of even the strongest CAI programs, however, is that there is little or no opportunity for student discourse. The programs are so structured as to provide students with little about which to discourse.

Simulations, Games, Laboratory Instruments

This category covers a wide range and includes some of the most ingenious and highly developed software to be found in schools. The common characteristic of these programs is that they generate information in response to actions by the learners. Thus, in a broad sense, they are tools for inquiry. A distinction should be made, however, between ICT that provides direct contact with "nature" and ICT that provides contact only with simulations. Examples of the former are computer-based laboratory instruments, such as pH meters, and Lego Logo. Simulations are ubiquitous. Hundreds of small simulations, usually in the form of Java applets, are available on the Web. There are also more powerful simulations and simulation-building tools, which permit active exploration and experimentation. It is well to keep in mind, however, that in using such applications, students are not interacting with the real world; they are interacting with a theory about the real world. This has both virtues and drawbacks. A simulation based on Newtonian mechanics or Mendelian genetics is likely to represent a simplified world free of the complications that affect motion and inheritance in nature. This makes the theoretical principles easier to grasp, but it also means that how deeply the students can go into understanding motion or inheritance is limited to what the simplified world embodies.

Technology to Support Discourse

Many different kinds of software provide facilities for discussion, but this tends to be the weakest part of the application. Often the discussion facility is tacked onto or is a modification of an application designed for some other purpose: for conventional course delivery, for e-mail, for document management, or for virtual laboratory work. The facility provides for posting messages, usually in chronological order, and for responding to or commenting on these messages. But often there is no provision for commenting on comments, thereby limiting dialogue to two steps. Better developed applications provide for "threaded" discourse, which would better be called branching discourse because what it amounts to is comments on comments, comments on comments on comments, and so on to an indefinite number of branches. The result, however, is hierarchical decomposition. Students can work down from an idea to details, but they cannot work up from the idea to a higher level, more inclusive idea that would subsume existing branches. Neither is it possible to connect an idea in one thread to an idea in another thread, except by textual reference. Thus, the software militates against the kind of synthesizing, connecting, and intertextuality that are essential for the collaborative pursuit of deeper understanding. Such technology is well suited to the uses one finds in the typical Web forum—to question-answer and opinion-response dialogue. But it is radically unsuited to anything that could be called knowledge construction or idea development.

> It is well to keep in mind, however, that in using such applications, students are not interacting with the real world; they are interacting with a theory about the real world.

A facility that provides for superordination (creating a higher level node) as well as subordination and also for linking horizontally (such as across threads) is entirely feasible. In fact, Knowledge Forum®, technology created at OISE/UT, provides such facilities and more to encourage depth of learning. Superordination is provided by "rise-above" notes, which subsume a set of existing notes within a synthesizing or summarizing note. Any note may be linked to any other note. An even more versatile means of representing higher level organizations of ideas is the

> Many different kinds of software provide facilities for discussion, but this tends to be the weakest part of the application.

"view." A view provides a graphical background that can display categories and category relationships, with individual and linked notes appropriately placed on the screen in relation to this background. In particular, a view can represent graphically the big ideas that frame an inquiry. Views can be linked to other views and can be subsumed by still higher level views. A particular note can appear in more than one view. Thus, wherever students are in a Knowledge Forum database, they can move up to create a higher level object, down to create a subordinate one, or sideways to connect one note or view to any other note or view.

The World Wide Web and the Pursuit of Understanding

The World Wide Web has been heralded as a vast information resource, enabling students to pursue inquiries independently and in greater depth than was possible when they had to rely on local print resources. There is converging evidence, however, that use of the Web encourages the gathering of miscellaneous facts about a topic rather than pursuit of deeper understanding (Moss, 2000). This should not be surprising, given the nature of popular search engines. They are good for zeroing in on a topic and finding the most popular documents related to the topic, but not for finding answers to "why" questions.

Problem-driven as opposed to topic-driven search is a theoretical possibility, but perhaps not an economically realistic one. For the present, teachers can refrain from assignments and projects that encourage topical fact-gathering. This means abandoning the time-honored research report or project, with its emphasis on collecting, organizing, and creating attractive displays of topical information. The alternative is genuine inquiry, driven by problems of understanding. When such inquiry is pursued collaboratively, students can share relevant findings from the Web, thus partly overcoming the limitations of Web searches. They can also share words and phrases that have proved useful to enter into Web search strings.

Toward More Sophisticated Software

Knowledge building (Scardamalia & Bereiter, 2003) is a process of sustained idea improvement fostered by communities, in which participants take responsibility for the advancement of community knowledge. Learning scientists, along with historians, philosophers of science, and other knowledge scientists, have studied the history of thought and its evolution, practices of novices and experts, and cultures of innovation. From this work, we know that deep understanding requires sustained idea improvement and that the knowledge building trajectory starts with the early, natural ability to play with ideas and extends to the not-so-natural and relatively rare intentional processes that serve to continually improve ideas.

> Deep understanding results when ideas become objects of inquiry and the discourse that surrounds them leads to their continual improvement.

Our expanded understanding of knowledge building has opened the possibility of knowledgeware that renders the hidden dynamics of sustained idea improvement transparent and embeds them in daily interaction between people and ideas. The surest way to support deep understanding is to make it integral to the day-to-day workings of classrooms. A new class of software, known as Knowledge Building Environments (KBEs), is designed to enable this (Scardamalia, 2003a).

In line with this requirement, KBEs make it possible to import any digital representation of an idea from any application into a community workspace. In the community workspace, the idea is built on, annotated, referenced, integrated into a higher order representation, reconstructed in multiple views, and so forth. KBEs additionally support users in generating and contributing ideas. All media types (text, video, graphic, scanned image, audio, and so forth) can become part of this community-constructed resource. As ideas are contributed, advances by one member precipitate further advances, at both the individual and group levels, so there is a continual movement beyond current understanding.

> The research is there and the prototypes are there to produce technology that supports rather than undermines the pursuit of deeper understanding. What is missing is market demand.

The design of KBEs is a major engineering task. Knowledge Forum, the environment mentioned above, is the original KBE; it currently provides the basic means for bringing work with all digital media into the knowledge building process. Users can import screen shots and various kinds of application output into Knowledge Forum notes and launch applications from within the environment, providing a basic means for bringing all kinds of work with digital media into the knowledge building process. And participants' self-generated ideas become objects of inquiry, to be explored and improved along with ideas created by others, bringing different worlds of knowledge work together into a coherent framework. It is thus possible to integrate the kinds of applications listed above, adding a meta-layer in which the outputs from these applications become objects of inquiry in the service of larger knowledge building objectives.

Toward a More Sophisticated Market

Educational software could be much better than it is. The research is there and the prototypes are there to produce technology that supports rather than undermines the pursuit of deeper understanding. What is missing is market demand. The most prevalent use of ICT in elementary classrooms is to provide digital versions of what used to be done with old magazines, scissors, and library paste. One kind of cut-and-paste has been replaced by another. It is absurd to talk about an educational revolution when that is the reality.

To serve purposes of deepening understanding, schools need (1) simulations that allow for deeper exploration, (2) discourse that supports sustained inquiry and idea improvement, (3) Web search tools that zero in on explanatory rather than merely topical information, and (4) KBEs that provide a coherent framework for use of the preceding technologies in pursuit of understanding. All of this can happen, but it will not happen until the school ICT market starts to demand it.

14

Knowledge Building in Elementary Science

Richard Messina

Richard Reeve

Richard Messina and Richard Reeve describe a three-year study of applying the principles of knowledge building and using the Knowledge Forum® software in a Grade 4 science class. They report on the success of the project in the final year in establishing a knowledge-building classroom community.

1. How could elementary teachers apply these principles in their classrooms?

2. Are there obstacles to using these teaching methods?

3. How could this structure be applied without access to the specific computer software?

The educational innovation of knowledge building refers to the construction of knowledge that is of value to a community (Scardamalia, 2000). In schools, knowledge building typically takes the form of a class of students building knowledge together around a shared problem of understanding. In their ideal form, knowledge-building classrooms have been likened to scientific research teams (Scardamalia & Bereiter, 1999). Scardamalia and Bereiter have indicated that to make the transition to a knowledge-building community requires a dramatic shift from an incidental focus on learning activities to a focus on the construction of collective knowledge (Scardamalia & Bereiter, 1999). As a result, knowledge building is not simply another approach to learning but is instead a new way of conceiving of the goal of education (Scardamalia, 2001). To make the shift to a knowledge-building community, teachers must progress from how they previously functioned as teachers to how they envision they need to function to make knowledge building a success in their classroom (Reeve, 2001).

This chapter reports on the design iterations that were implemented over a three-year period as three successive classes of Grade 4 students built knowledge about the concepts associated with the study of light. The research study took place at the Institute of Child Study Laboratory School at OISE/UT. Below we highlight key design features associated with the incremental shift toward a knowledge-building community, along with the improved conceptual understandings of the successive groups of students.

USING KNOWLEDGE FORUM®

In all three years, the communal software environment known as Knowledge Forum® was used to support the knowledge-building work of the classes. Knowledge Forum® is a networked database in which students create text notes on a problem they are investigating. It provides a medium for preserving questions and ideas in notes that are continually available for further discussion and revision. Other members of the class may "build-on" if they have information to add to the original note or are seeking clarification. Only the author of each note can modify/revise his or her own notes, but all notes are visible to everyone. Students are encouraged to state the problem they are addressing and to highlight the important vocabulary in their note. The identification of key words helps others find the note when a search by key words is conducted. Scaffolds are also available to help support and define the kind of writing and thinking that is being done in the note. For example, the Theory Building scaffold includes the following supports: My Theory, I Need to Understand, Evidence, A Better Theory, New Information, and Putting Our Knowledge Together. Authors can also create pictures and diagrams within their notes. Once titled and contributed, the note is automatically displayed in the view in which it was created. Views are spaces within the database where groups of notes can be arranged. Views are titled and may contain a background illustration created by the students to help organize the notes. Links from one view to the others can be placed throughout the database. Notes that deal with similar problems or investigations may be collected and placed within a new note called a rise-above. In rise-above notes, students summarize and organize the knowledge recorded in the collected notes, thereby representing a collective group understanding.

> Knowledge Forum® is a networked database in which students create text notes on a problem they are investigating. It provides a medium for preserving questions and ideas in notes that are continually available for further discussion and revision.

Year 1—Specialization

In the first year, the students were placed in groups based on their interests. Each group knew what its members already knew, had a sense of what they wanted to know, designed and conducted experiments to research their theories, and participated in reading groups with the other members of their group, using readings they often brought in themselves. However, students felt ownership only in their area of study. There were three essential components for the students:

1. Time to research/gather information

2. Opportunities for discovery through research and experimentation

3. Time on the computers to record findings and further questions that would be shared with the rest of the class

As there were 22 students and seven computers in the class, it made sense in the early stages of the study to divide the class into three random groups. The three-part cycle was created, consisting of 40-minute sessions, two to three knowledge-building cycles per week.

In previous implementations of knowledge building, it has been found that children's questions exceed the complexity of material available for their grade level (Messina, 2001; Reeve & Lamon, 1998). Therefore, an adapted version of reciprocal teaching (Brown & Campione, 1996) was introduced to the class to be used as a tool for groups to enhance their comprehension of important material that may be too difficult to understand without the support of other group members. In these groups, a leader would ask questions to clarify the core content of the material read.

The group would decide what information was important and understood. These points were recorded as dot-jot notes. Each student was given a black lab book (research journal) to record his or her notes.

> The experiment/exploration portion of the cycle was designed to support and promote the students' curiosity and questioning.

The experiment/exploration portion of the cycle was designed to support and promote the students' curiosity and questioning. Experiments were conducted on a designated table in the classroom. Often the students were asked to follow planned steps (teacher-designed experiments) and record the data in their research journals. The experiments were conducted by the students and were designed to complement the readings being done during reciprocal teaching. The students could be heard at the experiment table using the new vocabulary they had learned in their readings.

The cycle was made complete with time on the computers using Knowledge Forum®. This was the opportunity for the group members to state their research problem, offer their theories, and record their attempts to improve on their conjectures by writing the knowledge advances they experienced from experiments and readings. Because satisfying answers to their problems were often unattainable, new questions were added to the database, and the inquiry process would continue.

Within the database, students were expected to keep a note in their portfolio about their complete understanding of light. Based on the growth of these portfolio notes, it was clear that although they were being intentional learners, they were not acting as members in a knowledge-building community. The students were writing only about their own area of research. Students were exposed to the findings of other groups during knowledge-building talks, simply by being in the same environment while a group was conducting an experiment, yet they did not feel comfortable writing about any of the other concepts of light that they themselves had not investigated.

Again, the focus of this design study was to create a knowledge-building community. The first year can clearly be identified as a transition from a focus on intentional learners, organized into interest-based groups, to a whole group with a collaborative knowledge-building focus. Clearly each specialized group felt ownership of its aspect of the study of light, but there was little demonstration of view interrelationship. The community did not share the responsibility for the overall advancement of knowledge. This became the impetus for the following year's redesign.

Year 2—Sharing Knowledge

In the second year, the students organized themselves into six groups based on their interests. Although each group was in charge of a view in the database, the students were continuously encouraged to read and build onto notes in all of the views in the database. The

> The groups in the second year organized their views in ways that brought order to their knowledge.

goal was for the students to develop a breadth of understanding about the concepts associated with light. Data from pre- and posttesting and the students' portfolio notes about their understanding of light both indicate significant gains over the first-year group and suggest this strategy was successful.

It is believed that the creation of the class mission statement and frequent knowledge-building talks on the importance of developing a breadth of understanding of each other's views helped to create this dynamic. In addition, the community needed to approve the research interests of each group to ensure they were aligned with the overall class mission. Students were encouraged to see that sharing problems and knowledge was to advance understanding beyond the level of any one individual, that collective understanding surpasses the most knowledgeable individual. Situations where deeper understanding was created through the work of students working across views were highlighted and celebrated to encourage more cross-view interaction.

With students reading and contributing to all views while specializing in one area, the teacher felt that special attention needed to be paid to the principle of improvable ideas. The metaphor of a ball of clay to represent a theory during a knowledge-building talk was an attempt to prevent students from becoming emotionally attached to their theories, that is, to create a psychologically safe culture. Students needed to be comfortable receiving and giving criticism about theories on the database and during knowledge-building talks. It was stressed that the discourse needed to be about the advancement of knowledge. This empowered the students to think that the current accepted theories in science were simply the ones with the best supporting evidence but that there were many other, perhaps better theories that had yet to

IMPLICATIONS FOR TEACHING

The knowledge-building classroom takes on characteristics of the scientific community...

1. Experiment and explore to support and promote curiosity and questioning
2. Bring order to knowledge
3. Develop a breadth of understanding about the concepts under study
4. Discuss and review results

be supported with evidence. The students felt that they themselves might, through their own work, be able to prove the next new theory.

The groups in the second year organized their views in ways that brought order to their knowledge. Some wrote paragraphs in the background of their views, helping the other members of the knowledge-building community to navigate each view. Rise-aboves were created to achieve new syntheses and were used to notify members of other views about what the "big ideas" of each view were. Thus the children were creating their own curriculum, describing for themselves the key concepts in each view. Students used these notes in writing their portfolio notes. A review of the content of these notes suggests that the Grade 4 class identified problems and knowledge that were beyond those that are normally engaged in at Grade 4.

Year 3—Knowledge-Building Community

In the third year, the goal was to advance the classroom design in such a manner that the students would be building knowledge collaboratively, not just sharing it between views. Rather than have students decide on a focus for their study of light and commit to that area, the attempt was made to create an environment that was much more organic, fluid, and generative. Thus, although students demonstrated an interest in a particular area of light, no discrete groups were formed around those interests. Instead, views were created in the Knowledge Forum® database, and students were encouraged to work in any and all of the research views in the database.

Specific focus was placed on the knowledge-building principle of epistemic agency (Scardamalia, 2000). In the past two years, the teacher had previously decided the content of the year and creatively positioned the concepts so as to create the impression that the children were initiating the inquiry based on their interests. However, this year the teacher consciously avoided directing the learning and therefore did not impose a structure by directing the learning. Instead, as students began to work in the various database views and in their portfolio notes, the idea of "view masters" was created where groups of students adopted a view, read all the notes, and recorded the big ideas in the background of the view. This process seemed to encourage others to work on reciprocal teachings, to gather information, and thereby to support the knowledge building occurring in the weaker views. What evolved was a whole class working as a single research group with multiple subgoals under- and overarching the mission of being a knowledge-building community. Results from pre- and posttesting of the concepts associated with light also indicate that this third year was the most productive year in terms of both depth and breadth of coverage.

> Prior to receiving the data, the teacher indicated he felt the unstructured approach in the third year may have been developmentally too advanced for Grade 4 students.

Surprising Results!

Over the span of this three-year study, several database analyses were performed along with pre- and posttesting of the children's understanding of light concepts. The results suggest strongly that the technique of not assigning views in the third year led to the most productive knowledge-building community of the three years. It is compelling to note that in the third year, the students read extensively across the database views (82%), had significant improvements in their understanding of light

($p < .0009$ on 12 of 18 questions), produced the most notes per student, and worked on more problems than in the previous two years.

These results were surprising to the classroom teacher. Prior to receiving the data, the teacher indicated he felt the unstructured approach in the third year may have been developmentally too advanced for Grade 4 students. His theory was that the second year represented the ideal structure for knowledge building to proceed. Again, the design for the second year was small groups who were focused on a specialization, embedded in a larger community with the goal of sharing knowledge between groups. The teacher's previous experience suggested to him that children require tight arrangements of separate groups to make significant advances. In these arrangements, students are organized on the basis of interest, academic ability, and social or emotional needs. None of these factors were taken into consideration in the design of the third year. Also, in the first two years, it was a typical practice to identify clear goals for each of the groups with the belief that this would sustain the focus and contribute to internal group collaboration. The structural elements of knowledge-building talks, reciprocal teaching, student-designed experiments, and the use of the Knowledge Forum® database were present in all three years. However, in the third year, the students became a knowledge-building community through heightened agency over the processes by which knowledge was being created in their community. As a knowledge-building community, they created groups on a daily basis, made decisions about which problems of understanding required attention, and in turn produced knowledge that matched the breadth of the curriculum and exceeded its depth. But most important, as a knowledge-building community, they learned to produce knowledge of value to others.

15

Classroom Assessment for Deep Understanding

Lorna M. Earl

In this chapter, Lorna Earl discusses three purposes of assessment: (1) assessment of learning—reporting to parents and others about student progress; (2) assessment for learning—or diagnostic assessment used to give teachers information to modify teaching and learning activities; and (3) assessment as learning—to give students information to help them become active and engaged in their learning. This last purpose is key to ensuring deep understanding in students.

1. How do your assessment methods fit within this model?

2. Do you involve students in assessment as learning? How could you increase students' understanding of their learning to become more active in the process?

Author's Note: This chapter is excerpted and adapted from Earl, L. (2003). *Assessment as Learning: Using Classroom Assessment to Maximize Student Learning*. Thousand Oaks, CA: Corwin Press.

The history of assessment shows a long line of structural changes designed to inject quality control into education using a testing system designed to measure student performance and hold schools accountable. We have been consumed with more frequent and rigorous testing as an obvious mechanism for improving schools. Even well-meaning reformers offer testing as a politically feasible solution to the problems in schools. Unfortunately, criticizing educators does not improve schools, and higher test scores do not equal higher standards or better learning. Although policymakers often find ways to straddle the fence, teachers are independent actors who can wield their own influence in their classrooms and their schools. The time is right for rethinking assessment in schools.

Schools and districts are caught in the crossfire between contradictory purposes for education—"education for all" and "education as gatekeeper." Teachers and administrators are the instruments of these contradictory demands and are both recipients and perpetrators of the competing messages. In this confused and emotionally charged assessment environment, the stakes are high to get it right. Educators find themselves in a difficult position. They are part of the transition, laden with the burdens of the past, while contemplating the possibilities of the future. They know how it has always been and have a great deal invested in maintaining stability, but at the same time, many of them acknowledge that it just doesn't feel right. What better way to bring some clarity to a murky subject than to return to first principles—What is our purpose? What are we trying to accomplish? What is assessment for?

PURPOSE IS EVERYTHING

Paul Black (1998), in England, identified three broad purposes of assessment in schools—to support learning; to report achievement of individuals for certification, progress, and transfer; and to satisfy the demands for public accountability. He goes on to point out that there are tensions among the purposes that involve choices about the best agencies to conduct assessments and about the optimum instruments and appropriate interpretations to serve each purpose. It is not possible to use one assessment process for the many purposes that we want it to fulfill. Different purposes require vastly different approaches, and mixing the purposes is likely to ensure that none of them will be well served. It is becoming more and more obvious that we must first decide about the purpose and then design the assessment program to fit (Gipps, 1994).

> A vision of schools in which the purpose is deep understanding of ideas and concepts requires a dramatic change in the assumptions underlying education. . . .

A vision of schools in which the purpose is deep understanding of ideas and concepts requires a dramatic change in the assumptions underlying education, and it requires a different view of schools, schooling, teachers, teaching, and, particularly, assessment. In this conception, schools have the responsibility for preparing all students for tomorrow's world; teachers have the wherewithal to guide all students to high levels of learning and deep understanding; and assessment, first and foremost, is part of student learning. This seemingly straightforward shift requires dramatic changes in the way teaching and learning happen in schools.

RETHINKING CLASSROOM ASSESSMENT

Although most public attention is focused on the results of large-scale assessment programs, there is considerable evidence that classroom assessment—the assessment that teachers do in classrooms every day—has an immense impact on student learning and can be the lever for deep understanding.

IMPLICATIONS FOR TEACHING

Teachers who assess for deep understanding try to . . .

– Offer ongoing assessment and pertinent feedback to move learning forward

– Access students' existing beliefs and knowledge

– Identify incomplete understandings, false beliefs, and naïve interpretations

– Observe students' thinking over time, probe their understandings, and look for links between prior knowledge and new learning

– Teach students self-assessment

Black and Wiliam (1998) synthesized more than 250 studies linking assessment and learning and found that the intentional use of assessment in the classroom to promote learning raised student achievement. They also reported, however, that the characteristics of high-quality formative assessment are not well understood by most teachers and that this kind of assessment is weak in practice. Increasing the amount of assessment will not enhance learning. Assessment influences learning when teachers use it to become aware of the knowledge and beliefs that their students bring to a learning task, use this knowledge as a starting point for new instruction, and monitor students' changing perceptions as instruction proceeds. Students bring a range of prior knowledge, skills, beliefs, and concepts that influence how they will perceive, organize, and interpret the new task/learning environment. This makes assessment a major element in the learning process.

Classroom assessment has always been used for a variety of purposes, but the purposes are becoming more differentiated and complex. This means it is not easy to use one assessment process for the many different purposes. Assessment activities work best when the purpose is clear and explicit and the assessments are designed to fit that purpose.

Typically, teachers have three intertwined but distinct assessment purposes—assessment of learning, assessment for learning, and assessment as learning.[1]

Assessment of Learning

Assessment of learning is assessment used to confirm what students know, to demonstrate whether or not the students have met the standards, and/or to show how they are placed in relation to others. In assessment of learning, teachers use assessment to provide statements of proficiency or competence for students. Its purpose is summative, intended to certify learning and report to parents and students about their progress in school, usually by signalling students' relative position compared to other students. Assessment of learning in classrooms is typically done at the end of something (e.g., a unit, a course, a grade, a key stage, a program) and takes the form of tests or exams that include questions drawn from the material studied

---

[1]Some authors use assessment for learning to encapsulate the ideas described here in two categories—assessment for learning and assessment as learning.

during that time. In assessment of learning, the results are expressed symbolically, generally as marks or letter grades, and summarized as averages of a number of marks across several content areas to report to parents.

This is the kind of assessment that still dominates most classroom assessment activities, especially in secondary schools, with teachers firmly in charge of creating and marking the tests. Teachers use the tests to assess the quantity and accuracy of student work, and the bulk of teacher effort in assessment is taken up in marking and grading. There is a strong emphasis on comparing students; feedback to students comes in the form of marks or grades, with little direction or advice for improvement. These kinds of testing events indicate which students are doing best and which ones are doing poorly. Typically, they don't give much indication of mastery of particular ideas or concepts because the test content is generally too limited and the scoring is too simplistic to represent the broad range of skills and knowledge that have been covered. But this lack of specificity hasn't presented a problem because the teachers perceive the purpose of assessment to be the production of a rank order of the students and the assignment of a symbol designating the students' position within the group, whatever group it might be. Teachers maintain voluminous records of student achievement that are only used for justifying the grades that are assigned.

> ... there is considerable evidence that classroom assessment—the assessment that teachers do in classrooms every day—has an immense impact on student learning and can be the lever for deep understanding. ...

Assessment for Learning

Assessment for learning is designed to give teachers information to modify the teaching and learning activities in which students are engaged in order to differentiate and focus how to approach the learning of individual students. It suggests that students are all learning in individual and idiosyncratic ways, while recognizing that there are predictable patterns and pathways that many students go through. The emphasis is on teachers using the information from carefully designed assessments not only to determine what students know but also to gain insights into how, when, and whether students use what they know, so that teachers can streamline and target instruction and resources. Assessment for learning shifts the emphasis from summative to formative assessment, from making judgments to creating descriptions that can be used in the service of the next stage of learning.

When they are doing assessment for learning, teachers collect a wide range of data so that they can modify the learning work for their students. They craft assessment tasks that open a window on what students know and can do already, and they use the insights that come from the process to design the next steps in instruction. To do this, teachers use observation, worksheets, questioning in class, student-teacher conferences, or other mechanisms to give them information that will be useful for their planning and their teaching. Marking is not designed to make comparative judgments among the students but to highlight each student's strengths and weaknesses and provide students with feedback that will further their learning.

Clearly, teachers are the central characters in assessment for learning as well, but their role is quite different than in the prior approach. In assessment for learning, they use their personal knowledge of the students and their understanding of the context of the assessment and the curriculum targets to identify particular learning needs. Assessment for learning happens in the middle of learning, often more than once, not at the end. It is interactive, with teachers providing assistance as part of the assessment. It helps teachers provide the feedback to scaffold next steps. And it depends on teachers' diagnostic skills to make it work. Before teachers can plan for targeted teaching and classroom activities, they need to have a sense of what it is that students are thinking. What is it that they believe to be true? This process involves much more than "Do they have the right or wrong answer?" It means making students' thinking visible and understanding the images and patterns which they construct to make sense of the world from their perspective.

Record keeping in this approach may include a grade book, but the records that teachers rely on are checklists of student progress against expectations, artifacts, portfolios of student work over time, and worksheets to trace the progression of students along the learning continuum.

Assessment as Learning

Assessment as learning emphasizes the use of assessment to help develop and support metacognition for students.

Assessment as learning focuses on the role of the student as the critical connector between assessment and learning. As active, engaged, and critical assessors, students make sense of information, relate it to prior knowledge, and use it for new learning. This is the regulatory process in metacognition. It occurs when students personally monitor what they are learning and use the feedback from this monitoring to make adjustments, adaptations, and even major changes in what they understand. When teachers focus on assessment as learning, they use classroom assessment as the vehicle for helping students develop, practice, and become comfortable with reflection and with critical analysis of their own learning.

ASSESSMENT PURPOSE IS PARAMOUNT

Assessment of learning, assessment for learning, and assessment as learning are all valuable purposes for classroom assessment. However, it is not always easy getting the balance right. If deep understanding is the purpose, assessment for learning and assessment as learning take on a much higher profile, and assessment of learning becomes more focused and less pervasive. At this time, most classroom assessment is assessment of learning, focused on measuring learning after the fact and using the information to make judgments about students and report these judgments to others. Teachers also use assessment for learning by building in diagnostic processes, formative assessment, and feedback at stages in the program, although this process may often be informal and implicit. Systematic assessment as learning, where students become critical analysts of their own learning, is rare. Some teachers incorporate self-assessment into their programs, but very few explicitly use assessment to develop students' capacity to evaluate and adapt their own learning.

> By shifting the balance away from assessment of learning, teachers and students can use the assessment process as a vehicle for learning about the progress and problems embedded in new learning.

Teach Students Self-Assessment

To fulfill assessment's promise as an aid to learning, it is necessary to rethink its purpose. By shifting the balance away from assessment of learning, teachers and students can use the assessment process as a vehicle for learning about the progress and problems embedded in new learning. When the goal is deep understanding, assessment is too powerful to waste by leaving it to the end. Teachers and students can use ongoing assessment and pertinent feedback to move learning forward and deepen the students' grasp of the ideas. Assessment allows teachers access to students' existing beliefs and knowledge and helps to identify incomplete understandings, false beliefs, and naïve interpretations of concepts that will influence or distort their learning. When it is frequent and varied, teachers can use classroom assessment to tell a great deal about a student. They can observe students' thinking over time, probe their understanding, look for links between prior knowledge and new learning, and use the information to provide the feedback loop in the learning cycle.

Clarke (2001) tackles the issue of how to give feedback on written work to guide students' learning. She suggests focusing feedback on a few things that are directly connected to the learning intentions for the task. She uses simple strategies: using a highlighter pen to identify examples of the learning intentions in the student's work; selecting a few of these highlighted elements and writing what she calls a "closing-the-gap" prompt—prompts for making changes to their work that are geared to learning intentions and to the particular student, influenced by what the teacher already knows about that student.

Closing-the-Gap Prompts Giving Feedback on Written Work

Learning intention: To effectively introduce a character at the start of a story.

Activity: Choose someone you know but the class doesn't to describe in a written paragraph.

We are learning to: Write about people's characters for our stories.

How will we know we've done it? (created with the class): We will have written something about their appearance, their likes and dislikes, their personality, their attitudes, and other things that help others know more about them.

The example: Let's assume that a child has written about someone he knows from a summer camp. After highlighting several phrases that successfully give information about this person, the teacher asterisks the phrase "This person is a good friend."

The arrow to the "closing-the-gap" prompt could take any of the following forms:

- A reminder prompt: Say more about how you feel about this person.
- A reminder prompt is most suitable for a student who probably has good command of figurative language but has not used it here, for whatever reason.

- A scaffolding prompt: Can you describe how this person is a good friend? (question) Or describe something that happened that showed you what a good friend this person is. (directive) Or, he showed me he was a good friend when . . . (finish the sentence)
- Scaffolding prompts work well with students who need more structure or some direction but are likely to carry on from there.
- An example prompt: Choose one of these sentences to tell me more about your friend. "He is a good friend because he never says unkind things about me." Or "My friend helps me do things."
- When students are struggling or don't appear to understand the concept, example prompts can provide them with actual models of the learning intention.

Earl (2003) adapted from Clarke (2001)

Students are very motivated by these closing-the-gap strategies, and teachers are astounded by how quickly and thoughtfully they respond. A number of exciting spin-offs have come from this approach to feedback in marking. Once students get the hang of it, the feedback process lends itself to self- and paired-student assessment. Students start to think about what the teacher would highlight; they develop arguments and reasons for their choices; they offer one another suggestions for improvement; and they revisit their own work with a critical eye.

Going deeper comes from ensuring that students are not only learning but also thinking about their learning by reviewing their experiences of learning (What made sense and what didn't? How does this fit with what I already know, or think I know?) and applying what they have learned to their future learning. Assessment gives students the feedback and direction that they need to review and reflect on their learning, to determine how it fits, and to make adaptations if they are necessary.

> Students are very motivated by these closing-the-gap strategies, and teachers are astounded by how quickly and thoughtfully they respond. A number of exciting spin-offs have come from this approach to feedback in marking. Once students get the hang of it, the feedback process lends itself to self- and paired-student assessment.

When students (and teachers) become comfortable with a continuous cycle of feedback and adjustment, learning becomes more efficient, and students begin to internalize the process of standing outside their own learning and considering it against a range of criteria, not just the teacher's judgment about quality or accuracy. This ongoing metacognitive experience allows them to monitor learning along the way, make corrections, and develop a habit of mind for continually reviewing and challenging what they know.

In this reconfigured assessment environment, assessment would make up a large part of the school day, not in the form of separate tests but as a seamless part of the learning process. There would still be tests, for example, when the decisions to be made require identification of a few individuals or groups or when a summative description is important for students and for others as a milestone or "rite of passage." But in the real world, these incidents are far fewer than school experience would lead us to believe.

PART IV

The Challenge of Teaching for Deep Understanding

16

What Teachers Think

Pat McAdie

Achieving deep understanding for our students through the provincial school curriculum depends, in no small measure, on a more precise appreciation of the starting point. And who better to provide such information than the teachers of the province? In this chapter, Pat McAdie reports on the findings of the Elementary Teachers' Federation of Ontario (ETFO) survey of public elementary teachers in Ontario on a range of issues related to curriculum, instruction, and teaching for understanding. The results reported in this chapter are especially representative of more experienced teachers in the province.

The first part of this book argues for the meaning and importance of deep understanding as a central goal for Ontario education while the next two parts review much of what would be involved for teachers in the classroom to achieve this goal. We think that few teachers would actually disagree with our view that deep understanding ought to be central to their work. Many, however, would question the feasibility of achieving this goal, given the conditions in which they find themselves working and perhaps their background and training, as well.

Author's Note: I would like to acknowledge and thank Doris Jantzi, Senior Research Officer, OISE/UT, for her work on the analysis of the survey results. I would also like to thank Ken Leithwood for his considered suggestions for the chapter.

Achieving deep understanding for our students through the provincial school curriculum depends, in no small measure, on a more precise appreciation of the starting point, and who better to provide such information than the teachers of the province. It is those teachers who eventually must implement those practices with which earlier chapters of the book have been so preoccupied if anything is to change. To get this information, we designed and administered a survey to a representative sample of the province's public elementary school teachers.

We asked teachers their opinions and practices about

- Curriculum policy and its implementation
- Assessment policy and its implementation
- Classroom practices
    ○ Cross-disciplinary classroom practices
    ○ Literacy instruction practices
    ○ Mathematics instruction practices
    ○ Science and technology instruction practices
- Teaching conditions

We relied heavily on the work that is reported in other chapters in this volume in developing the survey. In addition, we drew on much previous research on teaching for understanding (Bransford, Brown, & Cocking, 2000; Perkins, 1993a; Wilson, 1992).

We do not claim that the results of our survey provide the same information that would be collected were we to directly observe what teachers are doing. But direct observation of teachers' work tells us nothing about what teachers are attempting to accomplish, very little about which practices they consider key to those goals, and almost nothing about the challenges they face in their schools and districts in teaching for deep understanding: These were the key questions we needed to have answered. In addition, recent research supports the validity and reliability of survey work more strongly than in the past. Specifically, in comparison with classroom observation and teacher logs, self-report surveys have been demonstrated to provide valid and reliable measures of classroom instruction and teacher experiences (Desimone & Le Floch, 2004).

The survey was mailed to a random sample of 2,500 ETFO teacher members on April 29 and 30, 2004. Nine hundred were returned in time for our analysis: Of these, 882 provided usable results for analysis—a 35 percent response rate.

With such a return rate, it is important to ask just how representative the responses are likely to be. So we compared the characteristics of those who responded with characteristics of Ontario public elementary teachers as a whole (information already available in ETFO files). The results of this comparison are outlined in Table 16.1. As the table indicates, the sample was representative on gender, teaching level, and single or combined grade classes taught. It was, however, distinctly different from the whole membership on total years of teaching experience.

We have no way to assess the reasons for this discrepancy in years of teaching experience—it could be by chance, or it could be because members with less experience felt they did not have the time or indeed the experience to complete the survey. Nonetheless, this means that the results reported in this chapter are especially representative of more experienced teachers in the province.

Table 16.1   Comparison of Survey Sample With ETFO Teacher Members

	Sample	ETFO Membership
Teaching Level		
Primary	46%	44%
Junior	34%	33%
Intermediate	20%	23%
Type of Class		
Single grade	60%	67%
Combined grade	36%	33%
Gender		
Female	84%	80%
Male	16%	20%
Years Teaching Experience		
Less than 5	1%	16%
5 to 9	20%	20%
10 or more	79%	64%

CURRICULUM POLICY AND ITS IMPLEMENTATION

Findings in Brief...

- Curriculum expectations are not being taught in all subject areas and at all grade levels.
- Teachers do not believe that the curriculum is developmentally appropriate for their students, most notably at the junior level.
- Teachers do not agree that they are adequately prepared to teach this curriculum or have sufficient resources to do so.
- To deal with this situation, some teachers are assigning more homework to students than they would like.
- Very few teachers agreed that the curriculum represented the diversity within our society.

All of these observations point to serious problems with the curriculum in its present form.

The survey contained 13 questions asking teachers about their experiences and opinions on curriculum policy and its implementation. We considered these especially key questions because a major impetus for this project was teachers' growing concerns about the new curriculum that had been introduced in elementary schools starting in 1997. Whereas the previous curriculum, still in its initial stages, had specified curriculum expectations for each division, the new curriculum outlined a great many specific expectations for each subject area for each grade level (we describe these in some detail in Chapter 1). Concern had been expressed that the new curriculum was overloaded, provided much breadth but little depth, and was developmentally inappropriate for students.

Questions in this section were designed to test these concerns and to inquire about the ability of teachers to work with this curriculum. Teachers were asked whether they were able to cover the curriculum expectations in six key subject areas; whether they believed the curriculum was developmentally appropriate for their students and if they could adapt it to the differing needs of their students; and whether they were adequately prepared to teach the current curriculum and had sufficient resources to do so. The survey also asked teachers how much homework they needed to assign to work with the current curriculum and whether the current curriculum recognized contributions and systemic barriers of diverse groups in Canadian society. On a five-point scale, teachers were asked if they *strongly agreed, agreed, were neutral, disagreed,* or *strongly disagreed* with a number of statements. What did we learn?

Curriculum Expectations Are Not Being Met

As the top graph on page 129 indicates, teachers were more likely to disagree than to agree that they were able to cover the curriculum expectations in six subject areas. Only in language arts and in physical education and health were teachers more in agreement than disagreement; however, in no case did a majority of teachers agree that they were able to cover all of the curriculum expectations. In science and technology, mathematics, social studies, and the arts, teachers were more likely to disagree that they could cover all the curriculum expectations.

Junior Teachers Have the Most Difficulty

As the bottom graph on page 129 shows, junior teachers (Grades 4 to 6) were significantly less likely than primary teachers to state that they could cover the curriculum in all areas except for physical education and health. Intermediate teachers (Grades 7 and 8) were significantly less likely than primary teachers to say they could cover the curriculum in social studies and in the arts.

Classes With One Third to Two Thirds of Students Having Special Needs Are the Most Challenged

Teachers of classes with special needs had the most difficulty covering the curriculum expectations, particularly in science and technology and mathematics. Classes in which more than two thirds of students have special needs were likely to be stand-alone special education classes, where adaptations to the curriculum have been made.

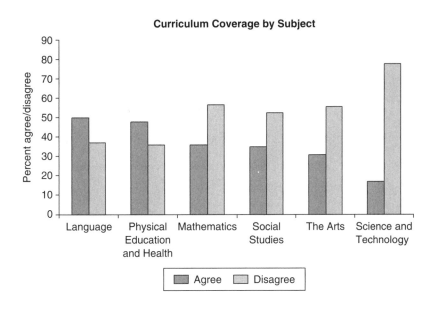

Curriculum Coverage by Subject

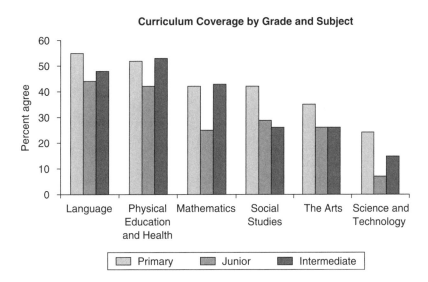

Curriculum Coverage by Grade and Subject

Teachers Are Assigning More Homework Than They Would Like

Sixty-three percent of teachers agreed that they had to assign more homework than they would like to cover the curriculum expectations. Junior teachers were significantly more likely to agree with this statement than primary teachers.

Teachers Believe the Curriculum Is Not Developmentally Appropriate

Sixty-one percent of teachers disagreed that the curriculum was developmentally appropriate for their students; only 27 percent agreed that the curriculum was developmentally appropriate. The lowest rating came from junior teachers—only 21 percent were in agreement and 68 percent disagreed. Intermediate teachers were more divided on the developmental appropriateness of the curriculum—39 percent agreed and 46 percent disagreed that the curriculum was developmentally appropriate for their students.

Is Curriculum Developmentally Appropriate?

	Agree	Disagree
Primary	28%	62%
Junior	21%	68%
Intermediate	39%	46%
All teachers	27%	61%

Only 15 percent of teachers agreed that the curriculum allows them to adapt to the differing needs of their students.

Teachers with fewer students with special needs were more likely to rate the developmental appropriateness of the curriculum higher, although these teachers were still in disagreement with the statement. In addition, these teachers had a slightly more favorable view of the adaptability of the curriculum to the differing needs of their students.

Only a Small Majority Feel Adequately Prepared

Only 57 percent of teachers agreed that they were adequately prepared to teach the current curriculum. Junior teachers (49 percent agreed) had a lower rating on this question than both primary (60 percent) and intermediate (63 percent) teachers. At the risk of being redundant here, this is a truly shocking result. Fully 43 percent of the province's more experienced teachers, on average, admit to feeling inadequately prepared to teach the current curriculum.

Few Believe They Have Sufficient Resources

Only 25 percent of teachers agreed that there were sufficient resources available to teach the current curriculum. Again, junior teachers were less optimistic about resources (19 percent agreed they had sufficient resources) than either primary (27 percent) or intermediate (31 percent) teachers. Schools, in their view, are clearly not equipped to achieve even the current curriculum, never mind the more ambitious one that we are advocating. No doubt the last eight years of provincial budget reductions has had a great deal to do with these opinions.

Teachers Are Split on the Recognition of Diversity in Curriculum

Teachers were fairly split on whether the curriculum recognizes the contributions of diverse groups and individuals to Canadian society—30 percent disagreed, 32 percent were neutral, and 38 percent agreed. There were no consistent differences by grade level taught or percentage of special needs students in classes. Forty-seven percent of teachers disagreed that the official provincial curriculum identifies systemic barriers faced by specific groups; only 13 percent agreed with this statement.

Results summarized in this section make it clear that curriculum expectations are not being taught in all subject areas and at all grade levels. Nor do teachers believe that the curriculum is developmentally appropriate for their students, most notably at the junior level. In addition, teachers do not agree that they are adequately prepared to teach this curriculum or have sufficient resources to do so. One strategy that some teachers are employing to deal with this situation is to assign more homework to students than they would like. In addition, very few teachers agreed that the curriculum represented the diversity within our society. All of these observations point to serious problems with the curriculum in its present form.

It should be noted that the Ministry of Education is currently reviewing the curriculum; however, major changes are not expected. For example, the social studies curriculum, which is being implemented in the 2005–2006 school year, reduces the number of expectations very little (78 over eight years of elementary education) and certainly not enough to affect the results reported in this chapter.

ASSESSMENT POLICY AND ITS IMPLEMENTATION

Findings in Brief . . .

- Provincial policies and practices do a poor job of assessment for the purposes of learning.
- Provincial policies and practices do a somewhat better job for the purposes of assessment of learning and assessment as learning.
- Classroom strategies are seen as more valuable than top-down assessment polices, including the provincial report card, the curriculum documents, and the Education Quality and Accountability Office (EQAO) tests.

Students will be more likely to achieve deep understanding when assessment is used as a tool for learning. Teachers need additional resources and skills if they are to use assessment in this way.

The next set of questions asked for teachers' opinions and experiences with assessment policies, including those in the curriculum documents, the standardized provincial report cards, classroom assessment strategies, and the province's EQAO tests. In Chapter 15, Earl discusses three purposes for assessment—assessment of learning, assessment for learning, and assessment as learning. These distinctions can be thought of as primarily providing assessment information mostly for parents and others, for teachers, and for students, respectively. Questions in this section are about the approaches and tools for assessment mentioned in relation to these three different assessment purposes.

The Majority of Teachers Don't Like the Provincial Report Card

Only 34 percent of teachers agreed that they liked the standardized provincial report cards. Fifty percent disagreed with this statement. Primary teachers liked the report card least—only 28 percent of primary teachers agreed they like it, compared with 38 percent for junior teachers and 40 percent for intermediate teachers. In addition, only 26 percent of teachers agreed that the provincial report card provides appropriate information to parents about the progress of their children; 62 percent disagreed. As a means of assessment of learning, it seems that the provincial report card falls short.

Like Standardized Provincial Report Card?

	Agree	Disagree
Primary	28%	56%
Junior	38%	44%
Intermediate	40%	45%
All teachers	34%	50%

Teachers Use a Wide Range of Classroom Assessment Strategies

An overwhelming majority of teachers (92 percent) agreed that they employ a wide range of assessment strategies in their classrooms. This did not vary by grade level, by class size, or by the fraction of students with special needs. Classroom assessment strategies would fall into both the assessment for learning and assessment as learning purposes.

Teachers Involve Students in the Assessment Process

Overall, teachers agreed that they involve their students in the assessment process. However, junior and intermediate teachers were more likely to agree with this statement than primary teachers—83 percent of junior teachers and 78 percent of intermediate teachers agreed whereas only 65 percent of primary teachers agreed with this statement. Involving students in assessment is an important aspect of assessment as learning.

Teachers Are Not Comfortable With Assessment Strategies in Curriculum Documents

Only 40 percent of teachers agreed that they are comfortable with the assessment strategies in the curriculum documents. Intermediate teachers (48 percent) were more likely to agree than primary teachers (37 percent). These assessment strategies are quite general and reflect the information required for an assessment of learning as reported in the provincial report cards.

EQAO Not Seen as Valuable for Assessment or Communication With Parents

Teachers were quite clear and unanimous in their opinion on EQAO tests. Only 6 percent agreed that the tests are valuable for assessing their students' progress, and only 4 percent agreed that they improved communication with parents, both aspects of assessment of learning. Only 12 percent agreed that the tests have a positive impact on how they teach as a means of assessment for learning. There were no differences by grade level, class size, or fraction of students with special needs in how teachers felt about EQAO. Although one of the purposes for these tests is often claimed to be the assessment of learning, Ontario's public elementary teachers give these tests a failing grade.

Educational Quality and Accountability Office Tests

	Agree	Disagree
Are valuable for assessing students' progress	6%	85%
Have a positive impact on teaching	12%	78%
Improve communication with parents	4%	87%

From the answers to our questions about assessment tools and practices, it seems that provincial policies and practices do a poor job of assessment for the purposes of learning, that assessment for learning and assessment as learning are somewhat better. However, classroom strategies that teachers employ are seen as more valuable than policies imposed by the provincial government through the provincial report card, the curriculum documents, and EQAO tests. As Earl points out in Chapter 15, students will be more likely to achieve deep understanding when assessment is used as a tool for learning. Teachers need additional resources and skills if they are to use assessment in this way.

CLASSROOM PRACTICES

Teaching for deep understanding involves allowing students to make connections within and across the curriculum. Deep understanding is acquired through the thoughtful exploration and discussion of ideas, not through the transmission of discrete facts, events, or bits of knowledge. Deep understanding has an impact on students' view of the world. The prior knowledge and experience children bring to class as well as their cultural values and beliefs influence the learning that takes place in the classroom.

Four sections of the survey probed teachers' classroom practices as they relate to teaching for deep understanding: overall or cross-disciplinary instruction practices; literacy instruction; mathematics instruction; and science and technology instruction.

CROSS-DISCIPLINARY PRACTICES

Findings in Brief . . .

- Teachers use instruction practices that promote deep understanding.
- They use collaborative activities, encourage discussion, and engage students to look beyond the discipline area to prior knowledge, other subjects, and their own experiences.
- The connection of the curriculum to culture does not appear to be a priority with elementary teachers.

Much has been learned over the past decade or so about how people learn (Bransford et al., 2000), and much of this is alluded to by Beck and Kosnik in Chapter 3. The questions in this section are intended to probe teachers' practices that take advantage of this knowledge.

Overall, teachers answered in the affirmative regarding their classroom practices supporting deep understanding. On a five-point scale, where 5 is *strongly agree,* 3 is neutral, and 1 is *strongly disagree,* the mean response for the questions in this section was 4.18, indicating that teachers believe themselves to be using techniques that develop deep understanding.

Teachers Support Collaborative Activities

Eighty-five percent of teachers agreed that collaborative activities are an important part of how students learn in their class. In addition, 94 percent agreed that their students acquire and construct knowledge collaboratively with them.

Discussion Is Encouraged but There Could Be More

Ninety-eight percent of teachers said they encourage students to talk about what they are learning in other subjects. Ninety-four percent agree that all their students have a voice in their classroom. Ninety-three percent agree that they provide opportunities for students to discuss ways to deal with differences of opinion. However, only 71 percent agree that they provide many opportunities for discussion and debate in their classrooms; 14 percent disagreed with this statement, and 15 percent were neutral.

Construction of Knowledge Is Encouraged

Almost all teachers (98 percent) agreed that students should be encouraged to talk about what they are learning in other subjects. No one disagreed with this statement. In addition, 94 percent of teachers agreed that students are encouraged to consider new material in relation to their own experience, one of the key tenets of constructivism and teaching for deep understanding. However, a smaller percentage agreed that students should compare and contrast new material with previously studied material, also a key component of constructivism and deep understanding; 78 percent of teachers agreed with this statement; 15 percent neither agreed nor disagreed, and 7 percent disagreed with this question.

Students Are Encouraged to
Think Beyond the Classroom

Virtually all teachers agreed that they want their students to think beyond the classroom. Ninety-nine percent of teachers agreed that students should be able to think about, explain, and apply their knowledge beyond the classroom. To a slightly lesser degree, 87 percent of teachers also say they encourage their students to discuss ideas in terms of their own and other people's culture and values.

Students Are Expected to Assume
Responsibility for Learning

Eighty-eight percent of teachers said that they expect their students to assume responsibility for their own learning. Eight percent were neutral about this question, and only 5 percent disagreed. This aspect of learning is also believed to be important in ensuring deep understanding.

The Role of Teachers Is to Ask Questions,
but Teachers Are Less Likely to Revisit Ideas

Ninety-seven percent of teachers see their role as one of posing questions, challenging thinking, and leading in the examination of ideas and concepts. Seventy-five percent of teachers say that they regularly revisit ideas and concepts previously discussed to work toward deeper or alternative interpretations. Although this is still a high percentage, it is about 20 percent lower than the responses to most questions in this section, possibly suggesting a problem with time.

The Connection Between
Curriculum and Culture Is Not a Priority

Only 46 percent of teachers agreed that they promote students' understanding of the relationship between curriculum and culture. Thirty-five percent were neutral about this question, and 19 percent disagreed. This is the weakest level of agreement in this section of questions.

In general, teachers agreed quite strongly that they use instruction practices that promote deep understanding. They use collaborative activities, encourage discussion, and engage students to look beyond the discipline area to prior knowledge, other subjects, and their own experiences. However, the connection of the curriculum to culture appears not to be a priority.

LITERACY INSTRUCTION PRACTICES

> ## Findings in Brief . . .
>
> - Teachers are using a range of instructional practices—having students make predictions, using graphic organizers, examining literary techniques, requiring inferences—that are important for actively engaging students with what they are reading.
> - When asked directly whether they focus on a topic in depth, less than half indicated that this was part of their literacy instruction—an interesting discrepancy.

We know from Booth (Chapter 6) that deep understanding in literature helps students gain knowledge in a myriad of areas—cognitive, personal, and social. Teachers help students by guiding their reading of a variety of texts and encouraging their use of graphic organizers and other tools to explore texts.

Teachers were asked to indicate on a five-point scale how often they used various literacy activities in their classrooms. Overall, teachers indicated that they generally used the practices listed, with an overall average rating of 3.76 (5 = *always*). Teachers of junior (3.82) and intermediate (3.86) grades rated their use of these practices higher than primary teachers (3.69).

Activating Prior Knowledge Is an Important Aspect of Literacy Classrooms

Eighty-seven percent of teachers said that they *sometimes* or *always* included activities that activated prior knowledge or made personal connections in their literacy instruction. Only 2 percent said they *rarely* or *never* used such activities.

Teachers Encourage Active Engagement of Students With Literacy Materials

Teachers generally used activities that encourage students to actively engage with literature. However, some activities are used more than others. Identifying with the author's purpose and techniques are not used as extensively as other active techniques.

Activity	Use Often or Always	Don't or Rarely Use
Making predictions	84%	2%
Summarizing details	83%	3%
Using graphic organizers	67%	9%
Examining literary techniques	58%	11%
Identifying author's purpose	58%	11%

Teachers Encourage Construction of Knowledge

Teachers do encourage students to construct knowledge in their literacy instruction, although less than they indicated in their general cross-disciplinary practices. Teachers were least likely to have students use data and text references to support their ideas.

Activity	Use Often or Always	Don't or Rarely Use
Requiring inferences	74%	6%
Produce original work	62%	9%
Supporting student's ideas	56%	12%

Direct Teaching for Depth Is Not Strong

When asked most directly about using activities that encourage depth of understanding, teachers indicated that such activities were not used as frequently as other techniques. Sixty-seven percent of teachers said they *often* or *always* included activities that went beyond the facts. Only 48 percent said they focused on examining a topic in depth rather than just covering the facts, concepts, or procedures. Given responses to other questions that indicate a stronger focus on activities that do encourage deep understanding, teachers may be responding here to an inability to both cover all of the learning expectations and go into a subject area in more depth. Given a strong provincial emphasis on literacy, including EQAO tests, there are more serious consequences if students do not cover expectations in this area. Even though only 50 percent of teachers agreed that they were able to cover the expectations in languages, this was the highest rating for all curriculum areas.

Collaboration Is Encouraged

Teachers claim to employ activities that encourage collaboration with other students but, again, less so than they indicated in the questions regarding cross-disciplinary activities. Seventy-two percent said they *always* or *sometimes* involved students in presenting their work to other students. Sixty-eight percent of teachers indicated that they had students work together in pairs or small groups.

Peer Assessment Is Not Used Frequently

Only 33 percent of teachers said that they engaged students in peer evaluation. Twenty-eight percent disagreed with this statement, and 39 percent were neutral about this activity.

Teachers' literacy instruction practices also are conducive to deep understanding. The activities that teachers are using in the classrooms—having students make predictions, using graphic organizers, examining literary techniques, requiring inferences—are important for ensuring that students actively engage with what they are reading to enhance learning and knowledge in all areas. When asked directly, however, whether they focus on a topic in depth, less than half of teachers indicated that this was part of their literacy instruction—an interesting discrepancy.

MATHEMATICS INSTRUCTION PRACTICES

Findings in Brief . . .

- Public elementary teachers are attempting to adhere to the approach to mathematics instruction described in Chapter 5—flowing between two ends of the spectrum, teaching for deep understanding at times and using more traditional math instruction techniques at other times.
- The weakest areas are integrating strands of mathematics and letting students construct their own mathematics knowledge.

We know from Chapter 5 by Ross and McDougall that deep understanding in mathematics comes from students working together on authentic problems, having access to all forms of mathematics, working as co-learners with their teachers, and gaining self-confidence to discover mathematics principles.

Teachers were asked to indicate on a five-point scale (5 = *highest*) how often various activities were the primary focus of math instruction in their classrooms. Overall, the average rating was 3.58, just above a neutral rating.

Process Is Emphasized Over Single Answers

Fifty-seven percent of teachers said that they used problems that could be solved in many different ways, indicating an emphasis on the process of solving problems rather than only getting the correct answer. Only 12 percent of teachers said they *rarely* or *never* used such activities. When asked more directly, only 7 percent said they put more emphasis on getting the correct answer than the process followed in solving math problems; 74 percent said they *rarely* or *never* did so.

Authentic Problems Are Used Sometimes

Fifty-four percent of teachers indicated that they were more likely to use authentic, real-life math problems. Although this was not a strong response, only 13 percent of teachers said that they *rarely* or *never* used such problems.

Viewing Students as Co-learners Is Not Strong

Fifty-eight percent of teachers said they had students share their strategies with each other. Only 41 percent said they learned from their students during math time; 26 percent said they *rarely* or *never* learned from their students.

More Than Two Thirds of Teachers Employ Active Learning Techniques

Math manipulatives are used *sometimes* or *always* by 69 percent of teachers. Sixty-six percent of teachers use activities to teach students how to explain their mathematical ideas.

Integration of Strands Is Not Used Extensively

Only 43 percent of teachers said that they *sometimes* or *always* integrated multiple strands of mathematics within a single unit; 25 percent *rarely* or *never* used such activities in math instruction.

Construction of Knowledge in Mathematics Rarely Focuses on Instruction

Letting students find their own solutions is not a strong focus in math instruction. Only 35 percent of teachers indicated that they *sometimes* or *always* used such activities; 21 percent said they *rarely* or *never* let students puzzle out things for themselves.

Ross and McDougall (see Chapter 5) talk about expert teachers flowing between two ends of the spectrum, teaching for deep understanding at times and using more traditional math instruction techniques at other times, depending on the specific curriculum and students. In most respects, public elementary teachers are at least attempting to adhere to this approach to mathematics instruction. The weakest areas are integrating strands of mathematics and letting students construct their own mathematics knowledge. Again, given the emphasis on numeracy and EQAO test results, teachers may feel they cannot afford to let students fall behind in covering all of the expectations in mathematics.

SCIENCE AND TECHNOLOGY INSTRUCTION PRACTICES

> **Findings in Brief . . .**
>
> - Teachers' responses to the questions regarding science and technology instruction practices were the lowest in promoting deep understanding.
> - Although teachers were still primarily in agreement with the practices probed in this section, their agreement was weaker than in other discipline areas.

In Chapter 7, Bencze explains the need for including the perspectives of other cultures in teaching science and technology. He also talks of the importance of knowing students' prior knowledge and of choosing practical, authentic content.

Teachers were asked to indicate to what extent they agreed with statements on their instruction practices in science and technology, from *strongly agree* (5) to *strongly disagree* (1). Overall, teachers are just above a neutral rating on this scale, at 3.47, indicating that teaching for deep understanding is not as strong in science and technology instruction.

Connection With Other Cultures Is Not Seen as Part of Science and Technology Instruction

Only 20 percent of teachers said that they agreed that they provide access to science and technology ideas from other cultures. Thirty-six percent disagreed with this statement, while 44 percent were neutral.

Most Teachers Take Account of Prior Knowledge

Sixty-four percent of teachers agreed that they know and take account of students' preinstructional understanding of science and technology; only 14 percent of teachers disagreed with this statement.

Direct Teaching Is Seen as Valuable

Almost all teachers agreed that they used some direct teaching to ensure all students had access to concepts and skills in the science and technology curriculum; only 3 percent disagreed.

Authentic Problems Are Used in Most Classrooms

About two thirds of teachers provide opportunities for students to apply science and technology concepts to problems that are relevant to the student; 10 percent disagreed that they used this approach in teaching science and technology.

However, only 54 percent of teachers agreed that they provide students the opportunity to do projects of their own choosing; 25 percent disagreed with this statement.

Understanding of Technology Is Not Expected

Only 47 percent of teachers said that they expect students to understand the scientific knowledge underlying technology. Twenty-one percent of teachers said that they did not expect students to gain such an understanding, and 32 percent were neutral. See Chapter 8 by Carl Bereiter for a discussion of the importance of understanding technology.

Historical Origins and Impact of Science and Technology Not Widely Taught

Only 46 percent of teachers agreed that they provided students with the opportunity to discuss the development of technology and its social effects, a quality of understanding promoted by both Bencze and Bereiter. Twenty-three percent disagreed with this statement.

A small majority of teachers (55 percent) agreed that they provided students opportunities to think critically about the intended and unintended consequences of science and technology; 17 percent disagreed with this statement.

Teachers' responses to the questions regarding science and technology instruction practices were the lowest in promoting deep understanding. Although teachers were still primarily in agreement with the practices probed in this section, their agreement was weaker than in other discipline areas.

COMPARISON OF TEACHING FOR DEEP UNDERSTANDING ACROSS SUBJECT AREAS

Although the questions were asked in different ways within each disciplinary section, they were all probing teaching practices that promote deep understanding. Are teachers more able or comfortable teaching for deep understanding in some areas than in other areas?

When asked in more general terms, teachers rated their teaching practices as conducive to deep understanding relatively high, 4.18 on average on a 5-point scale. However, when asked more specifically about their instruction practices in three areas of the curriculum—literacy, mathematics, and science and technology—they rated their use of these practices somewhat lower. Science and technology instruction practices received the lowest rating. Nevertheless, it should be noted that for all subject areas, teachers were more in agreement with the statements regarding their instruction practices, indicating that teachers are more inclined toward teaching for deep understanding than not. It is interesting to note that the average rating for ability to cover all of the curriculum expectations is highest for literacy and lowest for science and technology, with mathematics midway between these two.

	Average Rating	Average Rating for Curriculum Coverage
Cross-disciplinary practices	4.18	
Literacy instruction	3.76	3.09
Mathematics instruction	3.58	2.64
Science and technology instruction	3.47	2.01

TEACHING CONDITIONS

Findings in Brief . . .

- Teachers do not have sufficient time to meet with colleagues.
- They are not provided with sufficient professional development opportunities.
- Key working conditions for teaching for deep understanding are not being provided in Ontario's public elementary schools.

Teachers were also asked about their opinions and experiences related to a number of teaching conditions. We know from many of the chapters that teaching conditions affect the learning conditions for students. In addition, some teaching conditions restrain teachers' ability to teach for deep understanding.

Questions in this section use a 5-point scale from *strongly agree* (1) to *strongly disagree* (5).

Class Size Is Important for Effective Teaching

Ninety-one percent of teachers said that they found class size important for effective teaching; only 7 percent said that they did not find class size to be a barrier.

Few Teachers Have Sufficient Time to Meet With Colleagues

Only 3 percent of teachers said that they had sufficient time during the school day to meet with colleagues about curriculum issues; 96 percent of teachers disagreed with this statement. Many have pointed to the need for teachers to work in professional learning communities, which would require such time.

Professional Growth Opportunities Are Somewhat Lacking

Only 29 percent of teachers agreed that sufficient professional development opportunities are available; 56 percent of teachers disagreed. However, two thirds agreed that there are many opportunities to learn in their jobs, and 61 percent agreed that their jobs provided them with continuous stimulation and professional growth.

Just more than half of teachers agreed that those assigned to evaluate their teaching know what is required to teach for deep understanding; nearly one quarter disagreed with this statement.

Technology Is Generally Not Available

Only 35 percent of teachers agreed that they had access to technology appropriate for working with the curriculum; 45 percent of teachers disagreed with this statement. Scardamalia (Chapter 13) points to the value of appropriate technology in helping students reach deep understanding. Only 38 percent agreed that they had access to technology appropriate for developing lesson plans; 39 percent disagreed.

Fifty-nine percent of teachers agreed that they had access to technology appropriate for preparing report cards; 27 percent disagreed with this statement. It should be noted that the provincial report cards are designed to be completed on the computer, using specific software.

Teachers Have Discretion in the Classroom

Eighty-two percent of teachers agreed that they had the discretion to teach the way they should. Only 9 percent of teachers disagreed with this statement.

School Conditions Are Generally Positive

Teachers were quite positive about the schools they worked in and the colleagues they worked with on a number of factors related to standards in teaching, indicating some degree of professional communities in schools.

Condition in School	Agree	Disagree
Staff maintain high standards	78%	8%
Supported by colleagues	78%	9%
Staff often evaluates programs	71%	13%
Encouraged to experiment with teaching	64%	12%
Principal encourages deep understanding	60%	16%
School close and cordial family	56%	24%
School solves problems	55%	23%

The School Board Is Not Seen in as Positive a Light as the School

Teachers generally did not see the school board that they worked for as a source of inspiration and satisfaction.

Board Condition	Agree	Disagree
Board source of satisfaction	52%	18%
Proud to tell others work for this board	44%	18%
Inspires best performance	34%	41%
Agree with board's policies related to teachers	27%	37%
Accept any assignment	20%	61%

Some key working conditions for teaching for deep understanding are not being provided in Ontario's public elementary schools. Teachers do not have sufficient time to meet with colleagues, and they are not provided with sufficient professional development opportunities.

WHAT THE EVIDENCE TELLS US ABOUT PROMOTING INSTRUCTION FOR DEEP UNDERSTANDING

The route, it seems, to fostering the use of classroom practices that develop deep understanding in most areas of the curriculum is to encourage teachers to use a common core of instructional strategies in all or most of their teaching.

Figure 16.1 Model of Teaching for Deep Understanding

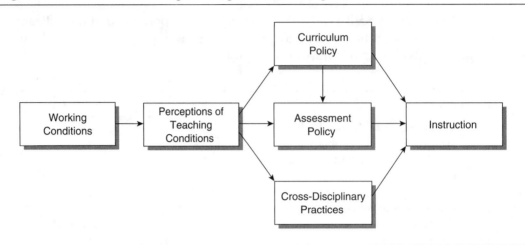

In the previous sections of this chapter, we reported teachers' views of many issues and variables related to teaching for deep understanding. To do this, we relied on fairly simple forms of data analysis and reporting, as the tables in the chapter indicate. In addition to these simple analyses, however, we also examined much more closely the apparent relationships among the many variables or conditions measured by the survey. Of these analyses we asked, What seems to account for variation among teachers in their use of instructional practices likely to foster deep understanding?

Our starting point was to make an educated guess about how the variables or conditions we measured might be related to one another. This educated guess is summarized in Figure 16.1. As this figure indicates, our hunch was that teachers' instructional practices for deep understanding would be most directly influenced by their perceptions of their school's curriculum and assessment policies, as well as the extent to which they were already engaged in cross-curricular forms of instruction. These perceptions, in turn, would be directly influenced by teachers' perceptions of teaching conditions in their classrooms and working conditions in their schools.

Our analyses tested these hunches. We conducted these tests across all areas of the curriculum for which we had collected combined information (literacy, math, science and technology), as well as within each of these three areas of the curriculum. In a nutshell, here is what we found:

- The single largest predictor of teachers' use of instruction that fosters deep understanding was their engagement in cross-disciplinary practices. This was the case overall, as well as in all three curriculum areas.
- Neither a school's curriculum nor assessment policies made much of a difference in the likelihood that teachers would use instructional practices aimed at fostering deep understanding.
- Teachers' perceptions of both their classroom teaching conditions and the conditions of work in their schools contributed significantly but modestly to their engagement in cross-curricular practices.

The route, it seems, to fostering the use of classroom practices that develop deep understanding in most areas of the curriculum is to encourage teachers to use a common core of instructional strategies in all or most of their teaching. Such practices include, for example,

- Encouraging students to think about and apply their knowledge beyond the classroom
- Immersing students in debate and discussion in which they are required to justify their ideas
- Requiring students to compare and contrast new material with previously learned material
- Discussing ideas in terms of their own and other people's cultures and values

CONCLUSION

We asked public elementary teachers a number of key questions on their opinions and practices about curriculum policy and implementation, assessment policy and practices, instruction practices, and teaching conditions. Nine hundred surveys, of 2,500 sent to ETFO teacher members, were used in our analysis— a 35 percent return rate.

Some key information we learned:

- Teachers are not able to cover the current curriculum at any grade level in any subject area. Junior teachers (Grades 4 to 6) reported the most challenge. Almost two thirds of teachers report assigning more homework to try to deal with this.
- More than 60 percent of teachers feel that the curriculum is not developmentally appropriate for elementary students.
- Less than 60 percent of teachers feel that they are adequately prepared to teach this curriculum.
- Teachers do not like the standardized provincial report card, nor do they believe the EQAO tests are valuable for assessing students' progress, for improving communication with parents, or for providing information to help them in their teaching.
- Overall, teachers agree with practices that would promote teaching for deep understanding. This was strongest in questions probing their cross-disciplinary practices or teaching practices in general. Further questions regarding instruction practices in literacy, mathematics, and science and technology revealed a somewhat weaker commitment to deep understanding teaching practices, although always on the positive side.
- Teachers do not believe that they have enough time during the school day to meet with colleagues about curriculum issues or that they have access to sufficient professional development opportunities.
- Generally, teachers think the school they work in provides a positive climate for teaching. However, teachers feel less strongly about their school board.
- Path modeling tells us that to foster the use of classroom practices to develop deep understanding, teachers should be encouraged to use a common core of instructional strategies, such as encouraging students to apply their knowledge beyond the classroom, encouraging much discussion and debate within the classroom, and relating their ideas and knowledge to other cultures and values.

There are many reasons why some teachers are limited in their teaching for deep understanding. The curriculum and assessment policies currently in place in Ontario are not conducive to teaching for depth; the curriculum is too crowded and assessment policies are more focused on summative assessment of learning than on assessment that can assist teachers and students. In addition, some working conditions need improving—notably the ability of teachers to work within professional learning communities, with more time to meet with colleagues and more access to professional development opportunities.

Public elementary teachers are for the most part committed to teaching for deep understanding. Improved curriculum and assessment policies and key working conditions would increase their ability to do so.

PART V

Enabling the Teaching of Deep Understanding

17

Conditions That Influence Teaching for Understanding

Sandra Folk

In this chapter, Sandra Folk reviews evidence about factors that stand in the way of teaching for understanding. She warns that the greatest enemy of teaching for understanding is the pressure to cover the curriculum and the lack of time to do so.

Previous chapters have introduced a rich range of concepts and practices aimed at helping teachers foster deep understanding among their students within and across the school curriculum. This chapter begins to unpack the obstacles teachers face in using these concepts and practices, a focus of all the chapters in this section of the book. The obstacles discussed in this chapter include teachers' lack of knowledge about the content of the subjects they teach and how to teach them, as well as teachers' working conditions.

UNPACKING THE OBSTACLES

Teachers' Content Knowledge

Teachers' content or subject matter knowledge plays an important role in teaching (Ball, 1991; Wineburg & Wilson, 1991). Studies conducted with teachers in different subject areas (Ball, 1991; Hashweh, 1986; Wineburg & Wilson, 1991) support the view that teachers who possess a rich, integrated knowledge of the subject can influence instruction in a positive way. As Fennema and Franke (1992) point out, "What a teacher knows is one of the most important influences on what is done in classrooms and ultimately on what students learn" (p. 147). Ball (1991) also tells us that teachers' subject knowledge matters to instruction and students' learning. According to Hashweh (1986), teachers who are most knowledgeable about a particular subject are able to weave together their understandings of different aspects of the discipline. They are also able to recognize and deal with students' misconceptions. Griffin (1995) concurs that teachers must have a command of the subject; he also believes that they must have learned for understanding to be able to teach for understanding. McLaughlin and Talbert (1993) further suggest that

> teachers with only superficial knowledge of their subject matter will have little flexibility in their pedagogical choices and preferences and thus be effectively constrained to teach "just the facts," or to leave learning up to the students. (p. 2)

Teachers' Pedagogical Knowledge

Closely related to content knowledge is knowledge that allows teachers to transform what they know into "something meaningful for students" (Prawat, 1989). This knowledge, which Shulman (1986) defines as pedagogical content knowledge, is needed to teach for understanding (McLaughlin & Talbert, 1993). According to Shulman's (1986) conception, pedagogical content knowledge includes

> the most useful forms of representation of those [content] ideas, the most powerful analogies, illustrations, examples, explanations, and demonstrations—in a word, the ways of representing and formulating the subject to make it comprehensible to others . . . an understanding of what makes the learning of specific topics easy or difficult, the conceptions and preconceptions that students of different ages and backgrounds bring with them to the learning of those most frequently taught topics and lessons. (p. 9)

Working Conditions

Although teaching for understanding is affected to a large extent by teachers' content and pedagogical knowledge, the influence of context on teachers' thinking and practice cannot be neglected. Compelling evidence suggests that teachers' work is significantly influenced by the context in which they carry out their practice (J. Gallagher, 2000). In support of this view, McLaughlin and Talbert (1993) advise that multiple factors of context, which permeate teaching, include students in a classroom, subject matter, colleagues, school administrators, and school organization, extending to broader environments beyond school systems, to parents, the community, and institutions such as government. Although these factors can enable or promote the type of teaching that encourages deeper understanding of subject matter, they also have the potential to negatively affect teaching and learning.

> Even when teachers recognize the importance and value of promoting understanding, it may not take precedence because parents, politicians, and other stakeholders are concerned only with students' performance on standardized tests.

Gardner (1993) identifies the following obstacles that stand between schools and educating for understanding: the test-text phenomenon, the correct-answer phenomenon, pressure-for-coverage, institutional constraints, and disciplinary constraints. But the greatest enemy of teaching for understanding is the pressure for coverage and the lack of time to do so. Most teachers are limited by too little time for exploring new instructional models, curriculum, and ways for assessing student performance (Good, McCaslin, & Reys, 1992).

Newton (2001b) also views time as a barrier to understanding. She is also of the opinion that understanding may not be a classroom priority, and there can be a silent compact of understanding avoidance between some teachers and some children (Newton, 2001a). Even when teachers recognize the importance and value of promoting understanding, it may not take precedence because parents, politicians, and other stakeholders are concerned only with students' performance on standardized tests. J. Gallagher (2000) also tells us that there are instances where students resist teachers who attempt to teach for understanding.

According to Anderson and Roth (1989), research in science reveals that students themselves may be obstacles to teaching for understanding as a result of the task environments to which they have been conditioned. Textbooks and other materials, including management and curricular demands, are factors that work against the development of classroom environments and instruction that promote understanding. These findings are consistent with Newman (1988), who reported that external pressures on social studies teachers to cover prescribed amounts of curriculum, as well as tests, district guidelines, and textbooks, were major obstacles to teaching for understanding.

My experiences in the area of mathematics also fit with these findings. Teachers with whom I have worked as a consultant and teacher educator often expressed the urgency they felt to cover the long list of curriculum outcomes to meet school board expectations. They also talked about the time pressures they faced to ensure students' success on board and provincial standardized testing.

Some studies within the literature help illustrate how the interplay of context and classroom environments affects teachers' practice. In an experimental study with a second grade teacher, Wood, Cobb, and Yackel (1990) concluded that the teacher was able to change her mathematical practice, promoting meaning and understanding in students' learning, because of the ongoing support she received from researchers. However, in reading, where she received no support from researchers and was constrained in instruction by her obligations to administrators, she continued with her usual approach, moving children through the instructional materials at a set pace to prepare them for mastery skill tests.

In some environments, teachers are compelled to deal with conflicting messages about classroom instruction. Eisenhardt et al. (1993) noted in a study conducted with preservice teachers that the practicing teachers in the placement schools were presented with conflicting messages by central administrators. At the same time as these administrators expressed a commitment to teaching for conceptual knowledge, they mandated implementation of curriculum and testing programs that emphasized procedural knowledge.

CONCLUSION

How can we move forward to achieve greater understanding on the part of our students in the face of these obstacles? Clearly, one part of the answer lies with teachers themselves—continuing to expand their content and pedagogical knowledge. But there is much to be done by those whose jobs are to support the work of teachers. For example, Griffin (1995) suggests that teachers need a rich variety of instructional materials, "drawn from the larger culture." Teachers alone should not be expected to locate all such material themselves. Griffin also points to the need for noninstructional time, for connections with other school professionals, and for linkages with other schools and educational organizations. Creating conditions such as these will require effort on the part of administrators and policymakers who understand the tasks facing teachers aiming to develop deep understanding on the part of their students. Subsequent chapters begin to spell out more concretely what is needed from these other partners in the educational enterprise.

18

The Importance of Partnerships to Support and Sustain Teaching for Deep Understanding

Nina Bascia

Anne Rodrigue

Shawn Moore

Teaching for deep understanding requires a rich infrastructure of support for teaching and learning. In this chapter, Nina Bascia, Anne Rodrigue, and Shawn Moore sketch out what the various partners in education need to do differently to enable teaching of deep understanding in Ontario classrooms.

Who the partners are . . .

1. Schools of education
2. Teacher unions
3. School districts
4. School leaders
5. Parents
6. Teachers themselves

There is considerable evidence that conventional wisdom about what teaching is, how to improve it, and who has the right to make decisions about it has reduced the likelihood of teaching for deep understanding. In the past 10 years, we have come to think about teaching as a set of activities that, if correctly detailed and carefully monitored, could be prescribed through policy by remote control. Teachers have been viewed as technicians whose job is to implement relatively simple, uniform "treatments" for students, who are "processed" by schools as if they are all roughly the same (Bascia & Hargreaves, 2000; Darling-Hammond, 1997). Policy efforts have emphasized what must be done and who is responsible rather than building the capacity of teachers and schools (Bascia, 2001). Teaching has become more regulated through a hierarchical chain of command that extends from principals all the way up to state and provincial departments of education, neglecting the role of teacher unions, school board trustees, faculties of education, and other organizations.

We have also seen reduced support for teaching; even the understanding that supporting teaching is necessary has eroded. As many experienced educators retire and less funding is provided for education, school systems have become leaner, pared down to programs and services seen as essential to a technical conception of teaching. Teacher-teacher relationships have become restricted and rationalized, with little time, opportunity, or resources for teachers to collaborate and to teach well.

The belief that teaching is basically a matter of following well-laid-out rules is not the only way to think about it and does not allow for the range of skills or the commitments needed to teach for deep understanding. In contrast, conceptualizing teaching as intellectual work assumes that it involves a complex set of activities requiring sophisticated professional judgment. Opportunities for teachers to learn—reflecting on practice, talking and working with other teachers and educational partners, developing a wide range of expertise including planning, assessment, content knowledge, and developing the ability to be critical consumers (rather than passive recipients) of externally driven change—are fundamentally important. To enact a conception of teaching as intellectual work means helping individual teachers, but also whole school staffs, school districts, and others become more adept at initiating, maintaining, and making use of their learning. It suggests that teachers must have a central role in identifying the best conditions for their teaching and learning. At the same time, it means we must involve a variety of other people and organizations in identifying and providing the supports necessary for teaching for deep understanding. Teaching for deep understanding requires moving from a triage model of schooling, where there are never enough resources to do well and the chain of command is paramount, to a tapestry model of schooling, with a rich infrastructure of support for teaching and learning (Bascia, 2005).

The adoption of a technical view of teaching, the reduction of the educational infrastructure, and the centralization of authority over education are common around the world. In many jurisdictions, governments have become impatient in conflicts with organizations that have somewhat different goals, values, and perspectives than their own. We contend, however, that these different views are

> Teaching for deep understanding requires moving from a triage model of schooling, where there are never enough resources to do well and the chain of command is paramount, to a tapestry model of schooling, with a rich infrastructure of support for teaching and learning.

critically important; rather than imposing a single authoritative solution, supporting teaching for deep understanding demands a synthesis of different positions and expertise. Long-standing conflicts between organizations—for example, between teacher unions and state or provincial governments or between schools of education and educators in the field—are the starting points for conversations about how to share responsibility for sustained support of teaching for deep understanding. Such dialogue is based on a healthy respect for what different partners bring to their common goals.

SCHOOLS OF EDUCATION

Improving teacher preparation has been the focus of many education reforms as researchers and policymakers make the link between teachers' own learning and teaching quality. Schools of education can play important roles in teachers' development by creating professional growth experiences for teachers throughout their careers. These experiences can foster the cognitive scaffolding that allows teachers to think deeply about what they do and how they do it. But a "great divide" between academia and K–12 schools has kept teachers and professors of education from working easily together. On the academic side, universities tend to respect and recognize the work professors do in K–12 schools and with teachers less than their many other types of research. There is not enough time in initial teacher education programs for new teachers to integrate complex concepts that will allow them to teach for deep understanding, and this, coupled with new teachers' understandable anxiety about "what I should do in the classroom Monday morning," can lead to a real dissonance between what new teachers think they need and what their professors want to give them. On the school side (what teachers call the "real world"), a lack of time to think deeply about what's going on in the classroom, few rewards or opportunities for intensive professional development, little opportunity to spend time talking with other educators, and a culture that discourages the sharing of concerns about teaching practice make it difficult for teachers to recognize the value of what theory and research have to offer (Cochran-Smith & Lytle, 1992; Little, 1993).

> ## ENABLING THE TEACHING OF DEEP UNDERSTANDING
>
> What the partners need to do differently . . .
>
> - Academics need to work more closely with teachers.
> - Unions need to put the conditions for teaching for deep understanding on the table.
> - School districts need to form partnerships with union leaders and parents.
> - School leaders need to build shared commitment, strengthen capacities, and refine school structure to support the teaching of deep understanding.
> - Parents need to be concerned with more than test performance and get behind the innovative teaching and learning strategies that promote deep understanding.
> - Teachers themselves need to pursue their own subject knowledge and enhance their pedagogical practice and understanding of how students learn.

Models for Working Together

In some countries, governments have dealt with this divide by handing over responsibility for teacher learning to schools and school districts. But if teaching for

> ...a "great divide" between academia and K–12 schools has kept teachers and professors of education from working easily together.

deep understanding is supported by teachers' exposure to the kinds of learning experiences that faculties of education can provide, the two worlds should be brought more closely together. Around the world, there are a number of good examples of how this is being accomplished, and although we do not advocate any one of these models as being "best," they are useful illustrations of what might become more common.

Problems of Practice

One model involves bringing new teachers, practicing teachers, and academics together in school settings to work together on real, specific problems of practice. The professional development school model has become increasingly popular, especially in the United States (see Darling-Hammond, 1994). What's important is that all of the partners understand these projects in terms of their ability to focus on teaching for deep understanding. Marilyn Cochran-Smith (2004) has described the significance of student teachers' relationships and collaboration with teachers who "are themselves struggling to teach against the grain" (p. 29), of practicing teachers who "construct problems, wrestle with uncertainty, change their minds about long-established practices or assumptions, gather evidence and examples for analysis and interpretation, connect pieces of information to one another, and develop interpretive frameworks for the daily work of teaching" (p. 13). This is a very different understanding of what it is to teach, and learn to teach, than being exposed to "exemplary" lesson design and learning how to implement "expert" strategies. In these situations, university faculty are not official supervisors or outside experts. Rather, they take the role of linking specific problems of practice with understandings of the deeper, broader ideas and forces at work in teaching and learning.

Professional Development

A second model centers on professional development projects that link teachers and academics interested in fostering teaching for deep understanding. Some of these projects focus on subject areas or literacies such as mathematics, science, or writing (Lieberman & Grolnik, 1996); others on larger school reform initiatives (Yeatman & Sachs, 1995). For teachers, discussions about practice with others outside their own schools makes it possible to step back from specific situations, to think more abstractly, to compare and contrast, and to generate strong, deep understandings about teaching. Communities of practice are valuable in and of themselves for participants; talking about teaching is understood as an integral part of what it is to be an "expert performer" (Lave & Wenger, 1991). Involved university faculty are also learning, not dispensing special expertise; learning is reciprocal, not one-way.

Research and Debate

University faculty also can and should play more active roles in supporting teaching for deep understanding beyond their direct interactions with teachers; they have special roles to play in improving infrastructure support for teaching. Studying aspects of education policy and practice, identifying the existence of emerging issues or recurrent problems, and interacting with other stakeholder groups can foster debate or lead to new solutions. Academics spread ideas, provide alternative perspectives, evaluate programs, and can advocate for teachers (Sachs, 2003). Their work is crucial to ensuring that teaching for deep understanding has a strong footing at classroom, school, district, and state or provincial levels.

TEACHER UNIONS

Teacher unions have long played an important role in enhancing teaching quality. The mission statements of many teacher unions demonstrate their commitment to the provision, protection, and enhancement of quality education (Rodrigue, 2003). Focusing their efforts on improving teaching conditions and professional learning is a lot of what teachers' organizations have been about, but these efforts have been undervalued and unrecognized. Of equal importance is the role they play as providers of professional development (Bascia, 2000, 2004).

Championing Teaching for Deep Understanding

Teaching for deep understanding requires specific discipline knowledge, coupled with powerful pedagogical knowledge and practices. In some Canadian provinces, such as Prince Edward Island and Nova Scotia, teacher unions cooperate with university partners to establish the selection criteria for candidates and the content of B.Ed. programming; they have instituted courses that emphasize reflective practice for inservice teachers. In the United States and Canada, teacher unions have also been significantly involved in the development and implementation of teacher induction programs, whether solely administered by the teachers' union or cosponsored with departments/ ministries of education and districts (Bascia, 2003). In Ontario, teacher unions provide support for beginning

> Unions may wish to consider further developing articles in collective agreements that promote the conditions to support teaching for deep understanding, such as time for collaborative planning and differing formats for professional development.

teachers with "Survive and Thrive," an online conference where new teachers interact with experienced teacher monitors, are linked to teaching resources, and discuss issues ranging from classroom management to reflective practice. Whereas some topics respond to new teachers' desire for "how-to" support, others help them develop the skills and habits necessary for teaching for deep understanding.

Unions have consistently provided for teacher learning in the settings identified by Lieberman (1996): direct teaching (through their provision of conferences, courses, and workshops); learning in schools (peer coaching, critical friends, action research); and learning out of schools (professional development centers, specialist councils, and teacher networks). Teacher unions have also been responsible for the production of resources to either support or expand the curriculum (Bascia, 2004). A look at Web sites of teacher organizations indicates the breadth of these resources, which often challenge the status quo and require teachers to focus on promoting stewardship and framing teaching and learning within a social context.

Teacher collaboration is an essential component of teaching for deep understanding, and many teacher unions provide programming in this area. The Alberta Teachers' Union, the Elementary Teachers' Federation of Ontario, and the virtual teachers' center of the Newfoundland and Labrador Teachers' Association help teachers develop the skills to work collaboratively, collect data, and engage in reflective inquiry. Many other organizations in both the United States and Canada have invested resources in developing teacher capacity to conduct action research.

As part of their organizational mandates, teacher unions seek to improve the working conditions of teachers. Union contracts (collective agreements) address issues such as class size, teacher autonomy in the selection of pedagogical materials, the scope and content of professional development, and support for curriculum implementation (Bascia, 2004; Rodrigue, 2003). Unions may wish to consider further developing articles in collective agreements that promote the conditions to support teaching for deep understanding, such as time for collaborative planning and differing formats for professional development.

Teacher unions can and do acculturate teachers to collegiality, autonomy, effective pedagogy, and the provision of quality education services (Bascia, 2000; Rodrigue, 2003).

By advocating for quality teaching conditions, negotiating for the time, space, and resources needed to effectively implement teaching for deep understanding, incorporating principles of teaching for deep understanding within professional development opportunities offered to teachers, and working with other partners to champion and support teaching for deep understanding, teacher unions can help change the face of Ontario's classrooms.

SCHOOL DISTRICTS

Bringing about teaching for deep understanding will require a wide range of stakeholders within and outside of school districts. To achieve this, senior district leaders must create organizational cultures that support partnerships and then model how they work in intense, demanding, and innovative reform environments. As Stein, Hubbard, and Mehan's (2004) research indicates, districts involved in systemic reform ignore or avoid involving union leaders, parents, and others at their peril. These groups will make their voices heard one way or another concerning reforms that they perceive will affect them directly.

Involving the Stakeholders (and Keeping Them Involved)

Partnership is a choice that district leaders must make: Do they involve external stakeholder groups in the reform process or not? The assumption seems to be that if the right policies and practices for implementation of reform are put into place and aligned from the superintendent's office to the classroom, then the key elements in successful change have been considered. The pattern is for district leaders to concentrate on relationships within the organizational boundary of the system itself (e.g., developing schools as learning communities; enhancing the role of principals as instructional leaders; focusing simultaneously on change at the system, school, and classroom levels).

For example, in San Diego, which initiated internally oriented, districtwide reform focusing on balanced literacy, external stakeholders made their presence felt. The teachers' association claimed that teachers had not been consulted; business leaders were critical that students did not possess the skills required to survive in the workplace; and an affluent group of parents forced the San Diego district to give their school "pilot" status on the grounds that the literacy reforms did not prepare their children for university.

> ...senior district leaders must create organizational cultures that support partnerships and then model how they work in intense, demanding, and innovative reform environments.

There are few studies of district reform where stakeholder partnerships were at the center of the planning and implementation of change. One notable exception is described by Togneri and Anderson (2003), who investigated five high-poverty districts in the United States that were improving student achievement to determine how these districts promoted reform in instruction. In all of these districts, the superintendents (directors) articulated a compelling vision of instructional reform and modeled distributed leadership that invited internal and external stakeholders to contribute their expertise, experience, and ideas to the reform process. Kent County School District (Maryland), for example, established a committee of teachers, principals, union leaders, university colleagues, board members, parents, and other interested parties to share in the process of development and implementation of curriculum reforms. In Minneapolis, the board, union, and central office leaders worked together closely and regularly on districtwide challenges to improving student achievement, working through any conflicts and barriers getting in the way of achieving this common goal, and collaborating on specific initiatives in professional development programs.

In these districts, reform efforts focused on improving student achievement in terms of the traditional, standardized curriculum, particularly "closing the gap" between minority and higher achieving student groups. This was challenging enough. Teaching for deep understanding is an entirely different matter because it takes us outside what many educators and external stakeholders have experienced and understand teaching and learning to be. In initiating a demanding undertaking like teaching for deep understanding across the system, partnerships between district senior administrators and external stakeholders become even more critical. The stakes are high for everyone, especially students.

Stakeholders can bring sharply differing views on whether proposed reforms are valuable and worth doing. There will be inevitable political differences concerning how reforms should be implemented and where the locus of control should lie. A central challenge to creating and sustaining stakeholder partnerships that promote teaching for deep understanding is to make deep changes to traditional educational management structures and processes so they are more inclusive and collaborative. School districts face many challenges in doing so, including bureaucratic insularity, where district leaders are not inclined to share power and decision making with external stakeholders and thus have little experience in creating and sustaining partnerships.

District leaders will have to do more than simply inform stakeholders that alternative perspectives and practices are needed to meet challenges in teaching and learning. This is only the first step. The point is not that district leaders should form partnerships with union leaders, business leaders, and parents because it is a nice thing to do, because it is politically correct, or because they hope it will avert antagonism, resistance, and sabotage down the road, but because partnerships, if managed properly, can enhance the teaching for the deep understanding agenda.

SCHOOL LEADERS

For many schools, teaching for deep understanding would constitute a significant, quite wrenching change from current practice. What would it mean to get the leadership conditions right? Leadership must be capable of fostering significant change toward teaching for deep understanding. In Chapter 5, Ross and McDougall refer to transformational leadership as fitting this bill. Considerable additional evidence has accumulated in support of this form of leadership. For example, transformational leadership has significant indirect effects on student engagement and participation in school, one important correlate of deep understanding (Leithwood & Jantzi, 1999). "Pedagogical" (Cavanaugh, MacNeil, & Silcox, 2004) and "instructional" (Hallinger & Heck, 2002) leadership are other forms of leadership that might foster the teaching of deep understanding in schools. Providing support to teachers—materials, access to professional development, models of successful practice, constructive feedback, and the like—will all contribute to the reorientation of teaching practices toward deep understanding. Such an approach to leadership concentrates on building shared commitment to a challenging vision for the school (such as deep understanding), building the capacities among members of the school to achieve such a vision, and continually refining school structure to ensure that it supports the teaching of deep understanding.

> For many schools, teaching for deep understanding would constitute a significant, quite wrenching change from current practice.

Resisting the Cookie-Cutter Approach

Transformative principals work with teachers, students, parents, and districts to develop a collective consensus that teaching for deep understanding is a goal worth pursuing. They recognize teaching for deep understanding as a complex undertaking and provide ongoing support, care, and recognition for those who commit to this philosophy. A transformative leader resists the cookie-cutter approach to teaching and learning, recognizing the contextual, institutional, and disciplinary constraints identified by Folk in Chapter 17 that stand between schools and understanding, and recultures the school in response.

Teaching for deep understanding requires students to explore connections with their learning and the world, to examine issues and topics of significance, to grow as individuals and as members of a community, and to engage holistically in their learning. To accomplish these goals may require a radical reconstruction of teaching and the space in which it occurs. Learning becomes more individualized and more fluid so that lesson planning, classroom setup, and the other norms that govern classrooms may need to be altered, revised, or abandoned.

To increase teachers' collective efficacy, principals need to possess pedagogical content knowledge, emphasize inquiry, recognize and encourage best practice, and set the conditions for continuous professional growth. Principals should seek out numerous and diverse opportunities for teacher learning and provide the space for teachers to collectively and individually examine their belief systems and pedagogical practices in a risk-free environment.

Transformative principals also focus on developing a culture of distributed leadership (Elmore, 2000) where various individuals within or attached to the school (as could be the case for education researchers) assume leadership roles, thus bringing individual strengths to a collective and dynamic vision of teaching for deep understanding.

PARENTS

Assumptions about appropriate closeness or distance between parents and teachers are shaped by deep-seated, enduring social, political, and institutional beliefs and practices (Lasky, 2000). These include the historical distancing of parents and teachers (Waller, 1932), notions of "teacher as expert" (Epstein, 1995), and parents' own experience of schooling (Hargreaves, 2001). As a result, parents are often marginal players in the school change and improvement process (Carey, Lewis, & Farris, 1998) in spite of two decades of evidence indicating that parent-school partnerships have positive benefits for students, parents, and schools (Henderson & Mapp, 2002).

> ...parents are often marginal players in the school change and improvement process in spite of two decades of evidence indicating that parent-school partnerships have positive benefits for students, parents, and schools....

Ontario's teachers perceive parents as "absolutely vital partners" (COMPAS, 2003). According to U.S. research, most families want to know how to enhance their children's learning (Sanders & Epstein, 1998). Parents are eager to work directly with their children (Cotton & Wikeland, 1989), particularly when teachers provide instruction and guidance (Dauber & Epstein, 1989) that individualize programs of home study to family situations.

Models for Teacher-Parent Partnerships

Teaching for deep understanding poses a difficult challenge for educators in terms of parent involvement: how to link classroom teaching and learning with parent support in the home in ways that promote instructional consistency and coherence. Parent education initiatives have been used to introduce parents to innovative teaching and learning strategies (Thiessen & Anderson, 1999). Elementary schools in Ontario (Onslow, 1992) and Ohio (Pourdavood, Cowen, Svec, Skitzki, & Grob, 1999), for example, have implemented Family Math Programs to educate parents about new instructional strategies. Teachers and parents at Brentmoor Elementary School attend the National Paideia Center to be trained together on the Paideia principles and instructional approach (Sekayi, Peterman, Stakich, & Caputo, 1999). Parents and teachers in a low-income, inner-city elementary school embraced a "family metaphor" to overcome cultural, economic, and linguistic barriers to parent involvement (Beck & Murphy, 1999). Parent centers can be a particularly effective strategy to involve parents, foster partnership, encourage collaboration between the school, home, and community, and improve student success (Johnstone & Hiatt, 1997). Cummins provides a good example of a school-home linkage and parent roles in Chapter 11.

Models of partnership help educators situate their efforts to bridge gaps between parents and the school. Epstein, Coates, Salinas, Sanders, and Simon (1997) formulate parent-school partnerships in a multidimensional framework: parenting, communicating, volunteering, learning in the home, decision making, and collaborating with the community. This model helps educators identify gaps and needs in their programs and also provides a framework for strategic planning.

Evidence suggests that the teacher-parent partnership model can support teaching for deep understanding and foster improvement in student learning. But significant social, political, and conceptual barriers stand in the way. Current reforms that stress standardization and accountability may actually discourage parents from being receptive to this approach to teaching and learning. As Sandra Folk suggests in Chapter 17, even if teachers recognize the importance and value of promoting understanding, it may not take precedence because parents, politicians, and other interested stakeholders are concerned only with students' performance on standardized tests. Traditional teacher-parent interactions (conferences, fund-raising activities, volunteer roles) tend to be scripted, narrowly defined, and paternalistic, just the opposite of an inclusive, collaborative model required for teaching for deep understanding. Teacher-parent partnerships are risky and demanding because they require educators to examine the adequacy of their own organizational structures and teaching practices, not simply resort to blaming student failure on parent "deficiencies."

Parents often are a child's first teacher. Moreover, the evidence shows that most parents will continue being involved in their child's learning, especially in the home, with a particularly strong interest, devotion, and motivation during the elementary years of formal schooling.

TEACHERS THEMSELVES

Teaching has been the subject of this entire book, so why focus on teachers in this chapter? Because if we don't think of teachers as partners, we run the risk of continuing to treat them as the objects of decisions made, however well-intentioned, by others who simply cannot understand what it is like to work with children in schools this term, this week, this day. If we don't consider teachers as partners, we reduce our ability to support them in appropriate ways; we continue to imagine teaching narrowly, as merely what happens within classroom walls, and undermine teachers' capacity to develop more robust, more collaborative, active engagement with partners, academics, decision makers, administrators, and others (Hargreaves & Fullan, 1998).

The accountability policy context increasingly faced by teachers has been characterized by conflicting ideologies of competition and inclusion, centralized control of curriculum and assessment, increased expectations and diminished resources, and a paradoxical focus on both external accountability measures and a call for renewed professionalism. McAdie reports on the results of the teacher survey in Chapter 16, noting that teachers grapple with a bloated curriculum, EQAO tests constrict their ability to teach for deep understanding, and they have little time for collaboration with colleagues.

> . . . if we don't think of teachers as partners, we run the risk of continuing to treat them as the objects of decisions made, however well-intentioned, by others who simply cannot understand what it is like to work with children in schools this term, this week, this day.

Acknowledging these less than optimal conditions may make us hesitant to challenge teachers to examine their practices in light of the principles inherent in teaching for deep understanding—critical thinking, productive pedagogies, dynamic and interactive student-teacher relationships, and curriculum, assessment, and pedagogy that draw from students' experiences, cultures, and home knowledge. Yet it is essential to do so.

Teachers as Practitioners, Researchers, and Critics

Teaching for deep understanding requires teachers to engage in a cycle of reflection and revision, to work on increasing individual and collective capacity. It involves taking risks. Teaching and learning for deep understanding obliges teachers to represent themselves as practitioners, researchers, and critics (Goodson, 2003), to challenge "norms of collegial loyalty" (Campbell, 2004), and to act as co-constructors, with other partners, of alternatives to present educational ideologies and practices.

Teaching for deep understanding obliges teachers to know their subjects in depth and to keep abreast of recent developments. Teachers must commit, throughout the course of their careers, to pursue their own subject knowledge, enhance their understanding of how students learn, refine pedagogical practice, and work collaboratively to improve instructional practice.

Teaching for deep understanding involves a shift from teacher as a compliant implementer of policy to teacher as active agent and creator of knowledge. It means rejecting the assumption that professionalism means having exclusive authority over educational practice; it requires teachers to collaborate with students, parents, education researchers, and other partners in the renegotiation of new roles and responsibilities. These relationships must be based on "reciprocity, where . . . parties meet on equal grounds, with the desire to improve student learning outcomes and teacher practice at its core" (Sachs, 2003, p. 65).

Teaching for deep understanding puts teachers at the center of educational practice. It responds to teachers' desires to be seen as professionals rather than technicians; it encourages collaborative curriculum design by administrators, teachers, and students. Yet teaching for deep understanding also implies a social and moral commitment on the part of teachers—a recognition that teaching for deep understanding is about wisdom and character development, connectedness to the world, promoting stewardship, and enriching class beliefs, attitudes, and behavior patterns.

Opening the classroom to other partners is a necessary component of teaching for deep understanding. External expertise must be infused and integrated within the education system, and partners must be included in the debates about education, its purpose, and its practice. To teach for deep understanding is highly complex and challenging; it is both exhausting and exhilarating. It is an individual endeavor crafted within a collaborative culture of consensus.

THE CHALLENGE OF PARTNERSHIP

Teaching for deep understanding depends on the involvement of multiple educational organizations and individuals. When they work against each other, the result is a fragmented and incomplete support structure for teaching. For example, when teacher unions and school boards take opposite corners—where the former is viewed as being concerned about trivial issues and the latter is seen as being interested in control for the sake of control—there are very real consequences that undermine teachers' ability to teach for deep understanding. When faculties of education and teachers square off over conceptual and practical approaches to teaching, the dichotomous results make it much more challenging for teachers to integrate concrete and abstract thinking about teaching.

When educators perceive parents as impediments, problems, and deficient partners, and parents view educators as professionally distant and unwelcoming, then it becomes extremely difficult, if not impossible, for parents to create home learning environments that support teachers' efforts to instruct for deep understanding. At the same time, the different perspectives and expertise that organizations and individuals bring to their understanding of how to support teaching are crucial because teaching is such a complex and important endeavor. The contrasts help provide a constructive critique on educational practices and identify the range of necessary supports.

> Supporting teaching for deep understanding requires an equivalent deep understanding of the necessity of multiple educational organizations' involvement.

Supporting teaching for deep understanding requires an equivalent deep understanding of the necessity of multiple educational organizations' involvement. They must embark on a continuous, evolving, and dynamic process to work through and beyond narrow, dichotomous thinking, to develop new understandings and new roles. This tapestry notion of support for teaching and learning is quite different from the concept of alignment, top-down control, or one-upmanship that has characterized educational politics over the last number of years. This understanding of educational partnership requires risk taking as organizations and positions are decentered from their traditional dichotomous relationships with each other; it requires patience, and above all an understanding that organizational interaction is a necessary part of ensuring the continuous improvement of teaching.

19

Teaching for Depth in Teacher Education

Carol Rolheiser

Mark Evans

In this chapter, Carol Rolheiser and Mark Evans note that teaching has become increasingly complex, challenging work, and teacher education equally so. They describe the strategies used to introduce the "teaching for depth" focus in the teacher education program at OISE/UT.

Four key challenges of teaching for depth in teacher education programs are as follows:

1. Tension may arise as instructors debate the merits of breadth versus depth.

2. Effective teaching requires attention to overlapping and interconnected knowledge bases that teacher candidates may not have when they enter the program.

3. Traditional individualistic learning environments do not support knowledge building, which is a social activity aimed at idea improvement.

4. Conceptual change and change in beliefs can lead to deeper knowledge, but such change is particularly difficult to accomplish in short teacher-education programs.

Authors' Note: We would like to thank our OISE/UT colleagues, Janette Pelletier, Elizabeth Morley, Lynn Lemieux, Kathleen Gallagher, and Ruth Sandwell for their contributions to this chapter.

S everal hundred studies contradict the long-standing myth that "anyone can teach" and that "teachers are born and not made." Cole and Knowles (2000) note that "the act of teaching has become increasingly complex, challenging work and is informed by multiple forms of knowledge and is representative of a variety of ways of personal, professional, and contextual knowing" (p. 7). According to Darling-Hammond (1998), "The most successful teachers not only have adequate preparation in their subject matter, they have also studied the art and science of teaching" (p. 7). Teacher education programs today face the challenge of preparing teachers for the classrooms of tomorrow. Teachers need to be responsive to continuous change and assorted pressures, mindful of the learners and communities they serve, and attentive to the multiple knowledge bases that inform effective practice.

THE COMPLICATED TASK OF TEACHER EDUCATION

Teaching for depth in teacher education programs needs to attend to those multiple forms of knowledge that both inform practice and encourage a spirit of critical inquiry. Research on teaching, according to Watkins and Mortimore (1999), has moved through four distinct phases in recent decades:

- A focus on different styles of teaching
- A focus on the contexts of teaching
- A focus on teaching and learning
- An emerging focus on an increasingly integrated conceptualization, which attends to technical competencies of teaching in relationship to critical knowledge bases and contextual forces

Early studies of teaching tended to focus on teaching styles, typically polarized (e.g., authoritarian/democratic, traditional/progressive, teacher-centered/student-centered). Empirical studies of teachers' pedagogy revealed that such polarized understandings were simplistic and, in practice, rare. Gradually, attention shifted to the relationship between contextual factors and teaching, introducing more sophisticated understandings. Attention to classroom contexts (e.g., inner city/rural) and how teachers orchestrated multiple learning activities within them added a layer of sophistication that went beyond studies of teaching style. How teachers make decisions about teaching extended to considerations of the realities of a live classroom. Studies during the 1980s and 1990s considered the intricate processes of teaching in relation to various theories of cognition (e.g., constructivism) and meta-cognition.

Recent attention to teaching for depth within some teacher education programs connects directly with emerging conceptualizations of teaching that attend to the relationships among the technical competencies of teaching, critical knowledge bases, and contextual forces (Bennett, Anderson, & Evans, 1997; Bennett & Rolheiser, 2001; Cole & Knowles, 2000; Hallam & Ireson, 1999; Turner-Bisset, 2001). Underpinning these conceptions is a sense that teaching has become increasingly sophisticated and ought to be approached in a way that respects the "relations between its elements: the teacher, the classroom or other context, content, the view of learning and learning about learning" (Hallam & Ireson, 1999). Turner-Bisset (2001), for example, has argued that while earlier studies of the qualities and processes of effective teaching were helpful, they were clearly just "tip of the iceberg" approaches because they ignored the many dimensions of knowledge required for effective teaching. Teaching for depth, for Turner-Bisset, requires attention to overlapping and interconnected knowledge bases such as substantive subject knowledge, syntactic subject knowledge, beliefs about the subject, curriculum knowledge, pedagogical knowledge, knowledge of learners, knowledge of self, and knowledge of educational milieu and learning goals.

Educational researchers and practitioners have recently taken up this call for more integrated and intricate understandings of teaching that can generate new and deepened understandings of teachers' practices.

TOWARD TEACHING FOR DEPTH AT OISE/UT

Each year, OISE/UT prepares about 1,300 teachers, more than any of the other 11 Ontario universities offering teacher education programs. At present, OISE/UT offers a nine-month consecutive program (B.Ed./Dip. Tech.) in elementary and secondary teaching, which is similar to that at other Ontario universities; we also offer distinctive and smaller two-year master's programs (master of arts in child studies and master of teaching), which lead to provincial teaching qualifications at the elementary level. We currently do not offer a concurrent program, although this is common at other universities in Ontario.

OISE/UT faculty have worked to strengthen a distinct vision for teacher education. Teaching excellence, coherent and substantive courses and cohort-based programs, faculty collaboration, strong school-university and field partnerships, equity, diversity, and social justice, and a research-informed orientation have emerged as important conceptual principles underpinning our program, enabling us to readily respond to changes in educational theory and practice. One of our central goals is to create and strengthen a foundation for professional learning for our graduates. As Howey (1996) says,

> It is essential given the complexity of teaching and learning and the number of years it takes for a teacher to fully mature as a professional that initial teacher education set a course wherein teachers learn to critically inquire into and reason about their practice throughout their career. This is the bedrock for learning to teach. (p. 149)

Yet, like other teacher education programs, we continue to grapple with the challenges inherent in the design and delivery of a high-quality teacher education program. Recently, we have highlighted teaching for deep understanding, or as we prefer, *teaching for depth,* to provide a strong professional foundation for our graduates in the face of significant change in the intellectual, policy, and contextual landscapes.

Introducing the Focus

Various strategies have been introduced at OISE/UT to create an impetus for teaching for depth. Because such a focus encourages the use of the latest research, it increases the chances of our program remaining meaningful and current.

Some of the initial strategies have included the following.

Academic Plan

The inclusion of teaching for depth in the OISE/UT seven-year academic plan has been a concrete way of communicating what we value. In addition, we have connected that focus to a broader goal that strives to ensure that what candidates learn in our teacher education program reflects the distinctive strengths of OISE/UT in research and scholarship.

Think Tank

The development of a think tank of diverse members of the OISE/UT community was an important mechanism for inquiry related to teaching for depth. This group met over the course of a year, engaging in activities that included reviews of research and theory (by group members and external authors), engagement in regular discussions, viewing of videotapes, development of a Web site, and strategizing of concrete actions for broader involvement.

Symposium

To jump-start the collective energy within OISE/UT and unpack the array of understandings and practices related to teaching for depth that were already under way, the think tank group planned a spring symposium for instructors, teacher candidates, and a few invited external guests. This full-day event also accomplished the goal of flagging the next phase of curriculum development and the important role teaching for depth would play. The community building that resulted from the different interactions throughout the day added another critical layer to this work.

Instructional Practices Presentations

To validate some of our existing instructional practices and to build on these practices, we invited a diverse group of instructors to present to their colleagues at the symposium. The public sharing of instructional practices and the underlying philosophies opened up the discourse around the varying ways instructors define teaching for depth.

Knowledge Forum® and Web Site

To enhance communication and promote knowledge building, Knowledge Forum®[1] was used to create a mechanism for both planning the symposium and continuing the discussion after it. Technical support was also provided for instructors new to this mode of discussion.

---

[1]Developed by Marlene Scardamalia and Carl Bereiter with a team of researchers, computer scientists, and educators, Knowledge Forum® is a virtual environment that puts the community in charge of its own knowledge building by providing the tools for groups to share information, launch collaborative investigations, and build networks of new ideas together. Based on research begun in 1987, Knowledge Forum was developed and is used in environments as diverse as K–12 schools, universities, and workplace settings, both in Canada and internationally.

International Conference on Teacher Education

As one strategy for infusing powerful external ideas into our own organization and to allow our own good ideas to be shared with others, we hosted an international conference entitled Teacher Education for the Schools We Need.[2] This conference supported our broader policy work and helped to strengthen the context for teaching for depth.

Creating New Leadership Roles

To develop a cadre of educators with the skills to lead teacher education reform (both internally and externally), new leadership roles were created. Program component coordinators, for instance, support instructors teaching specific program components such as School and Society and the Teacher Education Seminar. These leaders engage in overlapping and complementary change work, creating critical mass and broadening spheres of influence related to teaching for depth.

Other . . .

As our collective leadership develops, we will continue to add leadership strategies to our repertoire. We will constantly assess what actions will best move us toward our goal of teaching for depth.

EXPLORING DEPTH AND COMPLEXITY IN TEACHING

Ways in which OISE/UT teacher education instructors explore depth and complexity in their teaching were illustrated in various presentations at our recent symposium, Teaching for Depth in Teacher Education. We provide below brief excerpts from four presentations that highlight how instructors who teach for depth begin with a core set of learning principles. These examples show varying perspectives and technical competencies, as well as the theoretical sophistication used to guide and inform teaching in ways that are both current and purposeful.

Infusing Inquiry Across the Program—Janette Pelletier and Elizabeth Morley

These instructors in OISE/UT's two-year M.A. in Child Study and Education (MA CSE) program showed how teaching for depth is built into the mission and philosophy of a pedagogy based on the following principles:

- Teaching for depth means fostering deep thinking about children and curriculum.
- Thinking deeply about children means understanding them.

---

[2]*The Schools We Need* (Leithwood, Fullan, & Watson, 2003) is a review of Ontario education policy with recommendations for addressing a range of policy issues related to schooling in the province. Pointing out that neither the evidence nor the public supported further radical reform, the report called for ineffectual or negative policies to be revamped to meet five basic conditions for success—in the areas of vision, governance, evidence, support for teachers, and adequate and flexible funding.

- Understanding derives from systematic observation and interaction.
- Thinking deeply about curriculum means willingness to spend time acquiring and constructing ideas about a narrower range of expectations.

Central to their notion of teaching for depth is inquiry. One of the examples highlighted the comprehensive manner in which inquiry is infused across the program:

We begin by developing inquiring teachers, which in turn starts with the admissions process. We look for candidates who are interested in teaching for depth, who express interest in the teacher-researcher model. The process includes careful file review with attention to undergraduate grades, experience working with groups of children, and letters of reference from academic and professional referees, followed by a personal individual interview. Once the program begins, we encourage teacher candidates' participation in research activities and involve candidates in thinking about methodological and conceptual issues in research. Our courses support the focus on a teacher-researcher model; for example, we teach methods in child study and systematic observation. This entails understanding normative developmental progressions, systematic analysis of tracking, modifications for special needs, and issues in reporting.

Pelletier and Morley were careful to point out that teaching for depth reveals challenging issues. The following example illustrates one of these issues:

One issue concerns the contrast between depth and breadth. How can we teach for depth when breadth seems so salient in teacher education? Within the MA CSE preservice program, my particular course (Pelletier) is Introduction to Curriculum. It necessarily implies breadth—this is a survey course that gives only five to six weeks on each curriculum area, but serves the purpose of orienting the teacher candidates to the curriculum documents, of beginning to foster in them a critical stance towards expectations while simultaneously understanding that they must balance their beliefs about depth with the realities of policy and practice. Because our program aims to be integrated and coherent, we have chosen to devote our second-year curriculum courses to depth. In these courses, we select only two areas: language and math; teacher candidates are exposed to fewer areas and fewer expectations—they spend a great deal of time probing children's *minds* and carefully planning learning experiences built on their study of children. The child study method is taught and modeled in our Year 1 course on Child Study. Another related issue is time—we adopt the *slow schooling* approach, helping our teacher candidates to truly see that by going deep into fewer topics and allowing children the time to fully grasp a concept, children actually do learn more. Knowledge, attitudes, and skills that were not part of the original learning experience are called into play as children grapple with understanding.

Engaging in Reflection—Lynn Lemieux

This instructor in the Elementary Teacher Education program worked with a program coordinator to establish a common set of principles for teaching and learning in their cohort (the East Option), with research used to guide conceptual understandings, particularly in science education. One example that she provided discussed aspects of the program's integrative nature:

> As coordinators, we collaborate closely to ensure that the following principles of teaching and learning are reflected throughout the integrated program;
>
> 1. People construct meaning out of information and experiences by building on to and restructuring their existing knowledge and beliefs.
>
> 2. Learning is influenced by motivation, which is affected by a person's emotional state, beliefs, interests, goals, and habits of mind.
>
> 3. Effective learning requires effort and necessitates the active processing of experience in a way that is personally meaningful and conceptually coherent.
>
> 4. Learning is influenced by social interactions, interpersonal relations, and by communication with others.
>
> Candidates are engaged in reflecting on these principles, whether they are investigating ways to teach science and technology, mathematics, language arts, or social studies; therefore, many of the assignments we create are cross course in nature. For example, candidates are required to design a lesson sequence in mathematics using curriculum expectations in conjunction with instructional and assessment strategies from the Teacher Education Seminar course. They are also asked to reflect on the lesson in terms of the related psychological principles of learning and development.

Promoting the Social Health of the Classroom—Kathleen Gallagher[3]

Kathleen Gallagher, an instructor in drama education, believes that teaching for deep understanding requires attention to "Four Unremarkable Principles":

1. The process of learning (through drama) takes time.

2. (Drama) education is a dialogic art form productively powered by conflict and tied to the social health of the classroom.

3. Planning (in drama teaching) is not a lockstep activity that unequivocally dictates the actions of a classroom.

4. The (drama) classroom connects with the community and makes central the student's world.

For each principle, Gallagher outlined the theoretical bases underpinning it and also the challenges it presents for the classroom teacher. Her explanation of the

---

[3]See Chapter 10, this volume, for a fuller discussion of drama education.

second principle is illustrative: (Drama) education is a dialogic art form productively powered by conflict and tied to the social health of the classroom.

As education has, over the last 20 years, moved towards more co-operative modes of learning, research on the complex and often conflictual nature of group learning has not kept apace. The arts, and drama particularly, rely heavily on a group's ability to work co-operatively towards shared goals. Even the more traditional cognitive disciplines have recently favoured group strategies for content learning. Simultaneously, school systems have begun to pay greater attention to conflict as it arises in both classrooms and school communities. Controversial education policies such as "Zero Tolerance" and Ontario's "Safe Schools Act" represent attempts made by governments and policy-makers to combat what seems to be growing evidence of violence in our schools. These policies, and other attempts to manage conflict, have not always understood conflict between young people as well as they might. I would suggest that part of the problem is that these policies operate as though violence is the natural outcome of conflict. As a drama educator, however, my perspective on conflict, and its potentially rich relationship to the curriculum, is rather different. . . .

In drama especially, trust is required, but the idea of trust must be understood by teachers as a performative act. Trust is negotiated moment by moment; trust is not a state that can be achieved for all time. The negotiation of trust among peers has something to do with making the classroom, the school, and by extension, the world a safer and more humane place. If any progress is to be made, if we intend for students' engagement with subject matter to be strengthened, we must prioritize the health of the classroom environment and pay careful attention to the inevitable conflicts that will ultimately improve students' understanding of one another.

Introducing Students to the Constructed Nature of Knowledge—Ruth Sandwell

This instructor in the Intermediate/Senior Secondary Teacher Education program suggests that teaching for depth in history means that students are introduced to the constructed nature of historical knowledge, as well as the contingent products of that knowledge. She invites teachers and students to move beyond the 19th-century positivism that continues to have such a profound influence on history as it is taught in North American schools.

Positivism assumes that knowledge is fixed, certain, uncontestable, and the possession of privileged "experts." In history classes, this most often translates into lessons that simply require students to find the right answer by correctly finding what the experts have said, and telling it back to the teacher in a slightly different form. This kind of history ensures that history is boring and irrelevant to most students, not only because the range of facts, issues, and events tends to be small, but because the pedagogical possibilities of this kind of history tend to be limited to product knowledge. Taught in this way, history is largely a product to be consumed rather than a process of understanding and knowledge building to be actively engaged in. This school history, where history is reduced to facts, issues, and events to be learned, stands in marked contrast to the work of historians.

For the last 50 years or so, historians (in ways analogous to other scholars in the humanities) have been emphasizing that knowledge is not lying around waiting to be discovered. History is now widely understood as a dialogue among people, past and present, about how to best interpret evidence from the past. Learning how to responsibly construct meaningful, reasonable knowledge about complex social forms, in the context of other interpretations of the evidence and in the context of our contemporary concerns, is what historians do. Learning to think historically—to think critically about how evidence is constructed to create knowledge about the world, and parts of the world—arguably provides the best education for being a responsible person in a participatory democracy. This, to my mind, is why history should be taught.

CHALLENGES AND POSSIBILITIES

Initiating and sustaining a focus on teaching for depth in initial teacher preparation is not without its challenges. One such challenge is the tension that arises as instructors debate the merits of breadth versus depth. Although most support the value of a focus on depth, actions that align to this focus are more difficult to achieve. This is especially true when the demands and expectations from field partners and external policy requirements continue to grow. Because curriculum requirements are rarely reduced, faculties of education need to make hard decisions regarding what is necessary, realistic, and coherent.

> Teaching for depth in teacher education demands courageous decision making, purposeful planning, and thoughtful action, but we believe the potential outcomes for future generations of teachers and students are well worth the effort.

A second challenge is the knowledge base that teacher candidates bring to a program. This knowledge base will be influenced by the nature of their informal learning experiences and previous degree(s). Bransford, Brown, and Cocking (2000) make the case as follows:

Teachers must come to teaching with the experience of in-depth study of the subject area themselves. Before a teacher can develop powerful pedagogical tools, he or she must be familiar with the progress of inquiry and the terms of discourse in the discipline, as well as understand the relationship between information and the concepts that help organize that information in the discipline. But equally important, the teacher must have a grasp of the growth and development of students' thinking about these concepts. The latter will be essential to developing teaching expertise, but not expertise in the discipline. (p. 20)

A third challenge is the learning context created for teacher candidates during their teacher education program. Traditional individualistic learning environments do not support knowledge building, which is understood as a social activity whose object is the creation and improvement of new knowledge and the solution of knowledge problems (Bereiter, 2002; Scardamalia, 2002). One of its cardinal principles, the one that most sharply distinguishes it from other constructivist approaches, is idea improvement. When applied to problems of understanding, idea improvement entails going deeper, using all the knowledge resources available. In a knowledge-building context, it also entails epistemic agency—personal and collective responsibility for advancing the state of knowledge in the community. (See Bereiter, Chapter 2, this volume.)

A fourth challenge is time. Conceptual change and change in beliefs can lead to deeper knowledge, but such change is particularly difficult to accomplish in short teacher-education programs. Observing, experiencing, reflecting, dialoguing, and rethinking form a never-ending cycle. Candidates need multiple opportunities to grapple with the issues and examine their own dispositions if they are to develop new awareness and implement meaningful change.

Finally, various structural and organizational issues influence the capacity of teacher educators to teach for depth. Length and timing of classes, integration of practica and coursework, collaborative opportunities for course development by instructors, and other such factors play a role. Creative problem solving and attention to these factors will be critical.

Despite these and other challenges, focusing on teaching for depth holds tremendous possibilities for teacher education. By attending to the multiple knowledge bases that inform effective practice, and by fostering inquiry and using the latest research, we increase the chances that programs for aspiring teachers become solid foundations for future professional growth. Teaching for depth in teacher education demands courageous decision making, purposeful planning, and thoughtful action, but we believe the potential outcomes for future generations of teachers and students are well worth the effort.

20

Summary and Recommendations

Kenneth Leithwood

Pat McAdie

Nina Bascia

Anne Rodrigue

Shawn Moore

> The organization of our recommendations follows a "backward mapping" logic. We begin with recommendations for the classroom and back up from there to what the other parts of the system need to do differently to help create and sustain classrooms where teaching for deep understanding is the norm.

In Chapter 1, we made the case for why deep understanding ought to be the central goal for education. We argued that specific facts or disconnected pieces of knowledge, by themselves, have little meaning and, in any event, are remarkably unstable in most disciplines over time. Furthermore, we argued, the challenges and problems most people face throughout their lives demand the kind of intellectual, social, and emotional capacities developed through extended efforts to understand big complex ideas.

Even in the much more constrained world of formal schooling and its current preoccupation with testing for purposes of public accountability, teaching for deep understanding is clearly a strategy for success: Students who experience such teaching, most relevant evidence indicates, do at least as well and often better on the tests commonly used to hold schools accountable.

Chapters 2, 3, and 4 clarified what is meant by deep understanding and described the basic teaching and learning processes that generate such understanding. Chapter 2 grappled with what it means to understand something "in depth." Carl Bereiter suggests that "deep understanding means understanding deep things about the object in question." These deep things may be, for example, the underlying meanings of a poem, the fundamental causes of a historical event, the real issues behind a current controversy, and the like. In real life, we spend a good deal of time attempting to understand things deeply. We ask such questions as, Why did the U.S. government decide to go to war with Iraq? What can governments do to inform and involve the public about important policy decisions? What can governments and individuals do to protect the environment? What factors affect oil prices? Besides thinner ice, what does melting of the polar ice cap mean for the weather in North America? And even what makes a high-quality education system for all students?

Deep, as these questions suggest, means not obvious or superficial; it means getting to the heart of the matter; it might even mean becoming wise in some domain of human activity, as Ferrari suggests in Chapter 12. Teaching for deep understanding also means helping students weigh all sides of an argument and come to their own conclusions.

> Many teachers have been working at developing deep understanding among their students for many years, even with only weak official endorsement.

Adopting a constructivist view of learning, Beck and Kosnik provide us with an account of the cognitive, emotional, and social processes involved in acquiring deep understandings. Consistent with Ferrari's claim that wisdom entails much more than knowledge (he suggests character, as well), Beck and Kosnik demonstrate the multidimensional pathway through which one comes to a deep understanding of something. This is a process of making connections with one's own internal resources, as well as other related ideas "out there." Connections leading to deep understanding are not only cognitive. Understanding something deeply entails making connections, as well, to emotions, feelings, and values (connections that are particularly well fostered through drama and the arts curriculum, as Gallagher demonstrates in Chapter 10).

Chapter 4 described the range of meanings associated with *understanding* as a concept, pointing out, not surprisingly, that there is no single definition with which everyone agrees. That said, the degrees of difference among the meanings of understanding outlined in Chapter 4 seem relatively minor and certainly nothing that would stand in the way of acting on its development through the school curriculum. Some combination of "having sufficient grasp of concepts, principles, or skills so that you can bring them to bear on new problems and situations" (Howard Gardner's 1993 definition) and "being able to do a variety of thought-demanding things with a topic—like explaining, finding evidence and examples, generalizing, applying concepts, analyzing, and representing a topic in a new way" (David Perkins's 1994 definition) pretty much encompass the debate about how to understand the meaning of *understanding*.

Chapters 5 through 10 examined, in a much more detailed and domain-specific way the teaching and learning processes associated with developing deep understanding in a sample of the school disciplines. Chapters 11 through 15 examined these issues as they can be treated across the curriculum. The cognitive aspects of school need not be all that is considered. Indeed, Ferrari (Chapter 12) discussed the importance of including wisdom in our discussions. Others, such as Goodlad (2003/2004), stress equity and social justice as important aspects to be explicitly included in schooling.

One way or another, all of the remaining chapters aimed to help make deep understanding the central goal for education actually being pursued in *schools and classrooms.*

These chapters captured current elementary teachers' views about the challenges they face in teaching for deep understanding, and the authors also assess how the larger system surrounding the classroom—schools, districts, universities, governments—would need to work a bit differently to support teachers' efforts to teach for deep understanding. In the remainder of this chapter, we offer a small number of key recommendations for helping move the focus of the school system in the direction of deep understanding. These recommendations concern changes in the classroom, the school, and the district. In addition, we offer recommendations aimed at teacher education schools and state/provincial policymakers.

Developing deep understanding or critical thinking should not wait until students are older. We need to ensure that habits of mind are developed early while teaching early literacies.

The organization of our recommendations follows a "backward mapping" logic. According to this logic, the starting point for further developing students' deep understanding is to be clear about the kind of classroom instruction that is needed, such instruction being the most direct cause of deep understanding in formal education environments. With a clear picture of desirable instruction in mind, we are then in a position to consider the conditions that those in schools, districts, universities, and governments need to create to foster and support the implementation of such instruction.

> ...the main impediment to fully implementing significant reform in schools is not that teachers and administrators in schools are reluctant to change but that those people in districts and states surrounding the schools fail to do their part.

Each level in the school system should be accountable for creating the conditions required for the next level to do its work successfully. So those with school-level responsibilities are most directly accountable for creating conditions that support effective classroom practice. Those with district-level responsibilities are accountable for creating conditions for effective school practice. And so on.

RECOMMENDATIONS FOR THE CLASSROOM

We offer four broad recommendations in this section. At their most general level, many readers may think, these recommendations are already part of common instructional practice. The devil is in the details, however, and we remind you, again, that many such details are to be found in those earlier chapters focused on specific areas of the curriculum. The recommendations in this section identify practices effective in developing deep understanding common to most areas of the curriculum.

Some of these recommendations can be implemented (and are being implemented) in the context of many teachers' present working conditions; others, however, would require a change in those conditions. Those changes are the subject of recommendations in other sections of this chapter.

Classroom Instruction Should Build on Students' Ideas and Experiences

Extensive attention should be given to students' ideas, objections, and puzzlements. It is never too early to give such attention to students' ideas. Much of the purpose of such examination should be idea improvement. Improving on one's ideas and understanding them more deeply are synonymous, for our purposes. Topics selected for study should as far as possible be ones that relate to students' past or present experience as well as topics considered fundamentally central to the field of study or discipline at hand. As far as possible, topics studied should be relevant and interesting to the whole class and lend themselves to sharing in order to build a sense of community in the classroom.

Learning needs to be made a long-term, thinking-centered process so that students are thinking with and about the ideas they are learning. Explicitly teaching for transfer will be part of this activity and should be done quite systematically to help students connect ideas that they might not otherwise see as related and to help them cultivate mental habits of connection making.

Classroom Instruction Should Help Connect the Content of the Curriculum to Students' Values

The relevance of knowledge to one's own and other people's values should be a major topic of exploration in classrooms. This will increase students' interest in inquiry and also give them an opportunity to shape knowledge to their needs and circumstances and thus deepen it. In addition, the topics selected for study in the classroom should, as far as possible, be ones that are important for human well-being. Because not everything can be covered in school, we should help students focus on the more important topics.

Classroom Instruction Should Illuminate Ideas by Providing Significant Opportunities for Social Interaction Between Teachers and Students and Among Students Themselves

Teachers should engage students—and have students engage one another—in sustained talk about their ideas. By articulating their ideas, students become conscious of their thoughts and more able to subject them to explicit examination. Teachers should look for ways to ensure that the shared ideas in the classroom are deepened. To a large extent, students develop their ideas together; much of the focus, therefore, should be on enriching students' beliefs, attitudes, and behavior patterns.

Teachers also should work to ensure that the individual student's ideas and experience are made available to others in the class in an efficient manner. We need to enhance the effectiveness of collaborative activities in class. It is not sufficient that students are active and enjoy themselves, although this is important.

Classroom Instruction Should Help Connect the Content of the Curriculum to Students' Own Lives

Students should be encouraged to explore other dimensions of knowledge and life—not just the cognitive—in both the curriculum and the life of the classroom. This will deepen understanding in itself and also increase engagement, which, in turn, will further understanding because students will learn more. Topics and activities should be selected that will engage students in a holistic way. Some topics lend themselves more than others to being approached holistically; news and fictional stories, for example, stimulate students to think imaginatively and critically about difficult choices in complex settings, exactly what we mean by *holistically.*

Classroom assessment often provides information about how much students have learned and what the teachers' priorities for instruction should be. But it can also be a direct stimulant for student learning. A much greater proportion of classroom assessment should focus on the last of these purposes, assessment as learning. Such assessment should frequently focus on criteria for judging students' performances, feedback on those performances, and reflection through the learning process.

RECOMMENDATIONS FOR THE SCHOOL

Two sets of recommendations designed to help schools become supportive environments for teaching for deep understanding are outlined in this section. It needs to be said, however, that one size does not fit all. Each school will need to find its own way to implement the spirit and intention of these recommendations. We have learned this from mandated reform initiatives in many parts of the world that aim at the standardization of schooling.

Schools Should Develop a Strong Sense of Professional Community

This is wise advice, no matter the agenda for change, because a strong professional community in a school provides the accessible, practical, and trusted foundation of social relationships needed by staff to create, evaluate, and eventually implement new practices in their classrooms. Impressive evidence suggests that schools functioning as professional communities almost always do good things for students. This sense of community flourishes, for example, when teachers work with one another in teams on problems they consider to be educationally important and when experienced teachers provide peer classroom observations and coaching for new colleagues.

A sense of professional community is enhanced, as well, when teachers have a voice in decisions about the rationale and objectives for the school's programs and experience the challenges associated with implementation and sustainability. Norms within well-functioning communities of this sort encourage risk taking, promote peer collaboration, tolerate and promote learning from both success and failure, and acknowledge success. These norms are encouraged when teachers' professional development includes a focus on the challenges to traditional instructional practices in the classroom, critical friendships among colleagues, and support for teachers struggling with new approaches to instruction and assessment.

School Leadership Practices Should Be Aligned With the Expectation That Teachers Will Focus on Teaching for Deep Understanding

This recommendation means, for example, that those in school leadership roles, wherever feasible, should model the instructional skills and strategies that teachers are expected to implement in their classrooms and vis-à-vis which they will be evaluated and held accountable.

School leaders should also align administrative policies, routines, and procedures with the goal of teaching for deep understanding. These areas of administration include, for example, school budgets, criteria for the allocation of physical space in the school, and teacher appraisal procedures. Left unaligned, there is considerable potential for policies, procedures, and routines such as these to get in the way of teaching for deep understanding if that has not been a significant goal for the school until recently.

This recommendation also means that school leaders should anticipate and prepare themselves to respond to skepticism and lack of support on the part of some parents and other community members for a focus on deep understanding in their child's curriculum. This is certainly not the way many parents were taught themselves when they were in elementary school.

Other parents will be entirely in support of deep understanding as a goal for their children but not know how they can support this goal at home. Yet we know that parent involvement in the child's formative years can be crucial to both their orientation toward learning and their motivation for learning. School leaders need to open the schools to parents and the wider community, inviting, encouraging, and otherwise welcoming partnerships with parents in the development of deep understanding. These leaders will also need to become articulate apologists for, and advocates of, the importance of developing deep understanding.

RECOMMENDATIONS FOR DISTRICTS

Districts have the potential to play an important role in both encouraging and enabling teachers and school administrators to implement forms of teaching and learning that foster deep understanding. We offer four recommendations for districts.

District Leaders Should Articulate a Clear Vision of Teaching and Learning for Deep Understanding and Ensure That Most Members of the School System Understand This Vision and Are Committed to Its Achievement

As at the school level, it is important that district leaders engage all partners—teachers, school administrators, parents—in developing this vision.

Districts Should Provide Access to High-Quality Professional Development Aimed at Both the Instructional and the Leadership Capacities Needed in Schools to Develop Students' Deep Understanding

Such inservice programs may take many forms, for example encouraging principals and teachers to visit and observe schools in which teaching and learning for deep understanding is being well done; creating horizontal and vertical networks among principals and teachers within the system; and involving universities in districtwide professional development to help meet the challenge of integrating empirical research findings and theories of teaching and learning for deep understanding with existing teacher beliefs and practices.

Through such inservice or by other means, districts need also to ensure an ample supply of student learning material, input from subject experts, collegial interactions to explore classroom applications, and attention to teachers' beliefs about the subject matter.

Districts Should Give Teachers and Principals Substantial Control Over Instructional Decisions, Avoiding Policies That Overcentralize Governance, Finance, Supervision, and Curriculum Development and Assessment

As part of such control, districts should allow schools to undertake school improvement activities of their own designs aimed at enhancing schools' contributions to students' deep understanding.

Districts Should Encourage the Development of Transformational Orientations in the Selection, Training, and Supervising of School Leaders (Both Teachers and Administrators)

Transformational leadership, as Ross and McDougall describe it in Chapter 5, "is an approach in which principals encourage teacher development by engaging teachers in the creation of a school vision, by providing intellectual stimulation and support for individuals, modeling professional practices, setting high performance expectations, and sharing decision making." Such leadership builds many of the school conditions that encourage teaching for deep understanding.

RECOMMENDATIONS FOR STATE AND PROVINCIAL POLICYMAKERS

Our recommendations for policymakers concern the state or provincial curriculum, the state or provincial testing system, and implementation of policies that encourage teaching for deep understanding.

The Provincial Curriculum Should Do More With Less

As we pointed out in Chapter 1, the huge number of expectations in the current curriculum puts teachers under pressure to cover an enormous range of topics. This pressure should be reduced by focusing only on topics that are considered the essentials of the subject matter and have the potential to promote depth of understanding.

There should be sufficient room in the curriculum for teachers to engage students in ideas that interest them and are considered relevant to them. Such interest and relevance is vital for making those connections with students' existing beliefs, which are so necessary for developing deeper understandings.

If the state or provincial curriculum is to become both leaner and focused on more essential knowledge, as we argue it should, there will need to be greater oversight and coordination across individual curricula as they are being developed. When the curriculum in each subject area is developed with only loose or limited oversight, the outcome will inevitably be the overloaded set of expectations for learning that currently exists.

The Curriculum Should Take Into Account Diversity

Because students' understanding of, approaches to, and capacities for learning are shaped by their race, ethnicity, gender, and family, the curriculum should take into account such diversity, and students should be encouraged to explore their backgrounds, experiences, and values in relation to others inside and outside the classroom.

The Purposes for State- or Province-wide Assessments Should Be Clarified

At present, state and provincial assessments attempt to accomplish many purposes. One such purpose is assessment for learning; that is, schools and teachers are encouraged to use the results of the provincial tests for improving student learning. The tests serve this purpose very poorly and so have become a source of frustration and understandable confusion among many teachers. The most appropriate purpose for a provincial testing program, in our view, is the assessment of learning. Results of these tests might continue to be used to hold districts accountable for accomplishing provincial standards, although this could be done with less frequent testing than is presently the case and need not be done on an every-pupil basis. Districts and schools should be ceded the responsibility for assessments for learning and for assessments that become part of the learning process itself. The latter use of assessments is best suited to the development of deep understanding.

Processes Used to Implement Provincial Initiatives Intended to Foster Teaching for Deep Understanding Should Be Guided by Substantial Evidence About What Works

Change, we have learned, is complex and difficult. Mandated changes to policy, aimed at the core functions of teaching and learning, almost always underestimate

SUMMARY AND RECOMMENDATIONS **183**

the time and resources it takes for individuals and organizations to change. So the pace of implementation is critical to the success of a new program of teaching and learning for deep understanding. Administrators and teachers must be given sufficient time, support, and resources to learn and apply new instructional approaches and assessment techniques, as well as tools for measuring the achievement of objectives.

Implementation processes should be both bottom-up and top-down. That is, district leaders, principals, and teachers should have a voice, along with provincial policymakers, in decisions about whether or not mandated changes to curriculum and assessment are working as intended and whether the resources are sufficient to meet objectives.

RECOMMENDATIONS FOR TEACHER EDUCATION SCHOOLS

As Carl Bereiter argued in Chapter 2, students preparing to be teachers ought themselves to gain experience in the kinds of activities that will actually produce depth of understanding on the part of their future students. We offer three recommendations for teacher education faculties consistent with this argument.

Teacher Education Courses Focused on Pedagogy Should Identify the Big and Difficult Ideas in Education and Encourage Their Students to Seriously Grapple With Them in Ways That Build Deep Understanding

Teacher Education Courses Focused on the Subjects Future Teachers Will Teach Should Provide the Experience of In-Depth Study of Those Subject Areas Themselves

Teacher Education Courses Should Build Teachers' Understandings of the Growth and Development of Students' Thinking About Those Concepts Central to the Subject Disciplines

A FINAL NOTE

We have offered a small number of key recommendations in this final chapter. It would be foolish in the extreme to expect that a large proportion of them would be acted on quickly. This would be so even if our case for deep understanding, as the central goal for a state or province's curriculum, was unanimously endorsed.

But the more we act on these recommendations, the closer we come to achieving this goal. Many teachers have been working at developing deep understanding among their students for many years, even with only weak official endorsement. Changes in the conditions of work from year to year (for example, state or provincial legislative efforts to reduce class size) have the potential to significantly assist teachers to better appreciate the ideas and interests their individual students bring to the school curriculum. So we may be already moving forward, even if on a broken front. Any action on our recommendations will further these efforts.

Is one place better to start than another? Logically, it seems, we should start with classroom instruction. After all, that is where our backward mapping began. But this is not a logical business. The title of a recent study by Merideth Honig (2004) nicely signals our concern: "Where's the 'Up' in Bottom-up Reform?" This study found that the main impediment to fully implementing significant reform in schools is not that teachers and administrators in schools are reluctant to change but that those people in districts and states surrounding the schools fail to do their part.

If Honig's results are widespread, we should likely start by implementing our recommendations for the states or provinces and for faculties of education. It is likely to be very difficult for teachers to extend their teaching for deep understanding much further until the school, district, and provincial contexts in which they work provide much greater support for their efforts.

SUMMARY OF RECOMMENDATIONS

For the Classroom

At their most general level, many readers may think, these recommendations are already part of common instructional practice in most schools. The devil is in the details, however . . .

1. Classroom instruction should build on students' ideas and experiences.

2. Classroom instruction should help connect the content of the curriculum to students' values.

3. Classroom instruction should illuminate ideas by providing significant opportunities for social interaction between teachers and students and among students themselves.

4. Classroom instruction should help connect the content of the curriculum to students' own lives.

For the School

These recommendations are designed to help schools become supportive environments for teaching for deep understanding. Each school will need to find its own way to implement the spirit and intention of these recommendations. One size does not fit all . . .

1. Schools should develop a strong sense of professional community.

2. School leadership practices should be aligned with the expectation that teachers will focus on teaching for deep understanding.

For the District

Districts have the potential to play an important role in both encouraging and enabling teachers and school administrators to implement forms of teaching and learning that foster deep understanding. We offer four recommendations for districts:

1. District leaders should articulate a clear vision of teaching and learning for deep understanding and ensure that most members of the school system understand this vision and are committed to its achievement.

2. Districts should provide access to high-quality professional development aimed at both the instructional and the leadership capacities needed in schools to develop students' deep understanding.

3. Districts should give teachers and principals substantial control over instructional decisions, avoiding policies that overcentralize governance, finance, supervision, and curriculum development and assessment.

4. Districts should encourage the development of transformational orientations in the selection, training, and supervising of school leaders (both teachers and administrators).

For State or Provincial Policymakers

Our recommendations for policymakers concern the curriculum, the testing system, and implementation of policies that encourage teaching for deep understanding.

1. The curriculum should do more with less.

2. The curriculum should take into account diversity.

3. The purposes for state- or provincewide assessments should be clarified.

4. Processes used to implement provincial initiatives intended to foster teaching for deep understanding should be guided by substantial evidence about what works.

For Teacher Education Schools

Teachers ought themselves to gain experience in the kinds of activity that will actually produce depth of understanding on the part of their future students. We offer three recommendations for teacher education faculties consistent with this argument.

1. Teacher education courses focused on pedagogy should identify the big and difficult ideas in education and encourage their students to seriously grapple with them in ways that build deep understanding.

2. Teacher education courses focused on the subjects future teachers will teach should provide the experience of in-depth study of those subject areas themselves.

3. Teacher education courses should build teachers' understandings of the growth and development of students' thinking about those concepts central to the subject disciplines.

References

Aikenhead, G. S., & Jegede, O. J. (1999). Cross-cultural science education: A cognitive explanation of a cultural phenomenon. *Journal of Research in Science Teaching, 36*(3), 269–287.

Alexander, C. N., & Langer, E. J. (Eds.). (1990). *Higher stages of human development.* New York: Oxford University Press.

Allen, J. (2002). *On the same page: Shared reading beyond the primary grades.* Portland, ME: Stenhouse.

American Association for the Advancement of Science [AAAS]. (1989). *Science for all Americans: A Project 2061 report on literacy goals in science, mathematics, and technology.* Washington, DC: Author.

Amsterdam, A. G., & Bruner, J. (2000). *Minding the law: Culture, cognition, and the court.* New York: Harvard University Press.

Anderson, C. W., & Roth, K. J. (1989). Teaching for meaningful and self-regulated learning of science. In J. Brophy (Ed.), *Advances in research on teaching* (Vol. 1, pp. 265–309). Greenwich, CT: JAI.

Anderson, R. C., & Pearson, P. D. (1984). A schema-theoretic view of basic processes in reading comprehension. In P. D. Pearson (Ed.), *Handbook of reading research* (pp. 255–292). New York: Longman.

Arendt, H. (1958). *The human condition.* Chicago: University of Chicago Press.

Bailin, S., Case, R., Coombs, J., & Daniels, L. (1999). Conceptualizing critical thinking. *Journal of Curriculum Studies, 31*(3), 285–302.

Ball, D. L. (1991). Teaching mathematics for understanding: What do teachers need to know about subject matter? In M. M. Kennedy (Ed.), *Teaching academic subjects to diverse learners* (pp. 63–83). New York: Teachers College Press.

Baltes, P. B., & Staudinger, U. M. (2000). Wisdom: A metaheuristic (pragmatic) to orchestrate mind and virtue toward excellence. *American Psychologist, 55,* 122–136.

Bandura, A. (1986). *Social foundations of thought and action: A social cognitive theory.* Englewood Cliffs, NJ: Prentice Hall.

Barthes, R. (1977). *Image, music, text* (S. Heath, Ed. & Trans.). New York: Hill & Wang.

Barthes, R. (1982). *Empire of signs* (R. Howard, Trans.). New York: Hill & Wang. (Original work published 1970)

Bascia, N. (2000). The other side of the equation: Teachers' professional development and the organizational capacity of teacher unions. *Educational Policy, 14*(3), 383–404.

Bascia, N. (2001). Pendulum swings and sediment layers: Educational policy and the case of ESL. In J. Portelli & P. Solomon (Eds.), *The erosion of the democratic tradition in education: From critique to possibilities* (pp. 245–268). Calgary, Canada: Detselig.

Bascia, N. (2003). *Triage or tapestry? Teacher unions' work toward improving teacher quality in an era of systemic reform* (Prepared for the Center for the Study of Teaching and Policy, University of Washington). Toronto: Ontario Institute for Studies in Education of the University of Toronto.

Bascia, N. (2004). Teacher unions and the teaching workforce: Mismatch or vital contribution? In M. Smylie & D. Miretzky (Eds.), *Developing the teacher workforce* (pp. 326–347). Chicago: University of Chicago Press.

Bascia, N. (2005). Triage or tapestry: Teacher unions' contributions to systemic educational reform. In N. Bascia, A. Datnow, & K. Leithwood (Eds.), *International handbook of educational policy.* Dordrecht, The Netherlands: Kluwer.

Bascia, N., & Hargreaves, A. (2000). Teaching and leading on the sharp edge of change. In N. Bascia & A. Hargreaves (Eds.), *The sharp edge of educational change: Teaching, leading, and the realities of reform* (pp. 3–26). London: Falmer.

Beck, L. G., & Murphy, J. (1999). Parental involvement in site-based management: Lessons from one site. *International Journal of Leadership in Education, 2*(2), 81–102.

Beers, K. (2003). *When kids can't read, what teachers can do: A guide for teachers 6–12.* Portsmouth, NH: Heinemann.

Bencze, J. L. (2000). Procedural apprenticeship in school science: Constructivist enabling of connoisseurship. *Science Education, 84*(6), 727–739.

Bennett, B., Anderson, S. E., & Evans, M. (1997, April 17–21). *Towards an integrative theory of instructional expertise: Understanding teachers' instructional repertoires.* Paper presented at the Annual Meeting of the American Educational Research Association, Chicago.

Bennett, B., & Rolheiser, C. (2001). *Beyond Monet: The artful science of instructional integration.* Toronto: Bookation.

Bereiter, C. (2002). *Education and mind for the knowledge age.* Mahwah, NJ: Lawrence Erlbaum.

Bereiter, C., & Scardamalia, M. (1989). Intentional learning as a goal of instruction. In L. B. Resnick (Ed.), *Knowing, learning, and instruction: Essays in honor of Robert Glaser* (pp. 361–392). Hillsdale, NJ: Lawrence Erlbaum.

Black, P. (1998). *Testing: Friend or foe? Theory and practice of assessment and testing.* London: Falmer.

Black, P., & Wiliam, D. (1998). *Inside the black box. Raising standards through classroom assessment.* London: School of Education King's College.

Blair, T., & Jones, D. (1998). *Preparing for student teaching in a pluralist classroom.* Boston: Allyn & Bacon.

Bliss, M. (2002). Teaching Canadian national history (Address at the annual conference of the Association for Canadian Studies, Winnipeg, October 2001). *Canadian Social Studies, 36*(2). Retrieved January 18, 2006, from http://www.quasar.ualberta.ca/css/Css_36_2/ARteaching_canadian_national_history.htm

Bloom, B. (1981). *All our children learning.* New York: McGraw-Hill.

Booth, D. (2001). *Reading and writing in the middle years.* Portland, ME: Stenhouse.

Booth, D. (2002). *Even hockey players read: Boys, literacy, and learning.* Markham, ON: Pembroke.

Booth, D., & Barton, B. (2000). *Story works: How teachers can use shared stories in the new curriculum.* Markham, ON: Pembroke.

Booth, D., Green, J., & Booth, J. (2004). *I want to read!* Oakville, ON: Rubicon Publishers.

Bourdieu, P. (1983). The forms of capital. In J. G. Richardson (Ed.), *Handbook of theory and research for the sociology of education* (pp. 241–258). New York: Greenwood Press.

Bransford, J. D., Brown, A. L., & Cocking, R. R. (Eds.). (2000). *How people learn: Brain, mind, experience, and school.* Washington, DC: National Academy Press. Online at http://www.nap.edu/html/howpeople1/

Britzman, D. (2001). The arts of inquiry. *Journal of Curriculum Theorizing, 17*(1), 9–26.

Brophy, J. (Ed.). (2002). *Social constructivist teaching: Affordances and constraints.* London: JAI/Elsevier Science.

Brown, A. (1997). Transforming schools into communities of thinking and learning about serious matters. *American Psychologist, 52*(4), 399–413.

Brown, A., & Campione, J. (1996). Psychological theory and the design of innovative learning environments: On procedures, principles, and systems. In L. Schauble & R. Glaser (Eds.), *Innovations in learning: New environments for education* (pp. 289–325). Mahwah, NJ: Lawrence Erlbaum.

Bruner, J. (2002). *Making stories: Law, literature, life.* New York: Farrar, Straus & Giroux.

Byers, V. (1980). What does it mean to understand mathematics? *International Journal of Mathematical Education Science and Technology, 11*(1), 1–10.

Byers, V., & Herscovics, N. (1977). Understanding school mathematics. *Mathematics Teaching, 81,* 24–27.

Cajas, F. (1999). Public understanding of science: Using technology to enhance school science in everyday life. *International Journal of Science Education, 21*(7), 765–773.

Campbell, E. (2004, April 12–16). *Challenges in fostering ethical knowledge as professionalism within teaching communities.* Paper presented at the Annual Meeting of the American Educational Research Association, San Diego.

Capitalism [Computer software]. (1996). Triangle Park, NC: Interactive Magic.

Carey, N., Lewis, L., & Farris, E. (1998). *Parent involvement in children's education: Efforts by public elementary schools* (National Center for Education Statistics Statistical Analysis Report). Washington, DC: Government Printing Office.

Case, R., & Daniels, L. (2003). *Introduction to the CT2 [Critical Thinking Consortium]: Conceptions of critical thinking.* Retrieved from https://public.sd38.bc.ca/RTRWeb/PDFdocuments/CCIntro.pdf

Cavanaugh, R., MacNeil, N., & Silcox, S. (2004). *Beyond instructional leadership: Toward pedagogue leadership.* Paper submitted to the Australian Association for Research in Education, Auckland.

Chow, P., & Cummins, J. (2003). Valuing multilingual and multicultural approaches to learning. In S. R. Schecter & J. Cummins (Eds.), *Multilingual education in practice: Using diversity as a resource* (pp. 32–61). Portsmouth, NH: Heinemann.

Clarke, S. (2001). *Unlocking formative assessment: Practical strategies for enhancing pupils' learning in the primary classroom.* London: Hodder & Stoughton.

Claxton, G. (1991). *Educating the inquiring mind: The challenge for school science.* London: Harvester Wheatsheaf.

Clifford, P., & Friesen, S. (2004). *Readership and the new literacies.* Retrieved from www.gallileo.org/research/publications/leadership_new_literacies

Cochran-Smith, M. (2004). *Walking the road: Race, diversity, and social justice in teacher education.* New York: Teachers College Press.

Cochran-Smith, M., & Lytle, S. L. (1992). Communities for teacher research: Fringe or forefront? *American Journal of Education, 100,* 298–324.

Cohen, D., & Ball, D. L. (1990). Relations between policy and practice: A commentary. *Educational Evaluation and Policy Analysis, 12*(3), 249–256.

Cole, A., & Knowles, J. (2000). *Researching teaching: Exploring teacher development through reflexive inquiry.* Boston: Allyn & Bacon.

COMPAS, Inc. (2003). *The state of the teaching profession in Ontario, 2003: A report to the Ontario College of Teachers based on a survey of the province's teachers.* Toronto: The Ontario College of Teachers.

Cotton, K., & Wikeland, K. R. (1989). *Parent involvement in education* (School Improvement Research Series, Close-Up #6). Portland, OR: Northwest Regional Educational Laboratory.

Court Square [Computer software]. (1995–1997). New York: Classroom Inc.

Cummins, J. (2001). *Negotiating identities: Education for empowerment in a diverse society* (2nd ed.). Los Angeles: California Association for Bilingual Education.

Darling-Hammond, L. (1994). Performance-based assessment and educational equity. *Harvard Educational Review, 64*(1), 5–30.

Darling-Hammond, L. (1997). *The right to learn: A blueprint for creating schools that work.* San Francisco: Jossey-Bass.

Darling-Hammond, L. (1998). Teachers and teaching: Testing hypotheses from a National Commission report. *Educational Researcher, 27*(1), 5–15.

Dauber, S. L., & Epstein, J. L. (1989). *Parents' attitudes and practices of involvement in inner city elementary and middle schools* (CREMS Report 33.). Baltimore, MD: Johns Hopkins University, Center for Research on Elementary and Middle Schools.

Dennett, D. (2003). *Freedom evolves.* New York: Viking.

Derrida, J. (1978). *Writing and difference* (A. Bass, Trans.). London: Routledge & Kegan Paul. (Original work published 1967)

Desimone, L., & Le Floch, K. (2004). Are we asking the right questions? Using cognitive interviews to improve surveys for educational research. *Educational Evaluation and Policy Analysis, 26*(1), 1–22.

Dewey, J. (1916). *Democracy and education.* New York: Macmillan.

Dewey, J. (1938). *Experience and education.* New York: Collier-Macmillan.

Dewey, J. (1980). *Art as experience.* New York: Perigee. (Original work published 1934)

Dobbin, M. (1998). *The myth of the good corporate citizen: Democracy under the rule of big business.* Toronto: Stoddart.

Drake, S. (1992). *Developing an integrated curriculum using the story model.* Toronto: OISE Press.

Drake, S. (1993). *Planning integrated curriculum: The call to adventure.* Alexandria, VA: Association for Supervision & Curriculum Development.

Earl, L. (2003). *Assessment as learning: Using classroom assessment to maximize student learning.* Thousand Oaks, CA: Corwin Press.

Early, M., Cummins, J., & Willinsky, J. (2002). *From literacy to multiliteracies: Designing learning environments for knowledge generation within the new economy.* Proposal funded by the Social Sciences and Humanities Research Council of Canada.

Egan, K. (1986). *Teaching as story telling.* London: Althouse Press.

Egan, K. (1997). *The educated mind: How cognitive tools shape our understanding.* Chicago: University of Chicago Press.

Eisenhardt, M., Borko, H., Underhill, R., Brown, C., Jones, D., & Agard, P. (1993). Conceptual knowledge falls through the cracks: Complexities of learning to teach for understanding. *Journal for Research in Mathematics Education, 24*(1), 8–40.

Elmore, R. (2000). *Building a new structure for school leadership.* Washington, DC: The Albert Shanker Institute.

English, E. (2001). Teaching for understanding: Curriculum guidance for the foundation stage. *Evaluation and Research in Education, 15*(3), 197–204.

Epstein, J. L. (1995). School-family-community partnerships: Caring for the children we share. *Phi Delta Kappan, 76,* 701–712.

Epstein, J. L., Coates, L., Salinas, K. C., Sanders, M. G., & Simon, B. S. (2002). *School, family, and community partnerships: Your handbook for action, 2nd ed.* Thousand Oaks, CA: Corwin.

Erikson, E. (1968). *Identity, youth, and crisis.* New York: Norton.

Evans, M., & Hundey, I. (2000). Educating for citizenship in Canada: New meanings in a changing world. In T. Goldstein & D. Selby (Eds.), *Weaving connections: Educating for peace, social and environmental justice* (pp. 120–145). Toronto: Sumach Press.

Fennema, E., Carpenter, T., & Peterson, P. (1989). Learning mathematics with understanding: Cognitively guided instruction. In J. Brophy (Ed.), *Advances in research on understanding* (pp. 195–221). Greenwich, CT: JAI Press.

Fennema, E., & Franke, M. L. (1992). Teacher's knowledge and its impact. In D. A. Grouws (Ed.), *Handbook of research on mathematics teaching and learning* (pp. 147–164). New York: Macmillan.

Fensham, P. J., & Gardner, P. L. (1994). Technology education and science education: A new relationship? In D. Layton (Ed.), *Innovations in science and technology education* (Vol. 5, pp. 159–170). Paris: UNESCO.

Ferrari, M. (2003). Baldwin's two developmental resolutions of teen mind-body problems. *Developmental Review, 23*(1), 79–108.

Ferrari, M., Taylor, R., & van Lehn, K. (1999). Adapting work simulations for school: Preparing students for tomorrow's workplace. *Journal of Educational Computing Research, 21,* 25–53.

Fordham, S. (1990). Racelessness as a factor in Black students' school success: Pragmatic strategy or Pyrrhic victory? In N. M. Hidalgo, C. L. McDowell, & E. V. Siddle (Eds.), *Facing racism in education* (Reprint series No. 21, pp. 232–262). Cambridge, MA: Harvard Educational Review.

Fosnot, C. (1989). *Enquiring teachers, enquiring learners: A constructivist approach for teaching.* New York: TC Press.

Fosnot, C. (Ed.). (1996). *Constructivism: Theory, perspectives, and practice.* New York: TC Press.

Foucault, M. (1997). *Michel Foucault: Ethics, subjectivity, and truth* (P. Rabinow, Ed.). New York: The New Press.

Foucault, M. (1998). *Michel Foucault: Aesthetics, method, and epistemology* (J. D. Faubion, Ed.). New York: The New Press.

Freire, P. (1972). *Pedagogy of the oppressed.* New York: Herder & Herder.

Gallagher, J. (2000). Teaching for understanding and application of science knowledge. *School Science and Mathematics, 100*(6), 310–318.

Gallagher, K. (2000). *Drama education in the lives of girls: Imagining possibilities.* Toronto, London, Buffalo: University of Toronto Press.

Gardner, H. (1993). Educating for understanding. *The American School Board Journal, 180*(7), 20–24.

Gardner, H., & Boix-Mansilla, V. (1994). Teaching for understanding in the disciplines and beyond. *Teachers College Record, 96*(2), 200–217.

Gee, J. P. (2001). Identity as an analytic lens for research in education. In W. G. Secada (Ed.), *Review of research in education* (Vol. 25, pp. 99–126). Washington, DC: American Educational Research Association.

Gilbert, J. (2003). Inside out: Notes on theatre in a tenderized, 'mediatized,' tranquilized, society. In K. Gallagher & D. Booth (Eds.), *How theatre educates: Convergences and counterpoints with artists, scholars, and advocates* (pp. 106–113). Toronto, Buffalo, London: University of Toronto Press.

Gipps, C. V. (1994). *Beyond testing: Towards a theory of educational assessment.* London: Falmer.

Good, T., & Brophy, J. (1991). *Looking into classrooms* (5th ed.). New York: Harper & Row.

Good, T., McCaslin, M., & Reys, B. (1992). Investigating work groups to promote problem solving in mathematics. In J. Brophy (Ed.), *Advances in research on teaching* (Vol. 3, pp. 115–160). Greenwich, CT: JAI Press.

Goodlad, J. (1966). *The changing school curriculum.* New York: Fund for the Advancement of Education.

Goodlad, J. I. (2003/2004). Teaching what we hold sacred. *Educational Leadership, 61*(4), 18–21.

Goodson, I. F. (2003). *Professional knowledge, professional lives: Studies in education and change.* Maidenhead, UK: Open University Press.

Granott, N., & Parziale, J. (Eds.). (2002). *Microdevelopment: Transition processes in development and learning* (Cambridge Studies in Cognitive Perceptual Development). New York: Cambridge University Press.

Greene, M. (1995). *Releasing the imagination.* San Francisco: Jossey-Bass.

Greene, M. (2001). *Variations on a blue guitar: The Lincoln Center Institute lectures on aesthetic education.* New York & London: Teachers College Press.

Griffin, G. A. (1995). Slicing the system: Necessary conditions for teaching for understanding. *The Teacher Educator, 31*(2), 107–123.

Grumet, M. (2000). Foreword. In K. Gallagher, *Drama education in the lives of girls: Imagining possibilities.* Toronto, London, Buffalo: University of Toronto Press.

Habermas, T., & Bluck, S. (2000). Getting a life: The emergence of the life story in adolescence. *Psychological Bulletin, 126*(5), 748–769.

Hall, G. (1922). *Senescence: The last half of life.* New York: Appleton.

Hallam, S., & Ireson, J. (1999). Pedagogy in the secondary school. In P. Mortimore (Ed.), *Understanding pedagogy and its impact on learning* (pp. 68–97). London: Paul Chapman.

Hallinger, P., & Heck, R. (2002). What do you call people with visions? The role of vision, mission, and goals in school leadership and improvement. In K. Leithwood & P. Hallinger (Eds.), *Second international handbook of educational leadership and administration* (pp. 9–40). Dordrecht, The Netherlands: Kluwer.

Hargreaves, A. (2001). Beyond anxiety and nostalgia: Building a social movement for educational change. *Phi Delta Kappan, 82*(5), 373–377.

Hargreaves, A., & Fullan, M. (1998). *What's worth fighting for out there?* Toronto: Ontario Public School Teachers Federation.

Harvey, S., & Goudvis, A. (2000). *Strategies that work.* Portland, ME: Stenhouse.

Hashweh, M. (1986, April). *Effects of subject matter in the teaching of biology and physics.* Paper presented at the annual meeting of the American Educational Research Association, San Francisco, CA.

Henderson, A. T., & Mapp, K. L. (2002). *A new wave of evidence: The impact of school, family, and community connections on student achievement.* Austin, TX: Southwest Educational Development Laboratory.

Hiebert, J., & Carpenter, T. (1992). Learning and teaching with understanding. In D. A. Grouws (Ed.), *Handbook of research on mathematics teaching and learning* (pp. 65–97). New York: Macmillan.

Hirsch, E. (1987). *Cultural literacy: What every American needs to know.* Boston: Houghton Mifflin.

Hodson, D. (1998). *Teaching and learning science: Towards a personalized approach.* Buckingham, UK: Open University Press.

Holt, J. (1964). *How children fail.* New York: Dell.

Honig, M. I. (2004). Where's the "up" in bottom-up reform? *Educational Policy, 18*(4), 527–561.

Howey, K. (1996). Designing coherent and effective teacher education programs. In J. Sikula, T. J. Buttery, & E. Guyton (Eds.), *Handbook for research on teacher education* (pp. 143–169). New York: Macmillan.

Hurd, P. D. (1998). Scientific literacy: New minds for a changing world. *Science Education, 82*(3), 407–416.

Jobe, R., & Dayton-Sakari, M. (1999). *Info-kids: How to use nonfiction to turn reluctant readers into enthusiastic learners.* Markham, ON: Pembroke.

Johnstone, T. R., & Hiatt, D. B. (1997, March 24–28). *Development of a school-based parent center for low-income new immigrants.* Paper presented at the Annual Meeting of the American Education Research Association, Chicago, IL.

Jonson, A. R., & Toulmin, S. E. (1990). *The abuse of casuistry: A history of moral reasoning.* Los Angeles: University of California Press.

Joyce, B., & Weil, M., with Calhoun, E. (2000). *Models of teaching* (6th ed.). Boston: Allyn & Bacon.

Kozma, R. B. (Ed.). (2003). *Technology, innovation, and educational change: A global perspective.* Eugene, OR: International Society for Educational Technology.

Kuhn, T. (1970). *The structure of scientific revolutions* (2nd ed.). Chicago: University of Chicago Press.

Kuhn, T. S. (1981). A function for thought experiments. In I. Hacking (Ed.), *Scientific revolutions* (pp. 6–27). New York: Oxford University Press. (Original work published in 1964)

Lasky, S. (2000). The cultural and emotional politics of teacher-parent interactions. *Teaching and Teacher Education, 16*(8), 843–860.

Lave, J., & Wenger, E. (1991). *Situated learning: Legitimate peripheral participation.* Cambridge, UK: Cambridge University Press.

Layton, D. (1993). *Technology's challenge to science education.* Milton Keynes, UK: Open University Press.

Leithwood, K., Fullan, M., & Watson, N. (2003). *The schools we need: Recent education policy in Ontario & recommendations for moving forward.* Toronto: Ontario Institute for Studies in Education of the University of Toronto. Retrieved from http://schoolsweneed.oise.utoronto.ca

Leithwood, K., & Jantzi, D. (1999). Transformational school leadership effects: A replication. *School Effectiveness and School Improvement,* 10(4), 451–479.

Leoni, L., & Cohen, S. (2004, September). *Bringing students' identity to the fore of literacy.* Paper presented at the Conference on Cultural Diversity and Language Education, University of Hawaii.

Lieberman, A. (1996). Practices that support teacher development: Transforming conceptions of professional learning. In M. W. McLaughlin & I. Oberman (Eds.), *Teacher learning: New policies, new practices* (pp. 185–201). New York: Teachers College Press.

Lieberman, A., & Grolnik, M. (1996). Networks and reform in American education. *Teachers College Record, 98*(1), 7–45.

Little, J. W. (1993). Teachers' professional development in a climate of educational reform. *Educational Evaluation and Policy Analysis, 15*(2), 129–152.

Lyons, C. A., & Pinnell, G. S. (2001). *Systems for change in literacy education: A guide to professional development.* Portsmouth, NH: Heinemann.

MacDonald, A.-M. (2003). Intellectual passions, feminist commitments, and divine comedies: A dialogue with Ann-Marie Macdonald. In K. Gallagher & D. Booth (Eds.), *How theatre educates: Convergences and counterpoints with artists, scholars, and advocates* (pp. 247–267). Toronto, Buffalo, London: University of Toronto Press.

Martin, J. (1970). *Explaining, understanding, and teaching.* New York: McGraw-Hill.

Martusewicz, R. (2001). *Seeking passage: Post-structuralism, pedagogy, ethics.* New York & London: Teachers College Press.

Marzano, R. (1988). *Dimensions of thinking: A framework for curriculum and instruction.* Alexandria, VA: Association for Supervision & Curriculum Development.

Marzano, R. (1992a). *A different kind of classroom: Teaching with dimensions of learning.* Alexandria, VA: Association for Supervision & Curriculum Development.

Marzano, R. (1992b). *Dimensions of learning.* Alexandria, VA: Association for Supervision & Curriculum Development.

Marzano, R., with Pickering, D., Arredondo, D., Blackburn, G., Brandt, R., Moffett, C., Paynter, D., Pollock, J., & Whisler, J. (1997). *Dimensions of learning: Teacher's manual* (2nd ed.). Alexandria, VA: Association for Supervision & Curriculum Development and Mid-continent Regional Educational Laboratory.

Mascolo, M. F., Li, J., Fink, R., & Fischer, K. W. (2002). Pathways to excellence: Value presuppositions and the development of academic and affective skills in educational contexts. In M. Ferrari (Ed.), *The pursuit of excellence through education* (The Educational Psychology Series, pp. 113–146). Mahwah, NJ: Lawrence Erlbaum.

Maslow, A. (1999). *Towards a psychology of being* (3rd ed.). New York: John Wiley. (Original work published 1968)

McAdams, D. P., & de St. Aubin, E. (Eds.). (1998). *Generativity and adult development: How and why we care for the next generation.* Washington, DC: American Psychological Association.

McDougall, D., Lawson, A., Ross, J., MacLellan, A., Kajander, A., & Scane, J. (2000). *A study on Impact Math implementation strategy for the Ontario Mathematics Curriculum Grades 7 & 8.* Toronto: OISE/UT.

McLaughlin, M. W., & Talbert, J. E. (1993). Introduction: New visions of teaching. In D. K. Cohen, M. W. McLaughlin, & J. E. Talbert (Eds.), *Teaching for understanding: Challenges for policy and practice* (pp. 1–10). San Francisco: Jossey-Bass.

McMurtry, J. (2003, May 23). *Reclaiming the teaching profession: From corporate hierarchy to the authority of learning.* Keynote address at the annual conference of Ontario Teachers' Federation and the Ontario Association of Deans of Education, Toronto.

McTighe, J., & Wiggins, G. (1999). *The understanding by design handbook.* Alexandria, VA: Association for Supervision & Curriculum Development.

Messina, R. (2001, April 10–14). *Intentional learners, cooperative knowledge building, and classroom inventions.* Paper presented at the meeting of the American Educational Research Association, Seattle, WA.

Moll, L. C., Amanti, C., Neff, D., & González, N. (1992). Funds of knowledge for teaching: Using a qualitative approach to connect homes and classrooms. *Theory Into Practice, 31*(2), 132–141.

Moss, D. M. (2000). Bringing together technology and students: Examining the use of technology in a project-based class. *Journal of Educational Computing Research, 22*(2), 155–169.

New London Group. (1996). A pedagogy of multiliteracies: Designing social futures. *Harvard Educational Review, 66,* 60–92.

Newman, F. M. (1988). *Higher order thinking in high school social studies: An analysis of classrooms, teachers, students, and leadership.* Madison: University of Wisconsin, National Center on Effective Secondary Schools.

New South Wales Department of Education and Training (Australia NSW). (2003). *Productive pedagogy.* Retrieved from www.det.nsw.edu.au/inform/yr2002/mar/pedagogy.htm

Newton, D. (2000). What do we mean by teaching for understanding? In L. Newton (Ed.), *Meeting the standards in primary science* (pp. 191–203). London: Routledge Falmer.

Newton, D. (2001a). Helping children to understand. *Evaluation and Research in Education, 15*(3), 199–227.

Newton, L. (2001b). Teaching for understanding in primary science. *Evaluation and Research in Education, 15*(3), 143–153.

Nickerson, R. S. (1985). Understanding understanding. *American Journal of Education, 93,* 201–239.

Noddings, N. (1992). *The challenge to care in schools.* New York: Teachers College Press.

Norton, B. (2000). *Identity and language learning: Gender, ethnicity, and educational change.* London: Longman.

Nuthall, G. (2002). Social constructivist teaching and the shaping of students' knowledge and thinking. In J. Brophy (Ed.), *Social constructivist teaching: Affordances and constraints* (pp. 43–79). London: JAI/Elsevier Science.

Oatley, K. (1999). Why fiction may be twice as true as fact: Fiction as cognitive and emotional simulation. *Review of General Psychology, 3,* 101–117.

Oatley, K. (2003). *Fiction's sources: Conversation and imagination, Fiction's principal accomplishment: The idea of character.* Paper presented at the conference on Narrative: Art and Mind, Windsor Great Park, Windsor, ON.

Oatley, K. (in press). The narrative mode of consciousness and selfhood. In P. Zelazo & M. Moscovitch (Eds.), *Handbook of consciousness.* New York: Cambridge University Press.

Olson, L. (2005, January 26). Calls for revamping high schools intensify. *Education Week,* p. 18.

Onslow, B. (1992). Improving the attitude of students and parents through family involvement in mathematics. *Mathematics Education Research Journal, 4*(3), 24–31.

Ontario Ministry of Education. (2003). *Think literacy.* Ottawa: Queen's Printer for Ontario.

Pahl, K., & Rowsell, J. (in press). *Understanding literacy education: Using new literacy studies in the classroom.* Thousand Oaks, CA: Sage.

Pasupathi, M., Staudinger, U. M., & Baltes, P. B. (2001). Seeds of wisdom: Adolescents' knowledge and judgment about difficult life problems. *Developmental Psychology, 37*(3), 351–361.

Pedretti, E. (2004). Teaching science, technology, society, and environment (STSE) education. In D. Zeidler (Ed.), *The role of moral reasoning on socioscientific issues and discourse in science education* (Chapter 11). Dordrecht, The Netherlands: Kluwer.

Peel District School Board [PDSB]. (2001). *Science & technology, K–10: Enduring understandings, learning about the world around us.* Mississauga, ON: Author.

Perkins, D. (1986). *Knowledge design.* Hillsdale, NJ: Lawrence Erlbaum.

Perkins, D. (1993a). *Smart schools.* New York: Simon & Shuster.

Perkins, D. (1993b). Teaching for understanding. *American Educator: The Professional Journal of the American Federation of Teachers, 17*(3), 28–34.

Perkins, D. (1994). *The intelligent eye.* Santa Monica, CA: The Getty Center for Education in the Arts.

Perkins, D., & Blythe, T. (1994). Putting understanding up front. *Educational Leadership, 51*(5), 4–7.

Phillips, D. C. (1995). The good, the bad, and the ugly: The many faces of constructivism. *Educational Researcher, 24*(7), 5–12.

Piaget, J. (1932). *The moral judgment of the child* (M. Gabain, Trans.). London: Routledge & Kegan Paul.

Pinard, A. (1992). Metaconscience et métacognition [Metaconsciousness and metacognition]. *Canadian Psychology, 33,* 27–41.

Pourdavood, R. G., Cowen, L. M., Svec, L. V., Skitzki, R., & Grob, S. (1999). *A paradoxical path to reform: The case study of Lomond Elementary School* (Transforming Learning Communities). Columbus: Ohio State Dept. of Education.

Prawat, R. (1989). Teaching for understanding: Three key attributes. *Teaching and Teacher Education, 5*(4), 315–328.

Quantz, R. A. (1992). On critical ethnography (with some postmodern considerations). In M. D. LeCompte, W. L. Millroy, & J. Preissle (Eds.), *The handbook of qualitative research in education* (pp. 447–505). New York: Academic Press.

Reeve, R. (2001, April 10–14). *The knowledge building lab school: Principles to practice.* Paper presented at the meeting of the American Educational Research Association, Seattle, WA.

Reeve, R., & Lamon, M. (1998, April 13–17). *Factors to be considered: Overlapping communities of inquiry and a knowledge-building classroom.* Paper presented at the meeting of the American Educational Research Association, San Diego.

Reigeluth, C. M. (Ed.). (1999). *Instructional-design theories and models.* Mahwah, NJ: Lawrence Erlbaum.

Richardson, V. (Ed.). (1997). *Constructivist teacher education: Building a world of new understandings.* London: Falmer.

Rodrigue, A. (2003). *The conceptualization, production, and use of the rhizome of professionalism by Canadian teacher unions: Snapshots of the present, roadmaps for the future.* Doctoral thesis, University of South Australia.

Rorty, R. (1989). *Contingency, irony, and solidarity.* Cambridge, UK: Cambridge University Press.

Rosenblatt, L. (1978). *The reader, the text, the poem: The transactional theory of the literary work.* Carbondale: Southern Illinois University Press.

Ross, J. A. (1998). The antecedents and consequences of teacher efficacy. In J. Brophy (Ed.), *Research on teaching* (Vol. 7, pp. 49–74). Greenwich, CT: JAI Press.

Ross, J. A., & Bruce, C. (in press). Self-assessment and professional growth: The case of a Grade 8 mathematics teacher. *Teaching and Teacher Education.*

Ross, J. A., & Gray, P. (in press). Transformational leadership and teacher commitment to organizational values: The mediating effects of collective teacher efficacy. *School Effectiveness and School Improvement.*

Ross, J. A., Hogaboam-Gray, A., & Gray, P. (2004). Prior student achievement, collaborative school processes, and collective teacher efficacy. *Leadership and Policy in Schools, (3)*3, 163–188.

Ross, J. A., Hogaboam-Gray, A., McDougall, D., & Bruce, C. (2001). The contribution of technology to the implementation of mathematics education reform: Case studies of Grade 1–3 teaching. *Journal of Educational Computing Research, 26*(1), 123–140.

Ross, J. A., Hogaboam-Gray, A., McDougall, D., & Le Sage, A. (2003). A survey measuring implementation of mathematics education reform by elementary teachers. *Journal of Research in Mathematics Education, 34*(4), 344–363.

Ross, J. A., McDougall, D., & Hogaboam-Gray, A. (2002). Research on reform in mathematics education, 1993–2000. *Alberta Journal of Educational Research, 48*(2), 122–138.

Sachs, J. (2003). *The activist teaching profession.* Buckingham, UK: Open University Press.

Sanders, M., & Epstein, J. L. (1998). School-family-community partnerships and educational change: International perspectives. In A. Hargreaves, A. Lieberman, M. Fullan, & D. Hopkins (Eds.), *The international handbook of educational change* (pp. 482–504). Boston: Kluwer Academic Press.

Scardamalia, M. (2000). *Knowledge building principles* (Summer Institute 2000 Database). Toronto: The Knowledge Forum Project.

Scardamalia, M. (2001). Getting real about 21st century education. *The Journal of Educational Change, 2,* 171–176.

Scardamalia, M. (2002). Collective cognitive responsibility for the advancement of knowledge. In B. Smith (Ed.), *Liberal education in a knowledge society* (pp. 76–98). Chicago: Open Court.

Scardamalia, M. (2003a). Knowledge building environments: Extending the limits of the possible in education and knowledge work. In A. DiStefano, K. E. Rudestam, & R. Silverman (Eds.), *Encyclopedia of distributed learning* (pp. 269–272). Thousand Oaks, CA: Sage.

Scardamalia, M. (2003b). Knowledge Forum (Advances beyond CSILE). *Journal of Distance Education, 17*(Suppl. 3, Learning Technologies in Canada), 31–36.

Scardamalia, M., & Bereiter, C. (1999). Schools as knowledge building organizations. In D. Keating & C. Hertzman (Eds.), *Today's children, tomorrow's society: The developmental health and wealth of nations* (pp. 274–289). New York: Guilford.

Scardamalia, M., & Bereiter, C. (2003). Knowledge building. In *Encyclopedia of education* (pp. 1370–1373). New York: Macmillan Reference.

Schauble, L., Klopfer, L., & Raghavan, K. (1991). Student's transitions from engineering model to a science model of experimentation. *Journal of Research in Science Teaching, 28*(9), 859–882.

Schon, D. (1983). *The reflective practitioner.* New York: Basic Books.

Seixas, P. (2002). The purposes of teaching Canadian history (Address at the annual conference of the Association for Canadian Studies, Winnipeg, October 2001). *Canadian Social Studies* [online], *36*(2). Retrieved January 18, 2006, from http://www.quasar.ualberta.ca/css/Css_36_2/ARpurposes_teaching_canadian_history.htm

Sekayi, D., Peterman, F., Stakich, K., & Caputo, D. (1999). *A patchwork quilt of change: The case study of Brentmoor Elementary School* (Transforming Learning Communities). Columbus: Ohio State Dept. of Education.

Shen, V. (2001). Metaphor and concept in religious narratives. *Inter-Religio, 39,* 3–27.

Shulman, L. (1986). Those who understand: Knowledge growth in teaching. *Educational Researcher, 15*(2), 4–14.

Sierpinska, A. (1994). *Understanding in mathematics.* London: Falmer.

Simons, J. (1997). Drama pedagogy and the art of double meaning. *Research in Drama Education, 2*(2), 193–201.

Skourtou, E., Kourtis Kazoullis, V., & Cummins, J. (2006). Designing virtual learning environments for academic language development. In J. Weiss, J. Nolan, & V. Nincic (Eds.), *Handbook of virtual learning* (pp. 443–469). Dordrecht, The Netherlands: Kluwer Academic.

Stein, M. K., Hubbard, L., & Mehan, H. (2004). Reform ideas that travel far afield: The two cultures of reform in New York City's School District #2 and San Diego. *Journal of Educational Change, 5,* 161–197.

Sternberg, R. J. (2001a). How wise is it to teach for wisdom? A reply to five critiques. *Educational Psychologist, 36*(4), 269–272.

Sternberg, R. J. (2001b). Why schools should teach for wisdom: The balance theory of wisdom in educational settings. *Educational Psychologist, 36*(4), 227–245.

Sternberg, R. (2003). What is an "expert student?" *Educational Researcher, 32*(8), 5–9.

Sternberg, R. J. (2004). Wisdom and giftedness. In L. V. Shavinina & M. Ferrari (Eds.), *Beyond knowledge: Extra cognitive facets in developing high ability* (pp. 169–186). Mahwah, NJ: Lawrence Erlbaum.

Sternberg, R. J. (2005). Foolishness. In R. J. Sternberg & J. Jordan (Eds.), *Handbook of wisdom: Psychological perspectives* (pp. 331–352). New York: Cambridge University Press.

Taylor, C. (1995). *Philosophical arguments.* New Haven, CT: Harvard University Press.

Thiessen, D., & Anderson, S. (1999). *Getting into the habit of change in Ohio schools: The cross-case study of 12 transforming learning communities.* Columbus: Ohio Department of Education.

Tighe, J., Seif, E., & Wiggins, G. (2004). You can teach for meaning. *Phi Delta Kappan, 62*(1), 26–31.

Togneri, W., & Anderson, S. E. (2003). *Beyond islands of excellence: What districts can do to improve instruction and achievement in all schools.* Washington, DC: The Learning First Alliance.

Tovani, C. (2004). *Do I really have to teach reading?* Portland, ME: Stenhouse.

Turner-Bisset, R. (2001). *Expert teaching: Knowledge and pedagogy to lead the profession.* London: David Fulton.

Vadeboncoeur, J. A. (1997). Child development and the purpose of education: A historical context for constructivism in teacher education. In V. Richardson (Ed.), *Constructivist teacher education: Building a world of new understandings* (pp. 15–37). London: Falmer.

Van Engen, H. (1953). The formation of concepts. In H. Fehr (Ed.), *The learning of mathematics, its theory and practice* (Twenty First Yearbook of the National Council of Teachers of Mathematics, pp. 69–98). Washington, DC: National Council of Teachers of Mathematics.

Varela, F. J. (1999). *Ethical know-how: Action, wisdom, and cognition.* Stanford, CA: Stanford University Press. (Original work published 1992)

Vygotsky, L. S. (1978). *Mind in society: The development of higher psychological processes.* Cambridge, MA: Harvard University Press.

Waller, W. (1932). *The sociology of teaching.* New York: John Wiley.

Watkins, C., & Mortimore, P. (1999). Pedagogy: What do we know? In P. Mortimore (Ed.), *Understanding pedagogy and its impact on learning* (pp. 1–19). London: Paul Chapman.

Weglinsky, H. (2004). Facts or critical thinking skills: What NAEP results say. *Educational Leadership, 62*(1), 32–35.

Wells, G. (1994). *Changing schools from within: Creating communities of inquiry.* Toronto/Portsmouth, NH: OISE Press/Heinemann.

Wiggins, G., & McTighe, J. (1998). *Understanding by design.* Alexandria, VA: Association for Supervision & Curriculum Development.

Wilhelm, J. D. (2001). *Improving comprehension with think-aloud strategies.* New York: Scholastic.

Wilson, E. O. (1988). *Consilience: The unity of knowledge.* New York: Knopf.

Wilson, S. M. (1992). Deeply routed change. In D. K. Cohen, M. W. McLaughlin, & J. E. Talbert (Eds.), *Teaching for understanding: Challenges for policy and practice* (pp. 84–129). San Francisco: Jossey-Bass.

Wineburg, S., & Wilson, S. M. (1991). Subject matter knowledge in the teaching of history. In J. Brophy (Ed.), *Advances in research on teaching* (Vol. 2, pp. 345–393). Greenwich, CT: JAI Press.

Wolfe, T. (1975). The new journalism. In T. Wolfe & E. W. Johnson (Eds.), *The new journalism* (pp. 13–68). London: Picador.

Wood, T., Cobb, P., & Yackel, E. (1990). The contextual nature of teaching: Mathematics and reading instruction in one second-grade classroom. *The Elementary School Journal, 90*(5), 497–513.

Yeatman, A., & Sachs, J. (1995). *Making the links: A formative evaluation of the first year of the innovative links between universities and schools for teacher professional development.* Perth, Australia: Murdoch University.

Yee, P. (1996). *Ghost train.* Vancouver, BC: Douglas & McIntyre.

Index

**CORWIN
PRESS**

The Corwin Press logo—a raven striding across an open book—represents the union of courage and learning. Corwin Press is committed to improving education for all learners by publishing books and other professional development resources for those serving the field of PreK–12 education. By providing practical, hands-on materials, Corwin Press continues to carry out the promise of its motto: **"Helping Educators Do Their Work Better."**